PRAISE FOR THE NEW EDITION

[*Hype, Hypocrisy & Television in Urban India*] was a book way ahead of its time. Too many likely users who would benefit from it are deprived simply because it is such an old publication now. ... Nobody has done a comparable book on politics and sociology of Indian television. It would find an audience among journalists and television viewers bewildered by the fast evolving scenario. Media is now a huge industry and punches above its weight in terms of impact on our minds. There are too few serious books on the subject, barring the odd personalised memoir.

—Shekhar Gupta
Chairman and Editor-in-Chief
ThePrint

Shah is that rare writer who combines the topical energy of journalism with the reflective depth and breadth of scholarship. Her television book is, by the same token, that exceedingly rare approach to the subject that is neither superficial nor ponderous. This is a text that navigates seamlessly between reportage, social analysis and personal memoir. It brings policy debates alive and mines everyday experience for its structural significance.

—William Mazzarella
Neukom Family Professor Chair,
Department of Anthropology,
University of Chicago

PRAISE FOR THE FIRST EDITION

Her project is not the medium alone but an attempt to place it in its social context, to watch its effects on urban populations and to try and correlate changes in urban society with the impact of television. She makes a remarkably good job of it.

—The Times of India

Women, pre-marital sex, violence in schools, consumerism, MTV lookalikes, brand deluge, marital discord... and television... she maps the contemporary history of India.

—The Week

Telly-Guillotined

Thank you for choosing a SAGE product!
If you have any comment, observation or feedback,
I would like to personally hear from you.

Please write to me at **contactceo@sagepub.in**

Vivek Mehra, Managing Director and CEO, SAGE India.

Telly-Guillotined
How *Television* Changed India

Amrita Shah

YODAPRESS | **SAGE** | **select**

Los Angeles | London | New Delhi
Singapore | Washington DC | Melbourne

First published in 2019 by

SAGE Publications India Pvt Ltd
B1/I-1 Mohan Cooperative Industrial Area
Mathura Road, New Delhi 110 044, India
www.sagepub.in

YODA Press
268 AC Vasant Kunj
New Delhi 110070
www.yodapress.co.in

SAGE Publications Inc
2455 Teller Road
Thousand Oaks, California 91320, USA

SAGE Publications Ltd
1 Oliver's Yard, 55 City Road
London EC1Y 1SP, United Kingdom

SAGE Publications Asia-Pacific Pte Ltd
18 Cross Street #10-10/11/12
China Square Central
Singapore 048423

Published by Vivek Mehra for SAGE Publications India Pvt Ltd. Typeset in 10/16pt Georgia by Fidus Design Pvt. Ltd, Chandigarh.

Library of Congress Cataloging-in-Publication Data Available

ISBN: 978-93-532-8605-7 (PB)

SAGE Yoda Team: Amrita Dutta, Vandana Gupta, Arpita Das, Ishita Gupta and Tanya Singh

CONTENTS

Preface   vii

1. Coming Soon ...   1
2. The Big Leap   17
3. The Middle Class Strikes Back   32
4. The New Guerrillas   56
5. Star Trek   73
6. The Rath Yatra   87
7. Everything Must Go   117
8. Love for Sale   143
9. Let's Play Life   156
10. The Backlash   170
11. Indians in Blue Jeans   196
12. The Age of Infotainment   224
13. Angry and Addicted   243

Index   278
About the Author   285

PREFACE

LOUD, SENSATIONALISTIC, IRRESPONSIBLE, TRIVIAL, DANGEROUS—THESE
are some of the ways in which the Indian news media is
perceived by many in the country today. Terms like 'fake
news' and 'paid news' are freely and sometimes gratuitously
applied to journalistic output. Diminishing public respect
has rendered journalists vulnerable to pressures of various
kinds. Journalists are sacked en masse, heads of media
companies are raided for expressing anti-establishment
views, senior news staffers are fired for taking on powerful
politicians and attacked for exposing corruption and
wrongdoing. Even among crowds, while covering news
events, reporters and photographers are liable to be roughed
up and assaulted by random members of the public. How
did we get here? The avalanche of criticism, including sharp
rebukes from Justice Markandey Katju, as Chairman of the
Press Council in his four-year term starting October 2011,
suggests that the decline of the Indian news media, once seen
as a worthy pillar of Indian democracy and a rare example
of a vibrant, thriving press in a developing country, has been
sudden as much as it has been unexpected. But has it really?
In this book I suggest otherwise.

   Telly-Guillotined is a new version of my book, *Hype,
Hypocrisy & Television in Urban India* published in 1997.
In the latter book I took a journey through India observing
patterns made by the interplay of politics, economics,

society, communication technology and the electronic media. *Telly-Guillotined* connects that journey to the present, demonstrating how trends observed towards the end of the last century have intensified in the early decades of this one and assumed the alarming forms described above.

The book begins in the period immediately preceding the formal announcement of a structural reforms policy but at a time when socialist India had begun to move firmly towards economic liberalisation. Television was a prime driver in opening up the economy in the late decades of the twentieth century. Riding on infrastructural expansion, technological innovation and privatisation, television entered homes and pushed consumerism. I follow the widening trail, from decision-makers in their *sarkari* (government) offices in the capital to men who hooked up hundreds of households to a video set and called themselves cable operators.

New programming, unfolding over multiple channels and outlets, sent a lightning bolt of modernity into a conservative society the consequences of which were evident in rising materialism, increasing numbers of working women and greater permissiveness. The rapid, blinding pace of change produced widespread unease which was exploited by votaries of Hindutva to set up a clash between sundry modernisers and themselves as traditionalists upholding 'Indian culture'.

These culture wars, the homogenising effects of television programming and the opportunity presented by the electronic media for playing guerrilla politics contributed significantly to the rise of the majoritarian Bharatiya Janata Party as a political force at the national level. Narendra Modi leveraged the new mediatised environment to stage a colossal victory in 2014, as his predecessor Rajiv Gandhi had been able to do, on a relatively modest scale, 30 years before.

Meanwhile, the spread of neoliberalism globally was challenging the tenets which had once defined the news media's role in sustaining democracy. In 1987, US President Ronald Reagan repealed the Fairness Doctrine relieving licensed broadcasters of a public-interest obligation to represent opposing points of view. Almost a decade later, in 1996, the Telecommunications Act, coming into effect under Bill Clinton, deregulated the communications industry, enabling the consolidation of media companies. A market-oriented approach to editorial content propounded by Rupert Murdoch, the global media face of neoliberalism, began to reshape Indian journalism by commercialising the media and in more subtle ways by dumbing down content and influencing the choice of editorial formats.

'When capitalism strengthens, the media technology necessary to carry consumption to new groups is invented or acquired,' claims communication scholar Robin Jeffrey. Today, even as the emergence of extreme right-wing political leaders in countries across the world demonstrates the sway of a hyper-capitalist ideology, momentous technological shifts of the early twenty-first century have raised new issues of privacy and control within which journalism, following an older notion of ethics and a belief in citizens' rights occupies less space.

Hype, Hypocrisy & Television in Urban India came out at a time when there were few publishers and no funding avenues for books. A 1992 journalism fellowship from the K. K. Birla Foundation, though woefully modest (six thousand rupees every month for a year), provided the much-needed validation to take the project forward. The book was published and was widely reviewed but went out of print and remained so for several years, till now.

A great deal has changed since the publication of the 1997 book. Television viewership has grown, the number of television channels, including news channels, has exploded, the press has evolved in response to the audio-visual media as well as to the emergence of the Internet and social media. The proliferation of cell phones has transformed the way people receive news and entertainment. One could well wonder what a 20-year-old book might have to contribute towards understanding the media and society as it is today.

A great deal, I would contend. When a new edition of Neil Postman's provocative 1985 book, *Amusing Ourselves to Death: Public Discourse in the Age of Show Business*, was brought out in 2006, it evoked the comment that it was a 'twenty-first century book written in the twentieth century'. The remark revealed the problematic nature of timing in a scenario marked by a breathless pace of change. It is not in the minutiae of everyday developments or in the roll call of events immensely significant at the time of their occurrence then quickly forgotten, that one is likely to find explanations for our current predicaments. The answers to our concerns are in closely observed patterns over time. And this is what this new–old book sets out to provide.

I am deeply grateful to Yoda Press and SAGE for giving this book a new lease of life, especially to Arpita Das who understood the contemporary relevance of the book and steered the project with determination. My deepest gratitude goes to Shekhar Gupta and William Mazzarella for their support and encouragement, and also to Clare Arni for the cover photograph.

COMING SOON...

OCTOBER 2. THE DATE OF Mahatma Gandhi's birthday held little significance for us as children apart from the question of whether it would or would not be a holiday; the status of holidays changed each year depending on the vagaries of the government and school authorities. But this date in the year of 1972 is etched in my memory for quite another reason: it was the day television came to Bombay.

I remember the day well. I remember the excitement, the tense suspense with which we anticipated this seemingly magical phenomenon. But most of all, I remember the overwhelming but unspoken concern that this significant event would pass us by. For, nobody, at least nobody we knew in the middle class suburban locality where I grew up, had a television set. It was a fear that was restricted to us children. For our parents, preoccupied with more daily concerns, television existed, if at all, on the farthest margins of their consciousness.

As the evening drew closer our anxiety grew. Youngsters from the neighbourhood, all of us decked expectantly in going-out clothes met to discuss strategy. Our big hope, a cocky adolescent girl who had promised access to a family that owned a television set, now reported a problem. That option discarded, we were left with nothing.

Over and over we racked our brains for an answer but none came to our minds. Meanwhile, time was running out. The inaugural programme was scheduled to start, I think, at six or thereabouts and already we were half an hour behind time and no closer to a solution. Then, finally and hesitantly, someone came up with the information that at the end of our lane was a smuggler who lived alone and had a 'big, foreign television set'.

A smuggler! The suggestion sent us into a frenzy of nervous excitement. Tempted as we were, did the situation warrant such an extreme measure? And extreme it seemed for in our simple perception there were two kinds of crime. One kind was theft and murder, crimes usually committed by the poor out of desperation. And then there were things like tax evasion, black marketing, bribery, and of course, smuggling. And we who prided ourselves on our ability to do without had nothing but contempt for the second lot. Though secretly we might have envied the beneficiaries of white collar crime, as a group we scorned them for their weakness.

The choice then that confronted us was between the devil and the deep sea. Should we risk damnation by venturing into a smuggler's house, a certain den of vice? Would we not be guilty by association and, most important, what would our parents say? So we deliberated for a while till, eventually, desire triumphed over conscience and, stifling our apprehensions, we trundled off to our destination.

The alleged smuggler, a balding stout man, as ordinary a man as one could expect to find in the street answered the bell. Although he was taken aback at finding a dozen strange kids at his doorstep, he recovered quickly enough to welcome us into his tiny apartment. Requiring little encouragement we trooped in and settled down in front of the wide screen National Panasonic that was flickering with black and white images.

We had missed half the show. The television authorities had put together a variety entertainment programme for the evening. There was a pretty presenter, some skits, some dances and the mandatory speeches, all quite dull. Frankly, I remember very little of what I actually watched on television that day; I was more interested in detecting traces of felony around me.

The important thing was that television had arrived and we had been there to witness it.

When I think of that day now I am struck by our naiveté and the simplicity of the world we lived in. Partly of course, it was the ordinariness of our lives that made small matters such as a glimpse of a film star in a Chevrolet, the passing of a Jumbo jet or even a fire in a neighbouring slum assume proportions of immense significance. But more than that, I think, our determination to pay our respects to the new medium was born out of very limited expectations. We were like people who rush to marvel at the unveiling of a new monument without realising that from that day on it would be there every single day, to be admired, glanced at or even ignored by any passer-by.

On the other hand, if someone had told us that we would not have believed it. For television was an unheard of luxury. In fact, in those days, for salaried people like my parents and my friends' parents almost everything was a luxury. The purchase of a consumer durable by any family around us was a subject of immense speculation; children rushed home to inform their parents so that they could lean over balconies and watch its arrival. I could count the families who had a telephone and a refrigerator in the fifteen apartments in our building on the finger tips of one hand and still have a couple left over.

In the circumstances it was but natural that the appearance of the first television set in our very midst—in the flat across the landing—was considered a community event. And on its arrival everyone, grown-ups, children, servants, crowded in.

The owners, an old couple whose children lived in the United States, were close to my parents on account of which my family got to sit on the sofa while the others spread out on the floor, the balcony, the passage, anywhere that allowed even a postage-stamp-size glimpse of the screen. In this manner we watched the Sunday feature film, *Chaaya Geet,* the melange of Hindi film songs and the weekly film personality interview, *Phool Khile Hain Gulshan Gulshan.* In less suffocating conditions we also watched *The Count of Monte Christo, Here's Lucy* and the BBC rendition of *Pride and Prejudice.*

Over the weeks the audience thinned out. The women, embarrassed by the enforced proximity with men, were the first to leave. Presumably that put some pressure on the husbands. For, miraculously, a second television set appeared in the building, then another and another. And each new possessor in turn threw their doors open to accommodate the less fortunate.

As more antennae sprouted on the terrace however, hospitality receded. Old notions of pride and fears about television resurfaced. Parents who did not own a television set worried about how bad it looked for their kids to be seen at the neighbours'; those who did, complained about the effect it was having on their children's homework and eyesight. None of this proved to be a disincentive though. For, in no time at all, every flat in the building had its own television set.

And slowly and imperceptibly life changed. On Sunday evenings earlier we might have gone to the beach for camel rides and ice-cream; now we stayed home and watched the film on television. Our weekly visits to my grandmothers' were often abruptly curtailed to catch a particular show. Gradually we even stopped going to peoples' houses and fewer and fewer people dropped in at ours as conversation everywhere dimmed before the blue glow of the television set.

Not that it mattered, for television had brought the world into our homes. My mother who had nursed a lifelong desire to witness the Republic Day parade held annually in the capital was granted her wish in a remarkably simple way: the paramilitary units, the colourful floats and agile schoolchildren marched in splendid detail less than six feet away from her sofa as Melville DeMello's voice boomed from every window.

There were quiz shows, Origami lessons, How-to-do-it-yourself Bonsai and wildlife; Nadia Comaneci's triumphant debut at the 1976 Montreal Olympics and, of course, the cricket matches: Alan Knott's antics during the India–England series; India's dramatic clash with Clive Lloyd's boys in 1974.... Suddenly television was all around—in homes, behind shop windows, on hoardings, in cars. Some had it. Others dreamed endlessly about having it.

COMING SOON ...

Dreams, however, are prone to fade. And nothing fades faster than novelty. In our case, once we had acquired our television set, once it had become a part of our lives, as familiar as the carpet or the dent in the armchair, once we had grown accustomed to its unblinking visage, we were bored. The once glamorous visuals began to seem unutterably dreary. The frequent breakdowns grated ('Sorry For The Interruption!', children would screech at play quoting television's most repeated visual).

But crucially, once we had stopped exclaiming over the wonders of the medium, we realised there was nothing to watch. A large part of the limited broadcast was taken up by educational programmes. These were of poor quality and clearly of so little relevance to the actual audience that viewership was abysmally low. According to television audience figures at the time, documentaries on developmental themes were watched by 10 per cent of viewers. A weekly half an hour programme for industrial workers, *Hamare Kamgar Hamare Udyog,* had an audience of 3 per cent while only two to four in every hundred viewers turned on their sets for the daily rural programme *Krishi Darshan.* Entertainment consisted of three weekly film-based programmes which had a stupendously high viewership of over 80 per cent, a couple of foreign serials, grim features on classical dance and music and the infrequent sports event.

As the 1970s came to an end, television owners were a disgruntled lot. Like suitors in haste, we had looked long and hard at the object of our passion and found it wanting. What we had was not enough. We wanted more.

How much more?

Could India afford to spend its meagre resources on a costly medium like television?

On 15 September 1959, the Indian president, Dr Rajendra Prasad, had inaugurated a cultural programme at Delhi's Vigyan Bhawan which was to constitute the country's first television broadcast. For the programmers and technicians involved, All India Radio staffers who had no previous experience with television, the successful transmission of the evening's event was a phenomenal achievement. 'It was a day of tremendous euphoria,' recalled Shailendra Shanker, Officer on Special Duty at the time.

In actual terms, there was little to be euphoric about: India had yet to develop a separate infrastructure for television; the service was being operated from a single room on the fifth floor of Akashvani Bhawan, the headquarters of All India Radio. The programming, a UNESCO-sponsored educational service for Delhi schoolchildren and rural viewers was, at best, experimental. The audience too, was severely restricted by the lack of television sets. There was no indigenous television manufacturing industry at the time and most of the 150 sets that existed in the country were gifts from UNESCO and foreign donors. An attempt at expanding viewership through teleclubs proved successful but the number of viewers, by any standards, continued to be low.

The fact was that, despite the enthusiasm generated, the arrival of television in India was fraught with uncertainty. The new medium had commenced its revolutionary march across the industrialised world over a decade ago. But in India, newly independent and battling against endemic poverty, illiteracy and linguistic conflict, the overwhelming feeling was that television was a luxury the country could ill afford.

COMING
SOON ...

This was just one view though. In the West, communication scholars were propounding new theories regarding the impact of mass media on development, particularly for the Third World. David Lerner, a sociologist at the Massachusetts Institute of Technology maintained, on the basis of a survey in six Middle Eastern countries, that higher literacy rates led by increasing urbanisation would result in greater media exposure and consequently wider economic and political participation. In his significant book, *Mass Media and National Development,* Wilbur Schramm, a pioneer in communication science, stressed the importance of the mass media in disseminating information and claimed persuasively that backward nations could facilitate development by expanding the same.

This belief had many supporters in India. The most influential of these was Vikram Sarabhai. The famous physicist and visionary institution builder, Sarabhai, who laid the foundations for establishments as significant and diverse as the Indian Institute of Management in Ahmedabad, the National Institute of Design and the Indian Space Research Organisation, believed and passionately argued that television could accelerate social progress in India.

At his initiative, a National Satellite Communication Group (NASCOM) was instituted in 1968. And based on its recommendations the Indian government finally adopted the idea of a hybrid television network comprising communication satellites as well as ground-based relay transmitters, the aim being to disseminate messages across a wide audience at the lowest possible cost.

It was an ambitious scheme and for a country like India, an expensive one. But as luck would have it, the mid-1970s brought an opportunity for a dress rehearsal. The United States' National Aeronautics and Space Administration (NASA) under the guidance of Wilbur Schramm decided to grant India free satellite time on its Applications Technology Satellite-6 for a one-year pilot project.

The project which consisted of a special broadcast to six rural clusters (covering 2,400 villages) enabled policy-makers and communication experts to gauge the impact of television on areas such as health, agriculture, education and its potential use in furthering objectives such as family planning and national integration. It also allowed technicians to familiarise themselves with operational problems concerning satellite hardware, costs and management.

Despite the success of the SITE experiment, television continued to be of marginal significance in India. In 1965 daily broadcasts comprising educational and entertainment fare had commenced in Delhi. And between 1972 and 1975, spurred partly by the launch of Pakistani television, regular television service was extended to big cities and sensitive border towns.

Still, in 1980, two decades after its inception in India, television covered only 13 per cent of the country's area and reached a potential 25 per cent of its people. Ironically most of the stations had come up in the cities. And the relatively high cost of a television set (a black and white television set cost ₹3000, the equivalent of three months' wages for a mill labourer) ensured that the bulk of the viewership came not from the rural poor whose interests were a primary consideration in the introduction of television but the urban middle and upper classes.

And the fillip for television expansion when it came, was the result, not so much of a desire to spread development as much as the pursuit of power.

The broadcast media, unlike the press which was a free and thriving medium in India, was firmly controlled by the government. At the time of Independence, India's first prime minister, Jawaharlal Nehru, had insisted on state control of the broadcast media as a preventive measure against disintegration. And the tradition continued. Except that with the rise of Nehru's daughter, Indira Gandhi, state control became synonymous with the suppression of dissent and the creation of a personality cult.

News and current affairs programmes on television, such as they were during Mrs Gandhi's reign were pro-government. Criticism was blanked out. Opposition members were briefly, if ever, mentioned. On the other hand, television cameras faithfully recorded Mrs Gandhi's every action earning the medium the nickname, 'Devidarshan'.

According to Inder Gujral, minister for Information and Broadcasting in the early 1970s, Mrs Gandhi had seriously considered expanding the underdeveloped network to use for propaganda in preparation for the 1976 elections. In the absence of indigenous satellite technology, the exercise would have been prohibitively expensive and the prime minister was eventually persuaded to drop the idea.

Her desire to control minds did not fade away however. And in June 1975, she reacted to a nationwide agitation against her government by declaring a National

Emergency. The extraordinary powers conferred by the Emergency enabled her to jail Opposition members, bypass democratic conventions and silence the press. During the fearful 18 months that followed, all publications were censored, critical journalists were thrown into jail and dissent in any form was stamped out. Radio and television, meanwhile, continued to eulogise Mrs Gandhi and her government's achievements.

The repression invited a backlash and in 1977 when elections were called, a year behind schedule, the people decisively voted out the Congress government. Not surprisingly, one of the chief election planks of the triumphant conglomerate of Opposition parties, the Janata Party, concerned media autonomy. On assuming power, it appointed a commission to suggest ways of freeing the broadcast media (in April 1976, television had been delinked from All India Radio and established as a separate entity under the title Doordarshan which meant 'distant vision') from government control. The commission recommended the formation of the Prasar Bharati or Broadcasting Corporation of India which would be headed by an independent board of directors free from direct supervision of the Information & Broadcasting (I&B) Ministry.

The proposal remained on paper. By early 1980 the Janata Party, driven by strife and the competing egos of its leaders, had paved the way for Indira Gandhi's return to power. And in March when the bill for the formation of the corporation was introduced in Parliament it was thrown out by the Congress majority.

Plans for expanding the television network however still remained a low priority. The entire allocation for television expansion in the sixth five-year plan (1980–85) was a mere ₹210 million. Mrs Gandhi, now safely ensconced for another term, was not greatly inclined towards her new I&B minister Vasant Sathe's enthusiastic schemes for upgrading Indian television, a prime component of which was the introduction of colour.

COMING SOON ...

But Sathe was nothing if not persistent. 'Vasant Sathe was a visionary. When the history of television is written, Sathe's name should be in colour' claimed Shailendra Shanker who headed Doordarshan between 1980 and 1984. In retrospect, Sathe's role in the evolution of Indian television was significant. Yet, at the time, the ebullient minister with his grand plans for projecting television onto giant video screens in villages and his unswerving obsession with colour came across as a bit of a joke—a technicolour dreamer in a grey land of poverty.

Attitudes however underwent a sea change in the 1980s. The doubts, reservations and hesitations of earlier years were swept aside in a series of unplanned moves beginning with the Asiad.

In the early 1980s the Indian government had bid for and won the right to stage the IXth Asian Games. Many Indians perceived this as an unnecessary indulgence. The view was not without basis. The country lacked the infrastructure for an event of this magnitude and there were urgent problems that required the government's attention. Trouble was brewing in the prosperous northern state of Punjab. Militant Sikhs—Sikhs formed 2 per cent of the country's population and were the majority community in the state—had begun a separatist movement under the leadership of the fanatical priest Jarnail Singh Bhindranwale. The movement enjoyed the support of several UK- and Canada-based Sikhs and separatist leaders were determined to internationalise the issue (one plan entailed burning a copy of the Indian Constitution on the streets of Delhi to coincide with the inauguration of the Asian Games).

On the other hand, the chance to host the continent's most prestigious sporting event seemed to tap latent reserves of national pride.

India, post-Independence, had a rather dichotomous view of the West. There was on the one hand, the tendency to regard the West and everything about it as being vastly superior to the native; the elite, in fact, were heavily influenced by the West in terms of dress, manners and lifestyle. There was, on the other hand, a widespread suspicion often bordering on paranoia, of the West and its designs on India. This combination of adulation and hostility was a smokescreen for a visibly low self-esteem. Despite their repeated West bashing, what Indians particularly craved most from the West was respect. And the Games were perceived as a welcome opportunity for the country to improve upon its undistinguished presence on the global scenario.

Ultimately, sentiment won over pragmatism. And preparations for the event began on a war footing. By mid-1982 swirling concrete flyovers had materialised on the streets of Delhi, giving it the appearance of a well-planned modern city. Glitzy hotels had sprung up to accommodate the delegates expected towards the end of the year. Stadia, indoor swimming pools and restaurant complexes were hurriedly readied. A flurry of construction, organisation and planning was underway to put our best face forward.

The problem was: who was to convey it to the world? Who would prove once and for all that India was not just a land of bullock carts and sectarian violence but a thriving industrialised nation? Who would proclaim its journey into the 21st century?

Doordarshan?

The suggestion was received with scepticism if not outright mirth. It was no secret that Indian television was technically miles behind networks in the developed world. Second, thanks to the absence of a clear-sighted television policy and constant interference by politicians and bureaucrats, Doordarshan staffers were considered to be powerless supplicants without the experience or the capability to handle such an onerous responsibility. The information minister and Doordarshan officials on the other hand, were confident of delivering the goods and extremely keen on the opportunity.

Eventually a compromise was arrived at where Doordarshan would be given charge and a foreign backup crew kept at hand, just in case. And in view of the magnitude of the task, unprecedented concessions were made. When foreign networks refused to accept black and white clips for transmission, colour was introduced. Four outdoor broadcast vans and a few mobile cameras were acquired to cover 22 events that were to take place at 18 different venues. Doordarshan personnel were sent to Patiala where Indian sportsmen were training, and to Germany to learn about television. And, crucially, political interference was reduced.

Shiv Sharma, who went on to become Doordarshan's Director-General in 1988, was put in charge of operational control of the Games and was actually asked what powers he would like. 'I thought about it,' recalled Sharma, when I met him, 'and when I was ready with an answer, Shankaran Nair, the Director-General of the Asian Games who was from the Research and Analysis Wing (RAW, the Indian intelligence service) told me in RAW's typically secretive fashion to go into his office and dictate it to his secretary so that no one else would know what I had asked for.'

Sharma requested a ban on meetings in the I&B Ministry. Given the history of government interference in Doordarshan, Sharma's request was, to say the least, audacious. 'My attitude was this,' claimed Sharma: 'guillotine us later if you like, but right now leave us alone.' To Sharma's surprise, his wish was granted.

In large measure, the new sense of professionalism derived from the fact that the management of the Games was not in the hands of timid bureaucrats. The venture was being supervised by Indira Gandhi's son, Rajiv. In 1981, following the death of her younger son and chief political ally, Sanjay, in a plane crash, Indira had persuaded Rajiv to enter politics. Rajiv, an Avro pilot with Indian Airlines, was disinclined to follow in his brother's footsteps and after his reluctant initiation had kept a low profile. The organisation of the Asiad was his first public undertaking, and helping him were his old schoolmates, mostly professionals from the marketing or advertising industry. The team's indisputable clout and non-political background ensured that things got done quickly in a place where the smallest decision was usually kicked upstairs. It also infused the whole enterprise with a childlike enthusiasm. Shailendra Shanker, then Doordarshan chief, remembered being woken up at 2 am once for a crisis meeting with Rajiv Gandhi. 'Everyone was in their pyjamas' he claimed, 'and everyone had their calculators: Rajiv insisted that the organisers carry one at all times so that we could come up with instant

calculations.'

To the enduring surprise of all, Doordarshan, the underrated, underprivileged, much-maligned television network rose magnificently to the occasion. Its job was twofold: to prepare a 45-minute clip for foreign consumption and to cover the Games for Indian viewers. The second was critical for another reason. Having grown fitfully, in bursts and starts, Doordarshan was little more than a conglomeration of regional stations at the turn of the decade. But for the purposes of transmitting the Asiad throughout the country, 20 Low Power Transmitters had been installed in state capitals, with signals to be beamed down via a Russian satellite.

So when the fateful moment arrived for the flame to be lit at Delhi's Jawaharlal Nehru Stadium, millions of Indians from all parts of the country were able to watch the spectacle. 'We got calls and telexes from even remote places like Itanagar and Imphal describing the euphoria, the cheers that went up when people there saw athletes from their region on their screens,' recounted Sharma, 'It seemed like television had suddenly cut short distances.' It had done more than that. It had demonstrated to those in power the unparalleled ability of television to rally people behind a national cause.

THE BIG LEAP

ON THE MORNING OF 31 OCTOBER 1984, Prime Minister Indira Gandhi left her home on 1, Safdarjung Road to meet with a foreign television crew that was waiting for an interview in the adjacent lawns. As she reached the white iron gate separating the properties, two security guards stationed there, whipped out their guns. Before she could react, they shot her at point blank range.

The bleeding woman was rushed to the All India Institute of Medical Sciences (AIIMS). Around 25 bullets had been pumped into her frail body and the doctors made valiant efforts to save her life. But they were fighting a losing battle. By noon, the news had spread like wildfire. Crowds collected around the hospital, weeping and shouting slogans.

The mood was ugly. The assassins were Sikhs, and as Mrs Gandhi lay lifeless in a room at the AIIMS, talk of a reprisal against their innocent brethren in the rest of the country was in the air. The communal balance, fragile at the best of times, was threatened. India appeared to be on the verge of collapse. The dominant personality of Mrs Gandhi had long provided a semblance of control over the fractious and problem-ridden nation. But after Indira, what?

While the country wrestled with panic, senior Congressmen had decided on a successor to Mrs Gandhi: her 40-year-old son, the former Indian Airlines pilot and political novice, Rajiv Gandhi. By evening, the official media, which had maintained a stern silence all day, made an announcement about the new prime minister's address to the nation. At night, frightened Indians huddled around their television sets. *Sunday,* one of India's leading newsmagazines, described the scene:

> *The image still flickers in the television screen of the mind. Indira Gandhi lies dead. Mobs have attacked President Zail Singh's car. India hovers on the brink of chaos. Nobody is sure if the centre can hold.*
>
> *Then, late in the evening, the new prime minister addresses the people. His face, numbed by the shock of the last few hours, is taut but composed. His voice is deadpan but strangely assured.*
>
> *Indira Gandhi, India's prime minister, has been assassinated, he begins. 'She was mother not just to me, but to us all ... '*
>
> *Suddenly the dark seems to hold fewer terrors. Between the terrible uncertainty of the present and the hope of a stable future, is still the abyss. But now, that chasm appears less deep. The jump seems easier to make. Perhaps the nightmare will end soon. Things are getting better.*

In the days following the assassination, fears of an anti-Sikh backlash turned out to be justified. Reports of rioting filtered in from Madhya Pradesh, Uttar Pradesh, Bihar and Haryana. The worst hit was Delhi where armed thugs took over the streets, burning, looting and lynching thousands of innocent Sikhs. For three days madness gripped north India and then on 3 November, came the funeral of Mrs Gandhi.

Dignitaries had flown in from abroad, prominent Indians including film stars and other celebrities had congregated in Delhi, and crowds of admirers had made their way to the banks of the Yamuna where arrangements for a public cremation had been made. No soap could have competed with the real-life drama that was unfolding on television screens across the country that afternoon.

The scene was cathartic: flames licking the flower-bedecked body of the late prime minister, the sea of mourners in white, the sharp bursts of bugles mixing with the sad chanting of priests. There were some glitches, some moments of awkwardness, when Maneka, Indira's estranged daughter-in-law, dragged her son away from the pyre or when Congressmen fought among themselves to make gestures of obeisance to the body of their departed leader.

But for the large part, the mood was sombre and the nation's eyes were riveted on the late prime minister's family. There was Sonia, the grieving *bahu* who had held the bloodied body of her mother-in-law in her arms on the drive to the hospital; there was the granddaughter Priyanka affectionately wiping her mother's tears; grandson Rahul, still a child but restrained amidst the thousands of spectators. And at the centre of it all, was the son and heir: Rajiv.

The cameras did not leave his face for more than a few moments, capturing every fleeting expression. By turn pensive and solemn, the new prime minister conducted himself with rare dignity and poise. By his own admission, he was not a man given to public displays of emotion. But there was more on his mind than a personal loss. Four weeks later he was due to lead his mother's party to the polls.

A month later, I travelled to Gwalior, a former princely town in the state of Madhya Pradesh. Election fever was at its height and the whole town was festooned with buntings and banners proclaiming the merits of competing candidates. Elections in India's small towns and villages are always a lively affair but in this particular case the battle was not merely political.

In 1971, the government had abolished the privileges enjoyed by India's former princely rulers wiping out, in one fell swoop, the line dividing the ruler and the ruled. In the eyes of the people, nonetheless, the distinction remained. Some members of the royalty had attempted to legitimise their dominance through politics. Vijaya Raje Scindia, widow of the Maharaja of Gwalior, was one of them.

In the 1960s she had thrown her lot in with the Hindu revivalist party, the Jana Sangh, and was the party's candidate for the 1967 parliamentary elections from the Gwalior constituency. Her son and incumbent to the abolished throne of Gwalior, Madhavrao Scindia, had helped her campaign and himself contested on a Jana Sangh ticket from the neighbouring constituency of Guna. In 1979, however, he had changed his allegiance to the Congress thereby sowing the seeds of a family feud that was to continue unresolved for years to come.

At the time of the 1984 polls, Vijaya Raje Scindia had voluntarily relinquished her candidacy to support Atal

Bihari Vajpayee, former cabinet minister and president of the Jana Sangh's new avatar, the Bharatiya Janata Party (BJP). Ordinarily, Vajpayee's eminence and Vijaya Raje's backing would have been enough to ensure his victory. But this time the scales were equally weighted. Madhavrao, the young Oxford-educated scion of the royal family, had decided to contest the election from Gwalior. Given the circumstances, it was clear that this was to be no ordinary election but a true Hindi film-style confrontation between mother and son.

According to a local reporter I met when I arrived, the entire town was divided into enemy camps. I thought his claim was a trifle exaggerated till I sat in my hotel lobby leafing through a tourist brochure. One of the sights recommended by the brochure was the museum in the Jai Vilas Palace, which had, among other attractions, a model train used to carry post-dinner cigars and brandy around a dining table. It did not strike me as much of a draw, but the Jai Vilas Palace was virtually next door so I asked the receptionist if it would still be open. 'Closed madam' she said giving me an odd smile. 'Tomorrow?' I asked. 'Closed madam, everyday closed.'

I made some enquiries and discovered that due to the dispute between mother and son most of the royal family's treasures had been curtained off from public view. The hotel I was staying in, part of a palace that had been taken over by a hotel chain, was apparently another bone of contention.

I went up to my room, a huge chilly affair with massive four poster beds, and asked for a number. 'The palace madam?' the operator inquired. I asked for another number and again she appeared to know exactly who

I was calling. I replaced the receiver feeling increasingly like a fly trapped in a web of palace intrigue.

The next morning, I joined a team of reporters accompanying Atal Bihari Vajpayee on his campaign tour. Vajpayee, former external affairs minister in the Janata government, was among the most respected and well-liked figures in Parliament. Short, dark and unassuming, he was the rare exception that combined a talent for diplomacy with the ability to rouse crowds with his fiery speeches.

His election was a matter of prestige for local BJP workers who had gone to great lengths to organise a public meeting. The meeting was in a clearing between two villages where a *gadda* (mattress) had been laid out for the distinguished visitor. Curious villagers gathered in a loose circle to watch.

Vajpayee, hampered by a leg injury, took time to get started. But once he had been made comfortable, leg propped up before him, the famed orator launched into a stinging diatribe against the government, the likes of which had made him one of the most popular speakers in the aftermath of the Emergency.

The speech was vintage Vajpayee: raised arm, barely restrained fury, lisping delivery. The venue might have been an undistinguished village clearing but the BJP president spoke in the tones of an infuriated statesman addressing the United Nations. He spoke of Kashmir in the distant north where the Indira-led government had propped up a puppet regime; of Andhra Pradesh in the distant south where the centre had dismissed a democratically elected chief minister. He talked of authoritarianism, of nepotism and of a threat to the country's sovereignty.

The assembled villagers looked bewildered. An old man by my side turned to me with a beseeching expression and asked: 'Will this man bring television to our village?'

The day after, I hopped on to one of the many of cars transporting Madhavrao Scindia's impressive campaign machinery to the villages abutting the town. Smart, urbane and alert, Scindia presented a total contrast to his jaded opponent. He was, in fact, the ideal representative of the new-look Parliament that Rajiv Gandhi was hoping to put in place ('I want to attract a new breed of persons to politics,' he had told the British paper *The Sunday Times,* 'intelligent, westernised young men with non-feudal, non-criminal ideas who want to make India prosper rather than merely themselves'). Though surrounded by flunkies, Scindia displayed a disarming lack of hauteur. And as he talked with earnest authority about matters such as power shortages, bad roads and drinking water he came across as some sort of efficient mid-level manager rather than a king.

My perception changed however, as the cavalcade halted abruptly on the highway amid two open and empty fields. By the time the dust storm raised by the cars had receded, we were surrounded by people. Bent old men, women shielding their faces with grimy saris, sturdy farmers and children streamed out of nowhere, blowing bugles, carrying *diyas* and throwing flower petals in the air. The crowds gathered to stare, mesmerised by the royal presence among them. Scindia talked simply and humbly about the problems of his constituency; of the progress he had brought to Guna, and the progress he promised to bring to Gwalior. But each fresh offering of vermilion and garlands seemed to elevate him, to lift him to some indistinct point above the heads of common men, to a destiny prefixed and decided by the gods. I asked a young bystander who he was likely to vote for. 'I live on the land given by his father,' he said pointing at the young maharajah, 'how can I vote for anyone else?'

I returned to Bombay, as to reality; the bustling modern metropolis of offices, trains and factories was a far cry from the land of kings, castles and courtiers. I wrote a story predicting Scindia's victory, convinced that I had witnessed a vestige of India's feudal past, an aberration in an otherwise functioning democracy.

I was right about the result but wrong about everything else.

Over three decades of self-rule and the adoption of modern, democratic systems had not succeeded in stamping out feudalism. As the results of the Eighth Parliamentary election poured in, it seemed evident that the awe-struck farmer in Gwalior was no different from his counterpart in Banda, the fisherwoman in Cochin or, for that matter, even the businessman in Bombay.

The logic that stipulated that the sons of kings inherit the earth, echoed from all parts of India as Rajiv Gandhi, son of Indira, grandson of Nehru, led his party to power with a stunning majority. The Congress had merely selected a leader. The country had legitimately crowned its prince.

Ascension does not guarantee survival, however. At least it did not seem to in the India of 1985 with memories of political instability following the Emergency still fresh. The pitfalls were many: a hostile Opposition, a sceptical press, an electorate quick to cynicism as to hope, and opponents within the Congress party itself; any of these could conspire to bring about his downfall.

And Rajiv Gandhi, despite his resounding victory which he consolidated by immediately passing the anti-defection law making it difficult for members of parliament to defect, was far from invincible.

For one, his agenda which included liberalising the 25 economy, reducing poverty, curbing population growth, spreading literacy, ending corruption, protecting the environment, putting the brakes on secessionism, and, above all, ushering in a technological revolution that would prepare India for a glorious future in the 21st century seemed hopelessly utopian.

No leader in the past had succeeded in solving India's gargantuan problems. And there was even less reason to believe that Rajiv could do so. For one, apart from his illustrious ancestry he had no claim· to leadership. For 36 years he had lived the life of an average upper middle class Indian, and in the last four years, following his reluctant entry into politics, he had shown little understanding of the complex issues confronting modern India: he had once called the fanatical Bhindranwale a 'religious' leader and contradictorily labelled the more moderate Sikh faction 'secessionists'.

The actions he or his close buddies had been associated with had been either blatantly undemocratic, such as the engineering of a coup in Kashmir, or flamboyant and expensive, like the Asiad. Given his past cloistered life, there was no reason to believe that he understood conditions in non-urban India either. Nor did he surround himself with people who did. His arrogance within the Congress party had bred disaffection and a full one-third of his MPs were new faces, 88 of whom, in the words of one legislator 'had never seen the inside of a *panchayat'*. Rajiv Gandhi's initiatives reflected, as the country's prominent fortnightly *India Today* wrote in November 1984: 'the aspirations of an urban post-independence generation and its perceptions of how India should catch up with the rest of the world.'

Such a myopic vision—in a country wedded to socialism and inherently suspicious of technology and the West, talk of instant revolution could only be described as shortsighted—was bound to provoke a wave of protest. Except that Rajiv had a powerful weapon on his side: he had television.

Admittedly, Rajiv was not the first prime minister to have the mass media at his disposal. Indira, in fact had made unabashed use of television for government propaganda, a strategy that did not prevent its debacle in 1977. But by the time her son came to power much had changed.

Following the Asiad in 1982, television expansion had zoomed up the list of government priorities. Partly, the reasons were technical. The Low Power Transmitters commissioned during the Games had proved to be a cheaper and more feasible alternative to the capital-intensive High Power Transmitters used till then. This, coupled with the successful launch, in October 1983, of the Indian satellite INSAT 1B opened up a range of options. A Special Expansion Plan was put into motion on 1 July 1984. It heralded a growth that was unparalleled in the world. For nearly four months a transmitter was installed every day. By 1988 there were 220 transmitters in the country up from only 19 in 1981, and 62 per cent of the population was covered by television. 'It was the greatest explosion in the history of communication,' exulted S. S. Gill, a former secretary in the Ministry of Information and Broadcasting.

Sixty million people watched Rajiv's maiden appearance as prime minister on television. By 1986 the number had doubled. The total number of viewers still constituted just a tenth of the population. But it was a crucial segment. It consisted of businessmen, politicians, bureaucrats, journalists and readers of newspapers—people whose views, between elections at least, constituted critical feedback for any government. And this was the constituency Rajiv and his image builders, mostly an informal bunch of friends and handpicked members of his staff, set out to woo.

And if they were more successful than Mrs Gandhi had been, it was because they, unlike her, understood television.

In Indira Gandhi's time, coverage of the prime minister was dull and predictable: usually silent footage of her visit to a city or a village with a monotonous voiceover. The only times she actually spoke on television was when she addressed the nation or when Doordarshan televised her speech at some gathering. Consequently, she never came across as a real flesh-and-blood person on TV.

But in the more marketing-savvy times that her son assumed power, the old approach was discarded. The first thing his advisors realised was that television was, in Marshal McLuhan's term, a 'cool' medium: it did not lend itself to blatant propaganda. It needed a subtler, more visually oriented approach: a soft sell.

Accordingly, heavy-handed, non-visual mentions of the prime minister in news broadcasts were reduced and replaced by visuals that just showed him in action without singing his praises. Central to the success of this strategy was Rajiv's own personality. He was young, charismatic and spoke *to* the people rather than at them as his mother used to do. He was in the words of an admiring newspaper editor, Vinod Mehta: 'a TV natural'.

Rajiv's emergence as a TV natural was not accidental. His image builders realised early on that every time he read an address out to the nation on television, he came across as stiff and wooden. So he stopped reading. If he did speak, it was extempore, and therefore, more natural. Then his staff discovered that while he was not a good orator, he was best in conversational situations where he could respond to questions. So such situations were televised: his meeting with children, his lunches at press clubs in Washington and Delhi and the like.

His foreign visits, where he impressed hosts and the media with his charm and easy manner, were awarded saturation coverage to score brownie points with the home audience. And special care was taken in the presentation of Rajiv's visits to the backward areas of the country. In 1985, the prime minister visited places such as Rajasthan and Silent Valley in Kerala to get a first-hand account of the problems faced by the underprivileged. In each case, eight hours of film was whittled down to create a half-hour programme that showed Rajiv chatting with local people, sympathising with their problems and pulling up errant government officials. The films were edited, not by ham-fisted hacks at Doordarshan but by the minister's own secretariat. The unprecedented sight of a prime minister castigating his own officers combined with the scenic locations of his visits made these programmes primetime stuff.

Though the clever packaging and his own considerable charm made Doordarshan's obsession with the prime minister more diverting than it had been in Indira's days, it did not do much for the credibility of the medium. To counter the potential harm, cosmetic changes were made on television. A current news programme went on air for the first time, and in *Janvani,* the public was actually allowed to confront cabinet ministers. The prime minister also wrote a letter to his Information and Broadcasting minister that was cleverly leaked to the press. In the letter he complained that the news on TV read like handouts and too much time was spent on building up the image of the prime minister and his cabinet.

The elaborate exercise worked wonders. Twelve months into his term, the habitually cynical press was full of praise for the prime minister. Traditional Congress baiters such as Arun Shourie and M. J. Akbar had changed their tune (the latter ended up joining the party). The anti-Indira paper, *Indian Express* was eulogistic. Even the Opposition was charmed. 'Rajiv Gandhi comes across as a sincere and interested person who is keen to shed the confrontationist attitude of his mother,' claimed BJP's L. K. Advani. The man who, till a year ago, had been perceived, at best, as a nice guy who had entered politics to help 'mummy' was suddenly being described in embarrassingly laudatory terms: Mr Clean, A great conciliator, Inspiring leader, Twenty-first century visionary, brave, dynamic, self-assured....

Potential points of criticism too were cleverly deflected. Rajiv's privileged background, for instance, was projected as a plus point in that it enabled him to hobnob with foreign dignitaries on an equal footing and also made him a man of technological vision, someone with a 21st-century perspective; visuals of Sonia, his Roman Catholic wife, in Indian attire, demurely accompanying her husband on his tours around the country helped to give her the aura of a traditional *Bharatiya nari*. And many of Rajiv's measures, including a pathbreaking pro-rich budget, did not attract the flak they would have in the absence of an effective public relations policy.

Dangerously though, it also encouraged people to believe everything Rajiv did would work. By substituting style for substance, Rajiv's marketing strategy invited opinion makers to suspend disbelief and ignore the fine print.

A perfect example was the Assam Accord. For six years, the people of the Northeastern state of Assam led by a group of determined students, the All Assam Students Union, had been agitating against the growing infiltration of migrants from neighbouring Bangladesh. The impasse between the centre and the state had crippled the state machinery and led to several deaths.

Rajiv's move to reconcile with agitating leaders was justifiably hailed. But in his haste to reach an agreement that he could flourish before the nation on Independence Day, 15 August 1985, several ambiguities were retained in the wording of the agreement. The Accord proved ineffectual in dealing with the actual problem of illegal settlers and paved the way for the rise of a violent terrorist outfit, the United Liberation Front of Assam (ULFA).

By 1989, towards the end of Rajiv's tenure, it was clear that the 21st century was still a distant dream. Poverty had not been eradicated. More than half the population could not read or write. Terrorism raged in Punjab and Assam. In Kashmir, conditions had worsened.

The government's clever tactics with regard to television no longer worked. The news continued to read like handouts, giving the lie to Rajiv's purported desire for objectivity on television. And Doordarshan's obsession with the prime minister had finally led to overkill: one TV critic effectively described the public reaction by repeating two words in an entire review: 'Rajiv Gandhi'.

Power brokers still ruled the roost in the capital and elsewhere. The government that had prided itself on its conciliatory approach ended up laying the seeds of a communal confrontation that was to plague the country in the decade to come. And finally, Mr Clean himself, was voted out by the people following allegations of corruption. Things hadn't really got better. But for some time out there, they sure looked like they had.

THE MIDDLE CLASS STRIKES BACK

IN THE EARLY 1980s, THE most popular character on Indian television was a feisty young housewife called Rajni. Draped in the traditional sari, hair pulled back and a *bindi* on her forehead, Rajni could have passed off for the woman next door. In reality, far from being the demure, fatalistic stereotype of Indian womanhood, Rajni was a gutsy no-nonsense lady. Her problems were common, everyday obstacles faced by thousands of ordinary middle-class Indians. The difference was that she refused to be cowed down by them. Errant taxi drivers, corrupt civic officials, deceiving astrologers were all straightened out with a dose of her whiplash tongue. The fault, her conquering zeal seemed to suggest, was not in the stars but in ourselves. And Rajni was certainly no underling.

The Sunday morning serialisation of her exploits provoked a storm of indignation. Taxi drivers went off the roads in response to their negative portrayal in one of the episodes while TV critics condemned the quick-fix solutions provided to every problem as being typically 'escapist'. Television viewers, however, loved her. Ratings rose rapidly and Godrej, the company that was sponsoring the show registered a noticeable increase in sales. And so completely had she captured the popular imagination that in March 1986, when *Imprint,* a monthly features magazine decided to run a cover story on the Indian middle class, it put a Rajni look-alike aiming a red gloved punch at the camera on its cover. The article, titled 'The Middle Class Strikes Back' a forerunner of many to come also identified the key to Rajni's spectacular success: 'The show is successful,' the magazine claimed, 'because it embodies a rising middle class consciousness and the belief that it is possible to fight back now.'

Clearly, Rajni's appeal was that of a warmonger. Her audience was the middle class. (Market researchers would describe the middle-class person as someone earning between ₹12,000 and ₹60,000 per annum. But the term also had a more generic meaning that could take into its sweep both mill worker and industrialist: substantially anyone who was urban, literate and had an income above ₹12,000 a year. In the 1960s less than 20 million fell into this category, a miniscule segment of the population.) If Rajni's invitation to battle evinced such a strong response from this category of people more privileged than the country's starving millions it was because the perceived injustice among this class was equally great.

The rise of Indian nationalism which culminated in independence in 1947 was essentially a late 19th and early 20th-century phenomenon. It was around this time that a new class had begun to emerge in the cities. This class, characterised by its preference for western manners and education, sent many of its members abroad to study.

In the British universities to which most of them went, these young Indians were exposed to western liberal ideas which included concepts of political equality and liberty. Infused with the ideals of the free world, they returned home and flung themselves into the freedom movement against the British.

When independence was finally won, the country's leadership consisted primarily of lawyers, journalists, scholars and other members of the urban middle class. Even B. R. Ambedkar, the undisputed leader of the country's lower castes was to be shown later, in images and statues, dressed in a suit and holding books, both symbols of upward mobility.

Three decades later, however, the class that had been at the forefront of the country's freedom struggle was barely represented in parliament. The reason was simple: in its zeal to implement western liberal ideas, the urban elite had introduced the means of its own demise—universal franchise.

With a majority of the people living in villages, the middle-class politician had been quickly replaced by another kind of political animal—generally a less educated, rural personage. Traditional factors such as caste and community had assumed significance in elections and the more sophisticated city dweller found himself unable to compete. A right-wing party, the Swatantra Party, floated by some Congressmen, failed to win support. Others, like Jayaprakash Narayan, left politics to devote themselves to social work.

Added to the fact of political marginalisation was a sense of neglect. To a large extent this had to do with the emergence of Indira Gandhi as prime minister in 1966. Between 1969 and 1973 Mrs Gandhi had enacted a series of radical legislations aimed at freeing herself from the power lords in her party and winning support directly from the masses. The measures included the nationalisation of banks, general insurance and coal companies, and the enactment of the Monopolies and Restrictive Trade Practices Act (MRTP) which sought to curtail the activities of large industrial houses. These patently left-wing measures coupled with populist slogans such as 'remove poverty', 'free bonded labour', 'abolish rural debt' transformed Mrs Gandhi into a messiah of the poor and downtrodden and deepened the middle class's sense of isolation.

In actual fact, the urban elite had little to gripe about. The middle class, by virtue of its education, still firmly controlled the bureaucracy and the press—powerful institutions in democratic India. Politics may have become the preserve of peasant leaders but the coterie of unofficial advisors surrounding the prime minister was unmistakably middle class. The education system was geared towards producing lawyers and doctors rather than low skilled workers, and conditions in the country's towns and cities were infinitely better than in its villages. Crucially, Mrs Gandhi's populism turned out to be skin deep. Many of her laws, particularly those pertaining to big business, could be subverted by bribery, and thanks to the discouragement to competition provided by the Monopolies and Restrictive Trade Practices Act, big industrial houses ended up with a monopoly themselves.

In politics however, appearances matter. And the urban elite truly believed it had much to complain about. The one category that did seem to have legitimate grounds for complaint was perhaps the salaried middle class. The rate of direct taxation in India was unbelievably high: in 1970, Mrs Gandhi's government had pushed the highest marginal income tax rates to a penal 97.5 per cent and wealth tax rates to a minimum 5 per cent. While businessmen and employed professionals who filed their own returns could and often did evade tax authorities by doctoring their accounts (in 1985, the amount of black money, i.e., undisclosed income, was estimated to be as high as 18–21 per cent of the economy), the salaried class of teachers, company officials, government servants and others who had to pay taxes in full at source, were in a tight financial corner. The limited number of jobs further added to their frustration.

The middle classes the world over are distinguished by an all-consuming desire to better their lot. In India during the 1970s, the Indian middle class had reason to believe that it was deprived of its very *raison d'etre*. In just a few years, however, signs of change were evident.

In the November of 1982, at the time of the Asiad, I was in Delhi. Television broadcasts had gone colour a few months earlier and watching the Games on a colour set was considered a privilege almost equal to watching the event live. I got my first glimpse of colour TV at the home of a family friend in Karol Bagh. My host, a development officer with the Life Insurance Corporation, lived in some style. In addition to the colour television, he had a video cassette recorder, wall to wall carpeting, air conditioners and two cars. Some weeks ago, he had also invested in a second flat. The gains had not come from his public sector job but from a side business in jewellery export.

There seemed to be many like him all of a sudden. Several with far more successful stories to tell. A teenager who ran away from home to start a television and home appliance business; an adman who left the country's largest advertising firm to set up his own thriving agency; an executive in a fabric company who ended up owning a ₹75 million garment manufacturing concern. All these men, and a fair share of women, had certain characteristics in common: a good idea, enterprise and marketing flair; they also happened to be beneficiaries of the government's policy of encouraging small-scale entrepreneurs.

By the early 1980s the Centre's attitude towards business, even big business houses had undergone a significant change, for the Indira who came to power in 1980 after the collapse of the Janata Party government was a vastly different entity from the radical demagogue of the previous decade. Economic compulsion had aided in the transformation.

The country at the time was reeling from the combined effects of a disastrous harvest and the second oil shock. Grain stocks and foreign exchange reserves were fast depleting. Mrs Gandhi responded by going to the International Monetary Fund for a loan of ₹500 million, the largest in the country's history. And under the tutelage of the IMF, the government moved cautiously rightwards. Controls on industry and trade were relaxed.

Companies were allowed to expand production capacities and import duties on a range of goods including consumer items such as television sets and video cassette recorders were slashed. Populism had given way to pragmatism. The middle class was beginning to feel at home. Almost. Given Mrs Gandhi's characteristic inconsistency on economic issues no one was willing to bet on the long term.

The guarantee came suddenly and unexpectedly with the emergence of Rajiv Gandhi on the political scene.

Notwithstanding her apparent dominance, Mrs Gandhi had been extremely vulnerable to pressure from her sons. In the mid-1970s she had gone along with Sanjay's authoritarian programme of forced sterilisations and demolition drives. And in the early 1980s many of her right-wing initiatives such as the reduction of customs and excise on electronic items and upgrading the telecommunications system were a result of Rajiv's prodding.

With his election as prime minister, the middle class had reason to believe that the balance would shift more firmly in its favour. And it was right. In its very first budget, the Rajiv government announced a set of concessions for industry, pushed the growth of consumer goods and reduced the rates of personal taxation leaving the salaried class with spare cash to spend on the luxuries now entering the market.

But Rajiv did more than just open up the economy. For a nation weaned on the ideals of abstinence, denial and self-reliance preached by Mahatma Gandhi, Rajiv brought another kind of liberation. A liberation from guilt. Rajiv, the nice family man who flew planes and took photographs on holidays or Rajiv, the average guy who had flunked his degree at Cambridge and had listened to the Beatles in the 1960s, was a far cry from his predecessors. The men he surrounded himself with: corporate types in safari suits and jeans were also nothing like the *paan*-chewing, khadi-clad political stereotype.

In the changed political climate, the middle-class man could breathe easy. The years of camouflage and shame seemed to roll away. No more did he need to hide his materialistic aspirations. Not when the prime minister with his Dior sunglasses, Lacoste t-shirts and Gucci loafers himself seemed to say: it was okay to want, to covet, to have. The change was not just symbolic. Television was actively and aggressively driving the message home.

For three decades following independence, consumer products manufacturers had few ways of advertising their wares. The low literacy rate restricted the reach of the print medium. Radio had a limited non-visual appeal. And the scattered ownership of theatres and inconsistent projection facilities made cinema a highly unsatisfactory option. Doordarshan had aired its first commercial in 1976 but its miniscule viewership and dreary in-house programming attracted limited advertising.

Then, in 1982, Doordarshan amended its rules and invited advertisers to sponsor shows generated from private producers. The policy transformed the nature of programming on the national network and brought in a flood of advertising. In one stroke, the network boosted its earnings—from ₹112 million in 1981–82 to ₹933 million in 1986–87. Within this period Dooradarshan raised its rates many times and each time advertisers happily coughed up the enhanced prices. With reason, for sales of television sets were booming and by the late 1980s, advertisers had access to a whopping 17 million homes, resulting in a sharp increase in sales and spawning stories of startling success.

Karsan Patel, a chemist in a Gujarat-based government laboratory, for instance, had chucked up his job to manufacture a cheap detergent powder in a 12-square-foot shed in the 1970s. Initially, the going was tough. Over 90 per cent of Indian housewives used laundry bars to wash clothes and even Hindustan Lever Limited, manufacturers of Surf, the country's top-selling detergent, were content with a 5 per cent annual growth rate which came mainly from upper income households. Patel had to peddle his wonder powder, which he named Nirma, door to door on a bicycle. In the early 1980s, he got on to television with an ear-piercing jingle and sponsorship of the Sunday feature film. A few years later, half the country's housewives had switched from soap to detergent.

In 1984, Food Specialities Ltd, a subsidiary of the Swiss multinational, Nestlé, introduced Maggi 2-minute noodles in India. Given the miserable failure of packaged foods in the past the prospects for the new snack food were dim. Nevertheless, FSL's marketing team developed ads that countered the average Indian housewife's perception of convenience foods as an abnegation of duty by showing children actually *asking* their mother for Maggi. In July 1984, FSL began to sponsor *Hum Log,* Indian television's first soap on the travails of a middle-class family. The consumption of Maggi noodles jumped from 2,600 tonnes in 1984 to 5,000 tonnes over the next two years. And a host of imitators followed in its wake.

Though phenomenal, these were by no means isolated cases. 'With the commercialisation of television, billings rose overnight. Tons of cosmetics, detergents and toilet soaps were being sold without any additional effort,' claimed Srinivasan Raghavan of the market research agency, Mode. The connection between television advertising and consumer behaviour was not merely conjectural. In a nationwide survey conducted by the Operations Research Group in 1987, 53 per cent of the respondents said that they had purchased commercial products after seeing them advertised on television. Seventy-six per cent also claimed to be in favour of television advertising.

The approval was not restricted to the more prosperous classes. In 1989, in a Maharashtrian tribal village of dire poverty, where the only spot of colour was provided by yellow butterflies glancing off a pile of human faeces and the most expensive possession was a single battered transistor, I found villagers wistfully longing for television as a means of 'opening up the world for the children' and for the information it would provide on 'methods of farming, the right medicines for a headache, the best slippers and calendars to buy.'

The effects of television-led consumerism were clearly visible. Earlier, a mere handful of brands dominated the market. Lux toilet soap, Postman cooking oil, Tata Hair oil, Halo shampoo were the names consumers were familiar with and asked for at grocery shops. By the late 1980s, thanks to television, the market was deluged with brand names. The years between 1985 and 1990 experienced the biggest growth: brands of packaged tea increased from 31 to 80, shampoo from 23 to 53 and detergent powder from 26 to 44. A survey in 1990 found 34 hair oils being advertised on Doordarshan including both well-known names and small time, regional brands.

The dropout rate was equally high. Nine brands of shaving blades were introduced in 1985. By 1989, a total of 11 had dropped out of the race. In the talcum powder segment, a new brand was launched every month in 1991 even though the market was not large enough to sustain the growth. The message seemed clear: with television assuring access to the consumer, the manufacturer could afford to try new ways of attracting him or her rather than concentrating all resources on building up one brand alone.

The boom was most marked in the area of consumable products. But consumer durables were moving fast as well. The most coveted item of course was the television set. Between 1984 and 1990 the number of television sets owned rose from 3.6 million to 27.8 million. In 1988, five TV sets were said to be sold every minute and as many as 30 television brands were jostling for the buyer's attention. As far as these more expensive buys were concerned, television advertising was not the only driving factor. In response to the upsurge of demand for consumer goods, a variety of buy-now-pay-later schemes had come into operation.

The prominent players in this area were the banks. For foreign banks, hampered by government restrictions on expansion in India, consumer finance was a major growth sector. Citibank, the most aggressive of them all, set up a product development group and put a range of specific and all-purpose loans on offer. 'We are repositioning ourselves to meet rising consumer expectations,' claimed Citibank Vice President, Suren Khirwadkar.

Even nationalised banks, which had earlier focused on small scale entrepreneurs and the rural sector, jumped on to the bandwagon. The country's largest bank, the State Bank of India disbursed ₹400 million in less than two years (1988–89) for the purchase of TV sets, VCRs, washing machines, refrigerators, vehicles, sofa sets and so on. Thousands availed of 'Scoom', the bank's financing scheme for two-wheelers and 'travelcash' for holidays. 'The approach of nationalised banks was conservative earlier because funds were needed for growth,' explained Ramesh Khanduri, a State Bank officer, 'but now consumer banking is here to stay like any grocery shop.'

The neighbourhood grocery shop, in fact, had always traded on a monthly settlement to draw customers. But in the new environment its big brother, the department store was also offering attractive instalment schemes. The low rate of security required ensured wide usage; even a pavement dweller like Kalidas Mukherjee who earned a meagre living pulling a handcart through Bombay's busy streets had managed to acquire a black and white television set from one of the city's most popular department stores, Apna Bazar.

The spending spree was clearly reflected in changing urban lifestyles as well. Thousands of restaurants, health clubs, boutiques and fast food parlours sprang up in Indian cities. Department stores proliferated. Existing stores went upmarket with renovated interiors and higher prices. Sheetal, an ordinary garments shop in one of Bombay's most congested lanes, relaunched itself as an exclusive wear boutique with a new granite and marble look, a spiffy advertising campaign and an in-house team of designers. 'The new rich has spending power, if it wants to move upwards it needs classy clothes,' explained Sheetal's proprietor, Dhiren Shah.

The change percolated quickly to small towns. In Aurangabad, a town in the most backward part of Maharashtra, three five-star hotels, 10 new restaurants, 50 ice cream parlours, and innumerable fast food joints sprang up between 1985 and 1989. Vikram Naik is a former hotel executive and owner of Food Runner's Fast Food Centre, a well-lit, crowded eatery in the town , was one of the catalysts. 'It was too expensive for me too start anything in Bombay,' he claimed, 'so I thought I would come to an upcoming city and give it a taste of the new life.'

The most conspicuous evidence of change was perhaps the new architecture. All over the country, on the outskirts of cities, plain houses were giving way to a series of garish, heavily embellished concrete structures that the architect-writer Gautam Bhatia sarcastically categorised as Punjabi Baroque, Bania Byzantine and Marwari Modernism. In Bangalore a PVC pipe manufacturer had plastered the walls of his two-storey house with wallpaper on both sides. Cement baron M. S. Ramaiah took such elaborate pains over his mansion, filling it with stuffed tigers, wall-to-wall mirrors and curving staircases, that it had become a signpost for the entire neighbourhood.

For the less prosperous, but socially mobile middle class, a significant aspect of the new life was travel. In 1980, 1,017,000 Indians travelled abroad. By 1988, the number had more than doubled. The growth in internal traffic was even more dramatic. 'Colour films with their lush locales tempted people to travel in the old days,' reminisced Raja Patil, one of Bombay's oldest tour operators, 'with television, the temptation has become a daily affair.'

The price tag for the new life took its toll on the family nest egg; in *Probe* magazine, prominent economist V. A. Pai Panandikar estimated that the savings rate had declined from 24 to 22 per cent thanks to increased consumption. But though a large part of the bill was being footed through reserves and the new payment postponing schemes (credit cards, virtually unknown earlier, were now in common usage), Indians had woken up to a hitherto unexplored source of finance: the stock exchange.

In the old days Indians put their savings into gold. The nationalisation of banks changed attitudes only marginally; most people, particularly in villages, continued to view modern methods of investment with suspicion. By the mid-1980s a growing number of people were beginning to invest in stocks and shares. Buoyed by the trend, companies began to make rapid expansion plans and sought funding from the market in new innovative ways. Reliance Textiles Chairman, Dhirubhai Ambani, the first business magnate to exploit the potential of the Indian stock market, for instance, hired vans fitted with video recorders to disseminate advertisements of his public issues in crowded city areas and the rural hinterland. Public response justified expectations. One hundred and two companies floated new issues between April and October 1989 raising ₹35.61 billion (eight times the amount raised in new issues over the same period in the preceding year). And by the end of the decade, over 12 million Indians owned shares either directly or through funds.

The transformation was fuelled by the new acquisitive quality that was sweeping the country. I met Vinod Bhimani in a queue submitting an application form for a share in one of the new issues floated during the boom period of 1989. Till a few years ago, the 40-year-old bank officer maintained he had neither the 'knowledge nor the savings to invest in shares'. But five years before, after he was moved to a branch near the stock exchange he began to discuss stocks with friends on his daily train ride to work and was enthused enough to put a sum that amounted to eight times his monthly income into shares. 'The reason I was able to save so much is because my wife heard that you can make a lot of money from shares. She offered to save by cutting down on household expenses,' he explained.

As the decade of frenetic change was drawing to an end, every publication in the country and many abroad had taken note of the phenomenon. *Time* magazine wrote a cover story on the Indian Consumer Boomers in November 1989; *Probe* magazine quoted a New York consultancy firm's report on the Affluent Indian; economist Surjit Bhalla wrote in *Sunday,* 'After a comparitively slow process the incomes of the rich have suddenly reached credible international standards.' The big story of the decade was not famine, not poverty, not floods or political upheaval but money. And holding centre-stage, for once, was the class that publications estimated to have grown to somewhere between 100 and 200 million of brash, hustling, thriving spenders.

'Political power is closely related to size,' claimed economic commentator, Dr Jay Dubashi, 'a class that is small is diffident and survives by making adjustments with other groups.' This was no longer true of the Indian middle class. Rajni's people had come into their own. The boxing gloves were on. They were ready for battle.

A significant fallout of the phenomenon was the arrival of a new culture.

In the late 1970s, Shashi Kapoor, a popular Hindi film actor and his actress wife, Jennifer had set up a theatre in memory of Shashi's late father, Prithviraj, a stage and screen thespian. The theatre, a beautifully designed 200-seater, with special arrangements for lighting, panels and props, was established with the avowed purpose of encouraging professional theatre in Bombay. In a city where even the more successful language theatre was essentially an amateur activity, this was no mean ambition. Nevertheless, the low hiring charges and encouraging attitude of the management offered some incentive and in November 1978, Prithvi bravely came into being.

I remember going there, probably days after it had opened, to see a production of *Antigone*. The players, rank amateurs, gave a riveting performance and I took to going there often, sometimes for plays, sometimes for a meal—the adjoining kitchen run by a successful and eccentric photographer and his mother served a delectable crab curry and Irish coffee—and sometimes just to soak in the ambience of the picturesque open air cafe. It was the perfect place to hang out. The tea, served ethnic style in clay cups, was sweet and cheap. The stone seats were mildly uncomfortable but nobody cared how long you sat. And there was a lot going on.

Juhu, the beachfront suburb where the theatre was located, was Bombay's equivalent of Beverly Hills. There, along wide avenues cooled by the gentle sea breeze and sheltered by fortress-high walls lived the country's top film stars. A few kilometres northwards were the studios where over a hundred films were shot every year. This, in short, was the hub, the lodestar for millions of star-struck Indians. Tourists roamed the area hoping for a glimpse of Amitabh Bachchan or Hema Malini and hundreds of fresh-faced teenagers arrived daily from hick towns thirsting for cinematic fame. Most went away disappointed. But the rare stroke of luck kept the dream machine churning and the crowds continued to come.

Over the last few years, the traditional rustic sucker willing to stake his face or his fortune on the silver screen was joined by a different breed of hopefuls. These were actors from the Delhi-based National School of Drama and graduates from the Film and Television Institute in Pune. Trained in various departments of the medium, the entrants tended to be contemptuous of the commercial Hindi cinema as they were of the advertising world; but in lieu of an alternative, they opted for the former, and to their minds, lesser evil.

Supply however outstripped demand and the fortune seekers, many of whom shacked up in poky rooms as paying guests, were in for a long and painful wait. Against this backdrop, Prithvi, with its starry connections and ideal location somewhere between the studios and the film companies, was perceived as not just a theatre but a potential showcase for talent, a place to network or merely to swap hard luck stories, and in time it became a lounging pad for filmi aspirants.

Other kinds of people gravitated there as well. These were mainly dropouts from the established theatre world. Directors and actors who yearned to do something more meaningful than the adaptations of Broadway hits or of hits from other languages churned out by their peers.

Every evening the cafe was abuzz with characters: narcissistic would-be stars, angst-ridden actresses, confused, searching directors, adoring groupies, world weary souls, pontificators, postponers, ditherers and simple bums. Each round table played host to the same dilemma: art or commerce, theatre or film, creativity or money, Tarkovsky or Subhash Ghai. Everybody had a dream. Everybody was looking for a break. Not everyone sympathised. The bourgeois residents of Janaki Kutir, the colony around Prithvi, complained to the film magazine *Stardust* that the theatre was turning into a dope-scented scene of pick-ups and late-night brawls. The article, though damaging, did not pierce the idealistic haze that hung heavy over the chattering cafe.

And much of the passionate energy and talk found its way onto the 24- by 25-foot stage. Motley, a group comprising the fiery FTII graduate, Naseeruddin Shah, his then girlfriend, Ratna Pathak, Tom Alter, Benjamin Gilani and others picked playwrights ranging from John Mortimer to Harold Pinter. Dinesh Thakur, the bearded actor who had a brief fling with fame in a small budget film pitched his ambitions high with Badal Sircar's bleak *Baaki Itihaas*. Mahendra Joshi, the uncrowned king of the youth drama circuit directed then unknown actors Shafi Inamdar and Feroz Khan in *Ekshuf*, a chilling Hindi version of *Equus* and followed it up with a delightfully original musical, *Khelaiya*. The leftist Indian Peoples' Theatre Association brought its folk-street style theatre and Satyadev Dubey, the ageing *enfant terrible* of the Hindi stage, his irrepressible defiance. A local schoolteacher made an impressive debut as director with *Oedipus Rex;* a bunch of college students put up a series of freakishly witty plays and talented NSD students such as Anita Kanwar and Pankaj Kapur turned in sterling performances. Something was happening every day; something different, something new. There were moments of pretension and there were bouts of inspiration. Some productions reeked of amateurism, others of sheer brilliance. An evening at Prithvi was usually unpredictable but it was hardly ever dull.

A crucial factor in sustaining this heady mix of enthusiasm and eclecticism was the lack of expectations. To put it another way: the lack of an audience. Juhu was an hour's drive away from the city centre where Bombay's elite traditionally congregated for an evening out. Few were willing to make the long journey into the suburbs. This reluctance did little for the financial well-being of the groups but it did leave them free to follow their hearts. And over time Prithvi acquired a reputation for irreverence and for a different kind of theatre; different, that is, from the run-of-the-mill entertainment that was being dished out at other auditoria in the city.

Gradually, thanks to the scattering of film people that had taken to frequenting the theatre and the recognition achieved by some Prithvi regulars through their work in the emerging parallel cinema, it also became a fashionable place to be at. Curious spectators came to gape at screen celebrities in the flesh and shows began to fill up. An art-conscious tobacco company also came forward to help the Kapoors subsidise the losses the theatre continued to incur.

But in the mid-1980s, the fragile experiment faced a threat from a new and unexpected source. In 1982, following Doordarshan's amended policy on private sponsorship, a series of television programmes went into production. The new producers included ex-Doordarshan personnel, documentary producers, FTII direction graduates and some commercial film producers. In the absence of a television tradition, the new programmers borrowed formats from American TV. And to find actors for this sudden demand for software, the talent scouts descended upon Prithvi.

Soon, the cafe began to wear a deserted look as everyone including the hangers on and layabouts began to find work on the plethora of sitcoms, quizzes, popular music programmes, detective shows and soaps under way. The faces that seemed to have a place as fixed as the potted plants and tables in the restaurant were on their way to becoming familiar fixtures on the small screen. Many, in fact, became virtually indistinguishable from their small screen personae: Pankaj Kapoor turned into the carrot-chomping case-cracking detective Karamchand; Sushmita Mukherjee, his goggle-eyed assistant, Kitty; Anita Kanwar assumed the mantle of the compassionate Lajoji while Shafi Inamdar was transformed into the henpecked husband of *Yeh Jo Hai Zindagi.*

The new colourful programming on television diminished the audience for plays as well. In 1984, Doordarshan had begun airing India's first and longest running soap, *Hum Log.* The serial was started at the initiative of the then Information and Broadcasting secretary, S. S. Gill. In 1983 an Indian team led by Gill had visited Mexico to study the pro-development soaps of Miguel Sabido. These soaps were different from the regular commercial soaps aired on American television in the sense that they combined entertainment with specific messages to promote some aspect of development.

On his return, Gill commissioned a private producer, Shobha Doctor, to create a series that would combine a storyline with progressive messages on family planning, the status of women and so on and *Hum Log* was born. The first few episodes, in the best traditions of Indian television, were didactic and preachy. There was a demand to take the serial off the air. But Gill conducted a review and changes were made emphasising the story. And soon, *Hum Log* was climbing the charts.

The success of the serial indicated the existence of a huge market for well-made indigenous programmes. And the government's decision to go commercial laid the foundations for a new software industry. Doordarshan still held the reins. On paper at least, its approval for a programme was subject to the inclusion of pro-development messages in the content. Nevertheless, the focus had shifted clearly towards entertainment.

From a few hours of dull, education-heavy programming, Doordarshan expanded its telecast time with lively
fare that included *Khandaan,* a Hindi serial on the lines
of *Dynasty, Buniyaad,* a family saga beginning in pre-
Partition India, *Ek Kahani* on villagers struggling against
feudal oppressors and *Subah* on contemporary college
life. There were thrillers such as *Karamchand* and *Khoj;*
sitcoms such as *Yeh Jo Hai Zindagi, Mr Ya Mrs* and *Rajni*
set around ordinary middle-class couples in ordinary
middle-class homes. There were also serials for children
and sports programmes.

The appearance of diversity was somewhat deceptive.
Most of the new programmes, particularly the top-rated
ones, portrayed an urban elitist way of life that was alien to
the majority of the country's people. A study conducted by
Arvind Singhal and Everett Rogers in 1987 discovered that
60 per cent of low-income households felt that television
did not adequately project the difficulties and problems of
their daily lives; over 90 per cent of artisans and labourers
felt that the knowledge and skills of their occupational
category were not properly depicted; and 85 per cent of
low caste viewers felt their needs and aspirations had
no place on the electronic medium. Since the national
programme, on which the new serials were aired, was
in Hindi, an inevitably high percentage of non-Hindi
speakers (60 per cent) also felt alienated.

Despite inadequate representation, the new glossy look
immensely boosted the popularity of television in India.
And presented with a few hours of free, well-packaged
diversion every evening most television owners chose
to stay increasingly at home. This, predictably, took
audiences away from other media. The least accessible
of them all, theatre, was inevitably the worst affected.

At Prithvi, wads of tickets remained unsold. Television had taken away much of the acting talent. But even the die-hard performers that stayed on were battling against a powerful competitor for an audience.

Ironically though, theatre was more in the news than ever before. From the early 1980s onwards, a transformation had been taking place in the print media. Politics, the dominant theme of the Indian press, was giving way to light features on lifestyle, people, entertainment and so on. The reason for the change was an amalgamation of various factors: an upsurge in advertising, the arrival of various glossy magazines in the previous decade, the evolution of an upmarket audience, increased competition and the entry of professionals from other fields into journalism. Plays and theatre personalities were attractive subjects for soft stories and newspapers began to compete to give the best theatre coverage.

In late 1987 I was asked by *The Indian Post,* a smart new daily that was attempting to establish itself as a second newspaper to the invincible *Times of India* in Bombay to review Hindi theatre. The break-up of theatre by language was in itself a significant change; the earlier tendency being to lump all languages under a generic title. The assignment took me to the various playhouses of the city—the Tata, the National Centre for the Performing Arts' Experimental Theatre, the Nehru Centre—but mainly to Prithvi where Hindi theatre had truly come of age.

Much had changed at the little theatre by the sea. The cafe, cleared of its rag tag crowd, had a regular turnover of diners. The stage was booked months in advance and the House Full board was up almost round the week. Television had lost its charm, I thought, watching the crowds at the gate before a show. And Prithvi appeared to have worked its charm on a new kind of audience: not the eclectic mix of old but a homogenous sea of couples one may have seen at the screening of a Basu Chatterjee film in an earlier era. Men in *kurta pyjama*, women in crisp organza arriving in foursomes by car from the populous and increasingly prosperous suburbs around for a convivial evening enlivened by *samosas* and drama.

The plays too fitted the mood of its audience. Most of the old guard had left for the greener pastures of television and cinema but some, unswerving in their devotion to the stage, remained in a vastly changed form. Shafi Inamdar, star of the provocative *Ekshuf,* had a huge hit in *Chung Ching* a story of funny mishaps and misunderstandings set in a middle-class drawing room; Dinesh Thakur's big play of the season was *Hai Mera Dil,* a mishmash of comedy, slapstick and old Hindi film tunes based on the feel-good American play, *The Rainmaker;* Arpana, a group of Satyadev Dubey's students, had another light frothy hit based on, well, *The Rainmaker,* IPTA had taken a break from folk plays on feudalism to stage *Andhe Choohein,* an unintentionally funny attempt at remaking Agatha Christie's chilling *Mousetrap* and Ekjut, a group that I last remembered for its stab at a Hindi *Look Back in Anger* was back with a tedious, jerky comedy. There were a host of other similar plays performed by relatively unknown groups.

Most of the plays I saw over the next two years were feeble comedies. The rest, with a few exceptions, were thrillers. Production-wise, the plays displayed a marked improvement on the sparse appurtenances of the early days of Prithvi. The sets, costumes and sound revealed a certain amount of care and, more significantly, expense.

In fact, many of the units relied excessively on gimmicks: at one intercollegiate competition the winning production had fluttering birds, glittering stars and a huge glowing sun as props.

For all the slickness, the life had gone out of the theatre. The plays I saw did not move, they did not provoke or delight. Nor were they meant to. Their purpose, one they fulfilled well, was to entertain. And watching the typical living room, nagging housewife, bumbling servant, nosy neighbour, slapdash, gag-a-minute, freeze frame routine for the hundredth time, the source of inspiration became all too apparent. I could almost hear the canned laughter. Theatre had been televisionised.

It was perhaps inevitable for that was where the profits lay. And performers in other media were realising that as well. Travelling through south India some years later, I was to hear complaints about audiences that wanted timebound capsules of classical art: 'instant raga and instant natyam'. In December 1992, noted film critic Iqbal Masud describing the year's fare as 'quick wit, satire, heartbreak and social thrust which is at once theatrical and all knowing', concluded that the future of cinema lay in being 'more mediocre, more safe'.

Sometime around the turn of the decade *The Indian Post* shut down. Fortunately, for I had tired of thinking up new ways to describe the same play. I did go back to Prithvi a few times. On one occasion, I was early for a play. The cafe was almost empty. I asked for tea. It was given to me in a streaked mug. The bottom said 'Hitkari Potteries'. I took it and sat down. At the next table a group of young boys were deep in conversation. *'Yaar, achcha* play *to karna hain,'* one of them was saying, 'but where are the people?'

THE NEW GUERRILLAS

THE COMMERCIALISATION OF DOORDARSHAN OPENED up a whole new world for software producers. Advertising agencies set up full-fledged film units and a couple of modern well-equipped studios opened up in Bombay to service the advertising industry. The government also announced its openness to programming on issues of public interest such as family planning from private agencies. One person who responded eagerly to the offer was J. K. Jain. Jain, a short, energetic man with an air of unflappable calm about him, was a full-fledged doctor with his own medical establishment in the capital. He was better known, however, for his extra-curricular activities which included politics: he was an active member of the BJP and the Vishwa Hindu Parishad (VHP) and published a rabidly anti-Congress features magazine.

The widespread sympathy generated for Rajiv Gandhi through the televisation of Mrs Gandhi's funeral in 1984 had convinced the astute doctor that the future lay in the electronic medium. Acting upon his instinct and Doordarshan's open door policy he went ahead and set up a state-of-the-art studio on the outskirts of Delhi. His plan to produce documentaries for Doordarshan did not work out though. Thanks to his antipathy towards the ruling party, television authorities refused to touch him and Jain had to be content with renting out his studio facilities to other private producers.

Then, in 1987, he had an unusual customer. Chaudhary Devi Lal, the colourful Jat leader from Haryana admitted himself to the Jain Medical Centre for a minor surgery. Devi Lal, better known as *Tau* or elder brother in his state, was no ordinary politician. Tall, broad shouldered with a benign expression and a deep gravelly voice, the 73-year-old Devi Lal had an intimidating personality; he was also perceived as a potential threat to Rajiv's Congress Party in the forthcoming state elections.

Jain himself was present at the operation. As he waited for the anaesthesia to take effect, he struck up a conversation with the redoubtable leader. What did he think his chances were against the Congress, he asked the Chaudhary. 'Chances would be good if the Congress did not control television,' Devi Lal moaned, 'I just don't have an answer to something so powerful.'

'I do,' Jain murmured. The response was electric. The strapping Haryanvi almost leapt out of bed with excitement. Jain calmed him down and proceeded with the surgery. After he had recovered, Devi Lal again implored Jain for the magical solution to his dilemma. This time Jain had an answer: 'We can make videos,' he said confidently.

In 1982, along with television, the Indian government had liberalised imports of Video Cassette Recorders by lowering duties and allowing travellers to bring them in as part of their personal baggage. Knocked down versions of VCRs were also imported and assembled locally for the Indian market. Overnight, videos and colour TVs became the new status symbols among the rich. Those who could afford it returned from shopping expeditions in Hong Kong, Singapore and Dubai laden with bulky cardboard boxes. Others scouted around in the Indian market for the best deal.

Despite raging demand, however, the ownership of VCRs remained largely confined to the elite, giving credence to criticism of the government's pro-rich bias. What neither the government nor its critics envisaged was that, in no time, the canny entrepreneurial mind would devise a way to convert this new luxury toy into a cheap medium of mass entertainment.

In the West, video owners tended to be in the upper income strata using video to select from a mass of software or to pre-record and watch television programmes at a time more convenient for them; in other words, it was a means of controlling media flow. In areas such as the Middle East where affluence co-existed with a rigidly controlled media, video was more commonly used as a means to procure a diversity of programming.

In poverty-ridden India it became a tool for anarchy. Manufacturers used it to advertise products banned on the official media; political propagandists used it to disseminate information the government would have liked to hide and everyone used it to watch films they didn't have to pay for.

The crucial factor was access. At ₹10,000–15,000 with an additional ₹10 for every cassette rented, the VCR was an expensive investment, way beyond the reach of the ordinary Indian. That, however, turned out to be an easily surmountable problem. Rental agencies sprang up to service individual households and communities, particularly slumdwellers, who took to hiring a VCR on holidays and festive occasions; restaurants acquired sets to increase their clientele; and outstation-bound buses installed machines on board and sallied forth under the upgraded title, 'video coaches'. And ramshackle video parlours mushroomed all over the country. By 1987, there were an estimated 10,000 video parlours, 12,000 video coaches and 11,000 hotels with VCRs in India.

By the early 1980s, cable television had also made an appearance. In Bombay, a couple of enterprising young men led the way by using homemade splitters and amplifiers to connect several buildings in the upper-class residential areas of Malabar Hill and Cuffe Parade to a few strategically placed VCRs on which they showed films and foreign serials such as *Kojak* and *Three Is Company*.

Industrial groups like the Tatas and five-star hotels evinced an interest in the fledgling cable TV operation for their townships and customers respectively. And by 1983, many others had entered the business. The legal position on cable television was nebulous. The law did not permit the laying of cables across municipal roads. And in the early days, operators tried to avoid complications by restricting their networks to high rise colonies which were divided only by walls or private compounds. Bombay, with its dense population and cheek-by-jowl housing, offered ample scope within the ambit of this law.

As time went by, and the authorities did not come down on cable operations, as expected, operators got bolder. And soon more and more of the city came under cable.

By 1989, there were an estimated 1,000 cable operators in Bombay. Few of these were serious businessmen. In a suburban slum in Bombay, for instance, the sole video owner among 15 households connected his video to his neighbours' television sets by passing wires over the tin roofs and collected ₹50 from each house for showing two films a day. Unemployed youths, retired professionals and even housewives plunged wholeheartedly into this new, lucrative and low investment venture.

Though the trend spread like wildfire in Bombay, it was slow to catch on in other cities. The chief reason for this was a more scattered population in most other places. Added to this was the high level of risk in the operation for while the legality of the hardware was suspect, the software was clearly and indisputably illegal.

Almost all the video cassettes in circulation were pirated copies of Indian or Hollywood films. The source for the cassettes were the 50,000 video libraries that had emerged seemingly from nowhere to service video outlets. Circulating libraries, shops and even grocers, anyone with space to spare had taken to stocking video cassettes. In 1988, a nationwide survey by the Operations Research Group found that video libraries rented out 50 cassettes a day. And while Hollywood films, television serials from the West and Pakistan were immensely popular, 95 per cent of the stock of most libraries consisted of Hindi movies.

Piracy was rampant. Indian films were available on video on the day of their release in cinema halls, sometimes even a couple of days before. Most were copied from prints stolen from the laboratories or from prints made for overseas release. The latest Hollywood films also made an instant appearance in the Indian market mostly as blurred camera prints recorded surreptitiously on hand-held cameras.

The film industry made valiant efforts to curtail piracy. Hectic lobbying in parliament resulted in the strengthening of the Indian Copyright Act in 1984. The amendment to the Act made detection of pirated cassettes simpler and provided for harsher penalties for the offender. An implementing body, the All India Anti-Video Piracy Organisation, was also set up by representatives from the industry. All these efforts, however, failed to make an impact. And the industry was forced to reach a compromise. Instead of losing money to the pirates, producers agreed to sell video rights of their films at prices fixed according to pre-determined categories.

This decision had the odd effect of legitimising the video pirates since they were the ones with the duplicating machines, and the experience required to copy and distribute video cassettes on a mass scale; it also brought into existence the concept of video advertising.

But before the new system could take root cable television proliferated, changing the economics of the arrangement. 'Cable is like AIDS to us,' claimed a video library owner in a Bombay suburb. It was an apt description. With several households watching the same film at once on cable, video borrowings dropped and consequently fewer cassettes were bought, leading buyers of video rights to demand a lowering of the price. The beleaguered film industry went to court against the cable television operators.

The chaotic nature of the cable TV operation—there were hundreds of operators functioning without regulation or an overseeing body—coupled with the infighting in the film industry which was deeply divided over coming to terms with the new technology, made negotiations and the implementation of any settlement nearly impossible. And the situation continued unresolved.

But apart from films, other forms of programming were also in preparation. Companies such as Hindustan Lever began to make presentations for their dealers on video, a cheaper alternative to a 16 mm film (cost: ₹300,000) or an audio-visual (cost: ₹10,000–25,000). Video was not only more affordable at ₹10,000 a film but also far more convenient. Soon, even smaller companies were using it as an effective form of communication. 'Suddenly, there were so many video films being made—industrial documentaries, ad films, sales films—that a company had to make a film not only to sell itself but to keep abreast of the competition,' said film producer Roabin Mazumdar recalling the video rush of the 1980s.

Others came out with a range of video films on self-improvement, fitness, children's programmes and sports. Garware Plastics and Polyester Limited, one of the companies in the ₹5 billion Garware group actually commissioned a video tape manufacturing plant and set up facilities to duplicate 15,000 tapes a day.

A furtive and thriving industry also started up in blue films. Most libraries had acquired a stock of obscene movies from abroad which were given out to select clients. Another popular outlet was the video parlour, typically, a small room in crowded lower class areas where the audience, mostly children and men, watched films at a moderate rate of ₹2 or so per show. The widespread demand for blue films resulted in a few local attempts at imitation. The Indian BPs— the code name for pornographic films which stood variously for Blue Prints or *bhel puri*—consisted usually of a series of silent and inept shots of uneasy coupling in sleazy hotel rooms.

Far from being an innocuous gizmo in the hands of a few, video had spread far and wide. And a substantial number of initiatives on the medium were a result of the state's stranglehold over mass media. Despite the presence of over 20,000 publications in the country, the print media was no match for the sheer visual power of television. But video provided a cheap and handy alternative to anyone wishing to step outside the straitjacket of government restrictions or cock a snook at the establishment.

In the mid-1980s, links between criminals and the law were exposed by a video recording that showed senior police officers and a magistrate celebrating at a party hosted by gangsters; a series of video magazines came into existence bringing to life stories that the state television network would have never countenanced; a vegetable hawker with SEWA, an Ahmedabad-based women's organisation, shook up civic officials by putting conditions in the city's vegetable market on tape; independent filmmaker Anand Patwardhan turned to video when Doordarshan refused to telecast his award-winning documentary on the plight of slumdwellers.

Dr Jain and Devi Lal did end up making videos. The upbeat video commercial that showed the Chaudhury drifting through mustard fields and mingling with the common people was disseminated throughout the state by Jain's outfit, Video On Wheels, which consisted of a fleet of vans fitted with VCRs and screens. The commercial helped Devi Lal to win the elections and set off a new trend in political campaigning.

Video had cracked the state monopoly; and in doing so it had revealed the existence of an increasingly large group of people hungry for entertainment, leisure alternatives and information.

An influential medium, however, is apt to be misused, whether it is by power-hungry politicians or by greedy entrepreneurs.

***

One morning in April 1990, I boarded a train at Bombay's Gothic Victoria Terminus station headed for the suburbs east of the city. The train passed through a bleak landscape of narrow streets and drab apartment blocks. At each stop a swarm of chattering young women alighted from the second class ladies' compartment in which I was travelling to be replaced by a noisier contingent all similarly dressed in colourful polyester saris and *salwar kameez* with a red hibiscus or a drooping *gajra* carelessly tucked into the hair. Some carried large, plastic set squares and notebooks, others appeared to be on their way to dusty typewriters in hole-in-the-wall offices.

My destination was Ulhasnagar, a township 65 kilometres outside Bombay. I had never been there before but in press reports it appeared as some sort of wild frontier town of 500,000 —mainly Sindhis who had fled Pakistan after Partition—liquor bars, cinema halls, video parlours, illegal buildings and guns. In two years over 60 murders had taken place in the satellite town, many a result of the internecine rivalry between Ulhasnagar's most prominent denizens: the Kalanis and a builder-cum-land shark, Gopal Rijhwani.

This however, was a more recent picture. In my mind and, in the consciousness of most Bombayites, Ulhasnagar had long enjoyed another kind of notoriety.

In Ulhasnagar, or so the story went, it was possible to copy just about anything. Wrangler jeans, Lacoste t-shirts, Cross pens, Raybans, Panasonic tape decks, even local varieties of pickle, powder and perfume could be reproduced, brand logo and all. Cheap imitations of audio cassettes and foreign cigarettes that flooded the markets of the country were said to originate here. A bottle of bootlegged Scotch was liable to be dismissed as 'Ulhasnagari *maal'* and the joke was that the 'USA' in the 'Made in USA' label was actually an acronym for the Ulhasnagar Sindhi Association. In the average Bombayite's perception, it could be said that Ulhasnagar stood for something contemptible, something fake. It mattered little that the township's skewed reputation was perhaps ill-deserved; that stories of its boundless capacity for imitation were probably exaggerated and few had traversed the distance to discover the truth. In every mind there was the awareness that a few miles away there was a copy, a cheap copy of the real thing.

This aspect of Ulhasnagar however, had nothing to do with my trip there that morning apart perhaps from providing a somewhat unreal and make-believe setting for a very human tragedy. I was on my way there to write a piece about a gruesome murder. A week before, four armed men had forcibly entered a schoolroom and killed a fifteen-year-old girl by dousing her with kerosene and setting her on fire. The killing had horrified the community. Shopkeepers had downed their shutters and hysterical residents had collected outside the school and pelted stones at the police when it arrived.

The local police launched a manhunt and had managed to round up three of the killers. The fourth, the ringleader and the victim's alleged boyfriend, Haresh Patel, was found three days later, dead on the railway tracks a kilometre and a half from Ulhasnagar. There were burn marks on his hand. In his pocket there were photographs and a driving licence for two-wheelers. It appeared to be an open and shut case, a crime of passion, common enough except for the public and macabre nature of its execution. But the good burghers of Ulhasnagar were far from convinced. Why was Haresh Patel's body, if indeed it was his body, disposed off so hastily, they asked. Why was the victim's sister who happened to be in the classroom at the time of the attack, not invited for an identification? Was the police doing a cover-up job and where was Pappu Kalani?

The last mentioned, a key player in the battle for supremacy in Ulhasnagar, was president of the township's municipal council. He was known to be close to the state chief minister, Sharad Pawar and had recently won an assembly election on a Congress (I) (The Indian National Congress was split into two parts in 1967, where the 'I' stood for the Indira Gandhi-led half of the party.) ticket. Politicians in the Opposition scented an opportunity in Kalani's absence from Ulhasnagar at the time of the murder and arrived from Bombay to bemoan the prevailing lawlessness in Ulhasnagar and to collect information with which they could embarrass the ruling party back home.

So there I was, on a sloping street with rickety structures on either side. There were people and carts and hawkers like there are outside every railway station in India, yet Ulhasnagar in the bright morning sun seemed overhung with a thick pall of gloom. I looked around for some form of transport. An auto-rickshaw sailed towards me. 'Patrakar (reporter)?' the rickshaw driver asked expectantly. I nodded and asked him to take me to the police station.

We rode through the busy bazaar onto wide open streets, deserted save for the odd passerby, to arrive at Police Station No. 1 where ACP Jadhav was briefing a reporter from a Bombay tabloid. There were signs of weariness on the young Assistant Police Commissioner's face. He had gone over the same story a hundred times in the last few days. But for our benefit he repeated details of the investigation.

'How can you be sure it was a love affair?' I asked him.

He smiled resignedly and produced a packet. In it were letters. One was from Rinku. It began 'My dear husband Haresh.' The other, on pink paper patterned with roses and redolent with childish sentimentality and references to a 'marriage' was from Haresh to Rinku. There was also a photograph: a studio picture of a sullen faced young man and a delicately pretty girl poised against a painted backdrop. 'See,' he said triumphantly. I saw.

My rickshaw driver was waiting to take me to Rinku Patil's house which was fast becoming the best-known address in the small town. He stopped outside one of a series of identical buildings in a large, undistinguished middle-class colony. I climbed the stairs to the flat where the unfortunate schoolgirl had lived with her parents, sister and kid brother. The walls in the corridor bore splashes of colour still fresh from Holi. The door to the flat was open and flanked by *chappals*. I added mine to the pile and entered the small, sparsely furnished room. At one end, on a sofa an old man in rustic attire sat wordlessly and still. Across him from a laminated picture, collared with a fresh garland, Rinku Patil smiled confidently at the world.

A group of men were sitting in a circle on the floor surrounded by newspapers. At the centre, I recognised Rinku's father, Babulal Patil, a short stubby man. He was reading from an open notebook on which there were jottings in blue ink. He paused, as I sat down at the edge of the group.

I introduced myself. 'What would you like to know,' he enquired politely. I mentioned the police hypothesis of a romance turned sour. 'All rubbish, they are making up everything,' he said furiously. The old man in the corner spoke up, 'He is upset that they are making such allegations about his daughter,' he said quietly. Patil slapped his forehead. *'Ek to ladki ke jaane ka dukh, uspe yeh maha dukh'* ('My daughter is gone, now I have to put up with worse').

A murmur of sympathy went around the room. The other visitors, I gathered, were quasi-reporters: Ulhasnagar had nine vernacular newspapers and a variety of small publications that seemed to exist for no purpose but to boost the standing of its owners. It wasn't clear whether any of the congregation present actually wrote or merely professed to write. What was clear was that their presence in the house had been a daily affair since the murder. And from the conversation, which revolved around 'parallel investigations', the ineffectuality of the police, the suspicious absence of Pappu Kalani and so on, I deduced that they came not to condole but to build on the conspiracy theory that connected Rinku Patil's murder with sinister and mysterious centres of power.

The belief had been responsible for a wave of vigilantism in the small town: earlier, local people had beaten up two men, wrongly assumed to be connected with the killing.

While the discussion raged outside, Mrs Patil, heavily sedated and under shock, slept in the bedroom. Her son, a small boy in a school uniform ate lunch out of a *thali* watched by his sister who hovered uncertainly in the background, a frail, pale shadow of fear.

I sat among the group of visitors disconcerted by the gap between my expectations and the reality. If truth be told, I had come hoping to find some basis for the conspiracy theory, to unravel something, anything, that would connect the murder with an underworld or political racket and thereby elevate it to the status of 'serious' news.

But as I sat there listening to the conjectures, allegations and explanations that had drawn me there in the first place, I was suddenly sick. Sick of the politicians, the police, the screaming headlines, the humbuggery and my very own reasons for being there.

And worse was to follow.

A hush had fallen over the room. Casually, someone asked: 'Have you seen the video?'

Everyone turned to the speaker. Including me.

A bald thin man with a pinched face answered, 'It was shown on my cable TV last night'. Everyone looked at him.

'I tell you, the girl died not one, but a thousand deaths,' he thundered. 'Think about it. First the men lock the door. Then they corner her, step by step. Then they pour the kerosene. *Then*,' and here he paused dramatically, 'they set her on fire. And all this time she is thinking of her father, her mother. All this time she is in pain.'

The Kalanis had come to Ulhasnagar in the late 1970s. They had made a fortune from a liquor distributorship. Their rise was marked by allegations of shady deals with builders and murder. The family had close links with the Congress (I). Dhunichand Kalani had been president of the local Congress Committee and after his murder, the mantle had passed on to his nephew, Pappu.

Security guards with menacing firearms guarded the Kalani's centre of operations. Pappu was not in. But his brother, Narain, a stout *kurta-pyjama* clad man ushered me into his office, a vast room with a fountain gurgling outside. 'I rushed to the school the moment I heard the news,' he said, 'I was late. If I had got there just three minutes before I would have saved the girl.'

The telephone rang. As he got up to answer it, something fell from his pocket with a soft thud to the floor. He bent down to pick it up. It was a revolver in a brown leather case. He replaced it casually and continued. 'I went twice to the Patil residence to condole,' he said piously. 'People make us out to be *goondas,* but we are not violent people.'

I had been joined on my rounds by a motley crew which consisted of some of the people I had seen at the Patil household along with other local journalists. I asked my fellow busybodies if there really was a video of the incident. I was assured that one had indeed been doing the rounds on cable TV for the past week. I asked if I could see it. Arjun Arya, an oldish man with a slightly furtive air who had some minutes before handed me a garish visiting card with the introduction I had by now come to expect ('I have a local paper'), offered to show us a copy.

We followed him down narrow lanes. On either side were houses, one-storeyed structures with slanting roofs, set close to one another. Clothes fluttered from clotheslines and children's toys and a stray tricycle spilled over doorsteps. Arya's home consisted of one large multipurpose room, a kitchen and a bathroom shielded from view by a grimy curtain. An old woman watched us wordlessly while a younger one was dispatched to the kitchen. We arranged ourselves as best we could.

"Who shot the video", I asked.

'I did,' Arya said. There was a gasp of astonishment. Clearly, for all their *savoir faire,* the purported journos knew little about the much mentioned video.

'My tap was leaking and I had gone to get a plumber from outside the school,' he explained cautiously. 'I caught one of the men as he was running out. He hit me.' My companions looked incredulous.

'I didn't say it before,' Arya continued defensively, 'but I hear the police are giving a reward. If the police can get a reward for bravery, why not me?' Nobody answered. 'Anyway, I thought the man had robbed a chain, but when I heard what had happened, I came home and picked up my camera.'

'Who sold the tape to the cable operators,' I asked him. He shrugged. 'How do I know,' he said dismissively.

If the idea that a video cassette should find its way mysteriously to the cable distribution channels seemed absurd to everyone else as it did to me, no one mentioned it. Obviously, it was not important.

Other things were. Snacks arrived. Our host urged us to be comfortable. And once the processes of hospitality were set in motion, Arya proceeded to uncover the television set and pressed the video controls.

The room was dark. I could not see the faces of my companions. But there was an air of anticipation as the screen came to life.

The visual was jerky. The sound an incoherent babble. Images of a crowded street and a corridor filled with schoolchildren flashed by. And then, all at once, the camera was in the classroom. Slowly and deliberately it panned the walls. It crawled up to the ceiling, stopping pointedly to reveal a fan melted and distorted by the heat. It skated down to the floor, paused to focus on a *chappal* and then zoomed with relentless determination towards the charred body.

Around me, no one spoke.

Slowly the camera retraced its route—walls, ceiling, body. And then it was in the corridor zigzagging across a row of stricken faces. There were a few adults too. I recognised Narain Kalani in his *kurta-pyjama* and others standing behind him. And then it was back to the classroom, jerkily skating the blotchy wall, the ceiling with its melted fan, the floor and the *chappal* and the black, burnt corner. And then as abruptly as it had begun, it ended, in blackness.

The curtains were drawn to let in the light. As we finished our tea and biscuits a desultory chit-chat began.

By the time we wound up, it was evening. I went to the station and waited for the train that would take me home. Home to the real thing.

STAR TREK

ONE THING MUST BE SAID for the Non-Resident Indian; he is everywhere. As I negotiated my way down the sloping curves of Old Peak Road, one of the swankiest addresses in Hong Kong, I could swear I had never left home. The weather was balmy, not unlike a dry spell in the middle of a Bombay monsoon. Along the way I passed a cosy art gallery run by an attractive Indian woman. Two hundred metres down the road, a Mughlai eatery stood next to a Kashmiri carpet shop. Up the slope in the rarer reaches of Mid-Levels, I had bumped into an old friend I hadn't met for years from Bombay. And at a party hosted by an American marketing executive, the weekend before, half the guests had turned out to be Indian.

And these were just the newcomers. Indians had come to Hong Kong over five decades ago. Most of these early settlers were traders who had helped in the evolution of Hong Kong into a major trading post and contributed significantly towards establishing local institutions such as the Star Ferry and Hong Kong University.

Their descendants, most of whom spoke fluent Cantonese and considered Hong Kong their home, continued to play a dominant role in the island's affairs: earlier in the year, a trade delegation of Indian business-men had called upon Lu Ping, Director of the Hong Kong and Macau office of China's State Council in his Beijing office, in preparation for the Chinese takeover in 1997; and the people columns of the local newspapers were full of gossip about the Harilelas and the Sitals, the city's prominent Indian families.

But that, as they say, was that. Notwithstanding the prominent space occupied by the Indian community in Hong Kong, India, the land of their origin was as distant to the average Hong Kong resident as Siberia might have been to a redneck Texan. News items emanating from the subcontinent rarely got a mention in the local papers. Travel magazines searching far and wide for exotic holiday destinations did not spare a glance at the ancient civilisation a short two and a half hour flight away. The largest democracy with its rapidly liberalising economy was of little significance to the colony's glossy business magazines. 'India, no we don't really write about India much,' a business writer told me dismissively. What they did write about were the growling economic tigers of Asia; India did not figure in the list.

Other poor nations did not suffer the same fate. The mayoral race in the Philippines got considerable play, as did the incarceration of Burma's Aung San Suu Kyi. In fact, the country that occupied the most column space was China. Considering the imminent takeover of the island colony by its Communist neighbour, the pre-occupation was understandable. Except that the fascination had equally to do with money.

India, the land of 900 million people was not even in the race. China was indisputably the emerging market of the 1990s. The excitement was palpable. Businessmen talked glowingly of the thriving industrial district that had sprung up in Shenzhen across the border. The Hong Kong Foreign Correspondents' Club sported advertisements for Mandarin-speaking journalists. And a middle-aged couple I met at the Stanley Beach Market (the man was an editor with *The New York Times,* his wife, a freelance writer) were struck by spontaneous eruptions of free enterprise glimpsed on a recent visit to China, one being a barber plying his trade in the middle of a busy street.

Used to considering myself an Asian I found my sense of identity shifting in these new surroundings. For the longer I stayed in Hong Kong, the more I realised that Asia for some Asians stopped short of India and its western neighbours. Except in one place that was fast becoming the most familiar address in the continent: Star TV, Post Box 8422, Hunghom Bay, Hong Kong.

***

Half a century ago, science fiction writer Arthur C. Clarke introduced the concept of a communication satellite to the world. According to Clarke, a satellite positioned 22,300 miles above the earth would take 24 hours to orbit it. Since the earth spins on its axis once in 24 hours, a satellite at that height above the equator would appear stationary from the ground (even though moving through space at 7,000 miles per hour) making it a perfect platform for television broadcasting. Theoretically, his proposition seemed sound but even Clarke himself estimated that the realisation of his prediction was at least 50 years away.

He did not envisage the rapid pace of technological change in the years to come. The first low orbit satellite, Sputnik, was launched by the Russians as early as October

1957, setting off a space race between the USA and Russia. By the mid-1970s communication satellites were being used not only to transmit television broadcasts but also for long distance phone calls, and other communication functions. Satellite had also become cheaper and more powerful. By the late 1980s, even a two-metre dish could pick up signals from the sky.

With the SITE experiment in 1975–76, India became the first country to use direct broadcasting by satellite. By 1983 India had sent up her own satellite INSAT 1B which facilitated the massive expansion of television in the country. Six years later with a powerful dish antenna, Indians could access programmes from their neighbours, Russia and China. They could also catch shows in Arabic and western sitcoms relayed for American soldiers abroad.

By 1989, satellite dish antennae had begun making a discreet appearance in major Indian cities. These were not the smaller S-Band type dishes approved by the government for use in places where Doordarshan signals were unclear, but the larger 5 metre and 7.5 metre dishes.

Initially, the dishes were installed mainly by a few enthusiastic cable operators as an extension of their services and by rich individuals. Around this time, the Atlanta-based Cable News Network (CNN), Ted Turner's ambitious 24-hour news service leased a transponder on the Russian satellite Stationar 12. As a consequence, parts of India gained access to the service and five star hotels began to acquire dishes.

Compared to video, satellite television was slow to proliferate. In fact, till the Gulf war broke out in 1991, few Indians were even aware of its existence. But with the prominent role played by the network during Operation Desert Storm, CNN quickly became a household name in India's media savvy circuit. Still, the trend took time to catch on. For one, at ₹300,000, a large dish antenna was out of reach for most individuals. It made sense for cable operators to acquire them, but unclear signals and the paucity of programming meant that demand was low. The majority of cable viewers were happy with their quota of 3–6 films a day, and once the war ended, few were likely to be willing to pay extra for CNN and scattered programming on other channels.

All this changed with the arrival of Star TV. In April 1990, a Chinese Long March rocket put a refurbished Hughes HS 376 satellite into orbit over South East Asia. Richard Li, son of Hong Kong's richest man, Li Ka-Shing, hired seven transponders on the satellite, Asiasat 1, to launch Asia's first regional satellite service: Star TV. The service, conceived as an advertisement-based network started off with four channels: Star Plus, an entertainment channel consisting of sitcoms, soaps and talk shows; a sports-based channel called Prime Sports; MTV and the British Broadcasting World Service.

Star TV extended its service to India on 26 August 1991. Almost immediately the demand for dish antennae zoomed. Ten months later nearly 1.3 million households had acquired access to Star. The response took even Star's promoters by surprise. Li's original intention had been to tap the rich consumers of Taiwan and the burgeoning audiences of China. But by June 1992, India had outpaced the others and with 5,800 new homes being connected every day, it had one of the fastest growth rates in the continent.

Cars whizzed past dangerously as I stood at the busy intersection in Kowloon. Across the street was the squat, drab building that housed the creative and technical apparatus of Star TV. Within it, about a hundred people were engaged in putting together the news, views, action and entertainment package beamed daily to 11.4 million homes across Asia.

At noon the place presented a picture of chaos. On a television screen at one end, a monumental battle was underway on the newly launched Chinese channel. Somewhere else, MTV blared out its *Classic Hits* signature tune. Don Atyeo, the affable head of MTV trundled out of his cabin holding a dinky basketball court, a gift from an Indian fan. The Prime Sports team huddled in general manager Geoff Metzger's cabin for a meeting. Everywhere, there were people, informally dressed in shorts, jeans and colourful t-shirts, rushing from table to table shouting, chatting and brandishing papers.

Across the long uncarpeted corridor, the hands-on staff went about its work in quieter surroundings. In one of the many editing enclosures, American-Chinese veejay Nonie's unmistakable voice was being glided gently into a song for a 45-second teaser. In a larger room, close by, the graphics department was fabricating logos and titles for various shows. The familiar *Riviera* logo stared out of one screen. At the flick of a button it re-emerged in different shapes and sizes. There was little room to manoeuvre however. For the large part, graphics on Star TV were faithfully reproduced from the original and the fillers on various channels came from abroad.

In fact, almost all the software was acquired. 'With so much material available in the English-speaking world it did not make sense for us to produce our own,' claimed Celia Chong, Vice President Programming, Star Plus, from her tiny office crammed with tapes—hours of soaps, chat shows and sitcoms waiting to be sifted through. In another room, her assistant was glued to an Oprah Winfrey show.

The only channel that did produce its own shows, albeit with ready video clips, was MTV. The monitors next to the recording studio reflected multiple images of MTV Asia's most popular veejay Danny McGill: Danny standing, Danny pacing the floor, Danny chewing his nails, Danny bored, Danny clowning around.

From his fan mail it was clear that the smooth-talking veejay with red lips and a little beard was a big hit with Indian viewers. There were gush letters from girls describing him as the 'handsomest', 'cutest' creature to ever walk the earth. An admiring letter from a male fan suggested removing the beard might take him the last few inches to perfection and one from a girl in Bombay's Antop Hill who, while pledging her love to Danny, implored him to read her letter only after 11 p.m. because 'my pop is so strict you know'.

Back in the recording room, a petite girl called the countdown into a microphone. The *Top Twenty* signature tune came on and Danny McGill burst into an animated voiceover. The recording went smoothly. Ian, the producer, breezed in to watch. Danny read the last one with a deadpan expression and then stormed into the room demanding '*Splurts* onto the charts, what the hell is splurts?' Nobody had an answer. The booming sounds of Headbangers Ball thudded out of speakers and the recording staff went into a frenzy pounding the floor and strumming imaginary guitars.

Somewhere close to the studio was the high security transmission area—grey, carpeted, quiet and cold. Huge machines as grey as the walls silently performed the nitty gritty task of converting tapes onto VHS for the library and onto Betacam for transmission.

Each channel had a separate transmission room. In one, the technical operator was glued to the French Open as it came through live. In another, the news was being beamed from London. BBC, unlike Star's other channels, retained an independent existence with representative, Patrick Chalmers, operating from his own apartment and the software being fed directly to the transmission centre from the UK. All the little bits and pieces of the operation came together in the Master Control Room which was a bit like a vision from Star Trek: a stack of television monitors, wires and a row of forbidding machines performing various complicated tasks. Here, every signal was monitored. Men staring goggle-eyed at the screens checked picture quality, sound levels, and watched for breakdowns in transmission. From here the signals were transmitted to Star's uplink centre in Clearwater Bay and then sent out to receivers in Asia.

***

One early morning in November 1993, East West Airlines, one of the first of several private operators to emerge following the deregulation of the domestic airline sector in 1990, transported me to Cochin in the Southern state of Kerala.

Kerala, apart from being the first place in the world to freely elect a Communist government, had also long been the most progressive region in the country, in terms of land distribution, health and education. Cochin,

Kerala's biggest city, consisted of a cluster of sleepy islands and peninsulas: an unlikely setting for a pop concert. Nevertheless, the route from the airport on Willingdon island to the mainland, Ernakulam, that morning, was dotted with hoardings advertising precisely such an event. 'Welcome to Cochin' said one to the unusual visitor expected to enliven the city's humdrum existence that evening.

The visitor, Apache Indian, also known as Steven Kapur, was a Birmingham-based singer of Indian origin who had burst onto the British charts that year with a hit single, *Arranged Marriage*—a quirky look at the Indian custom of matching couples by qualifications. His unique style which blended the Indian *bhangra* with reggae had earned him the sobriquet, the 'Indian Ragamuffin', and some prestigious awards in his adopted home.

Fusion was a popular trend of the time. Progressive recordings by established artists such as the Beatles, Paul Simon and David Byrne had earlier introduced foreign sounds to a western audience. But the new trend was of ethnic artistes themselves displaying the particular appeal of their music to the world. These cultural crossovers which included Ethiopian crooner Aster Aweke, the Algerian-born, Paris-based, Arabic-singing musician Khaled, and Brazilian singer Margeret Menezes, had managed to sell thousands of copies of their music. New languages and new instruments such as the kora, the balaphon, Chinese cymbals, rattles and even Mexican donkeyjaws reverberated on the western charts.

Considering the competition, Apache's success was potentially a flash in the pan. With a new hybrid hit in the making every day, Kapur, despite his inimitable style, seemed an unlikely candidate for global stardom. That was, till MTV Asia stepped in. Apache's appearance on the continent's favourite youth channel transformed him into a household name on the continent. On his first ever visit as a pop star to India, the twentysomething singer was received like a hero. Reporters tracked his every move and crowds mobbed him at airports. His efficient publicity machine milked the adulation by organising, among other things, a tearful reunion with his 98-year-old grandmother in Jalandhar.

Some months and another hit *(Boom Shak-A-Lak)* later, Apache was back in India. On his previous trip he had performed in Bombay and Delhi. This time, his itinerary was focused on smaller cities such as Pune, Bangalore and of course, Cochin.

I dropped off my bags at the Hotel Sealord, an adequate but weather-beaten establishment with vast, airy rooms, and set out to explore the terrain. My first impression of Cochin consisted of wide roads, shopping complexes and construction. The city slick look turned out to be a façade, however, for just off the main road was a warren of little streets that resembled nothing more than a cosy village.

Men in *mundas,* women in saris and frequently, the north Indian *salwar kameez,* swarmed the narrow lanes. Fringing both sides were bookshops which appeared to stock mainly textbooks. Scattered between the bookshops were also the traditional south Indian coffee houses where the most popular item appeared to be *baida* (egg) curry.

Beyond the fluorescent lights and bustle of Ernakulam, however, lay another Cochin: a quieter place redolent with history. In some ways Cochin reflected more clearly than other Indian cities, the country's eclectic influences. Here, as the guide books proclaimed, it was possible to see

India's oldest church, a palace built by the Portuguese, an ancient Jewish settlement and a performance by Kathakali dancers.

I took the ferry to Matancherry and walked around the deserted pier, along the line-up of stalls serving fried fish, shops strung with hats of straw and banana leaf and quaint antique stores. I visited the 16th-century synagogue with its Chinese hand-painted willow pattern floor tiles, and the palace with its portraits, palanquins and lotus ponds. I walked through desolate afternoon streets, passing quiet houses topped by television antennae and lonely crosses. I stopped to admire the brilliant red stained glass window above the altar at St. Francis Church, where Vasco da Gama had been buried for 14 years. And finally, I took the boat northwards to Vypeen.

A light drizzle had started up. I sat on one of the park benches scattered along the embankment and watched the Chinese fishing nets that stood vigil over the placid waters. In the misty distance I could see the outlines of bulky merchant ships. Up close was lush greenery. All around me was a feeling of peace, contentment and prosperity— not of having too much but having just enough.

In the evening the brand new Regency hotel on M. G. Road was abuzz with excitement. Apache Indian, his wife, son, bodyguard (Milo), manager (Mambo) and the tour promoters had practically taken over the hotel. Young boys in baggy shorts and baseball caps rushed around the gleaming lobby bearing messages, organising transport, smoothening out last-minute hurdles. There was a hysterical edge to the frenzy. For while hundreds of ticket holders at that very moment were making their way to the Rajiv

Gandhi Indoor Stadium, where the concert was scheduled to be held, in a room back at the hotel, Apache Indian, the star of the evening, was refusing to go on with the show.

The reason was unclear. The buzz was that he was upset about the security arrangements. As the organisers tried to reassure him, the cars waited.

At the stadium, the scene was chaotic. The autorickshaw dropped me a few yards away and I made my way through the surging crowds on foot. The police were having a tough job keeping gatecrashers at bay; later a minor scuffle broke out on the street. In a while the melee cleared slightly. Many it seemed, had come not to see the show but to satisfy some common curiosity.

Strains of recorded music filtered out and the ticketless all-male bystanders in *mundas* and polyester trousers shuffled around like beggars at a feast, watchful and sullen. Eager hands reached out to grab me as I, the only female presence on the street, went past. Once inside I realised my folly. Unlike in Bombay where mixed audiences for rock concerts was the norm, the social mores of a town like Cochin implied gender segregation. There was not only a separate entrance for women, but also a special enclosure prominently marked 'LADIES SECTION'. There were women, incongruously dressed in traditional finery with children and grumpy middle-aged husbands in the 'Family Section'. The rest of the audience was male.

The fun had already begun. On the stage, a teenage brother and sister duo from Germany who went by the name, Noble Savages were singing their compositions in heavily accented English. The crowd gyrated happily to the unfamiliar tunes. The spotlight swung through the audience picking up a sari here, a *munda* there, but many of the young men who appeared to be between 15 and 25 were in jeans and seemed to have appropriated elements of fashion from the videos on MTV. Some wore drug fighter t-shirts, others sported baseball caps tweaked front to back. Several had taken their shirts off and were waving them around. One man had a leather jacket and a helmet on. The mood was rowdy.

The dancing got progressively frenetic. The Noble Savages were holding fort now with a number in German.

The crowd didn't seem to understand a word, nor did it seem to care. Clearly, the action on stage was unimportant; it was the audience that was on show. More shirts came off. Banners sprouted. A mutinous mob from the cheaper stands embarked on a descent to the more expensive standing area below, breaking bamboo barricades along the way. As they reached the bottom the insurgents let out a whoop of triumph and broke into a series of exertions: rolling on the floor, doing the grind, jabbing a finger in the air and forming a human chain.

The smell of booze was in the air; other intoxicants probably prevailed. But the human dynamos spinning around me didn't look like they needed external stimulation. They were high on the act of being high. Except at one point when MTV Asia's sultry veejay, Sophiya made an appearance in a pair of teeny shorts, a wild cheer went up in the crowd. And a stampede commenced as people vied to get before the camera that was recording the event for television.

Then, all at once, Apache appeared, a garish vision in black and red velvet, dark glasses and gold medallion. The zippy track of *Boom Shak-a-lak* rent the air and a troupe of female dancers in short body-hugging dresses commenced to wriggle their bellies according to Apache's nasal instructions.

In the ladies' section, a group of about fifty young girls swayed in what appeared to be choreographed unison. And as Apache went into the more familiar *Arranged Marriage,* an electric current zipped through the audience. Barricades came crashing down as more people descended to the floor. The police made feeble and unsuccessful attempts to stem the traffic. 'The cops here are usually quick with their *lathis.* I don't know what's happened to them today,' observed a press photographer who was gleefully aiming his lens at the crowd.

Indeed, the uniformed men did seem strangely torpid amid the bedlam, One bopped tentatively to the music but the sight of hundreds of youngsters reacting to the foreign sound, by now a mixed group of boys and girls had also appeared on the floor, seemed to have bemused his colleagues. Eventually they gave up altogether to sit in stupefied amazement in the press gallery.

Meanwhile, the concert continued. Apache, having discarded the velvet attire for a t-shirt launched into a new song on communal amity. But the listeners, unfamiliar with the tune, seemed to lose interest in the performance and resorted to their individual devices for amusement which consisted of jumping up and down, hugging each other and curling up on the floor. One man twirled an umbrella with gay abandon.

No one seemed to notice that Apache had left through a side exit. That Sophiya had said her piece for the camera, back to the audience. The show was over. The stage was empty. But the bewildered crowd stayed on listening to the beat that was now a part of them.

THE RATH YATRA

FOR 78 WEEKS BETWEEN 1987 and 1988, India, courtesy Doordarshan, was hooked on a heavenly opiate: the Sunday morning serialisation of the Hindu epic, the Ramayana. Variously termed, the 'religious serial', the 'soap opera of the gods' and so on, the television drama, had notched up a mind-boggling viewership of 85 per cent. Examples of its popularity were Legion: brides refusing to participate in wedding rites till the end of the episode; ministers turning up late for their own swearing-in ceremony; an entire train kept waiting while the driver and its passengers caught up with the latest instalment.

Familiarity rather than novelty appeared to be the key to its success. Rama, the hero of the serial and an avatar of the god Vishnu, was probably the best-known deity in the Hindu pantheon. Dussehra, the day he triumphed over his adversary Ravana, and Diwali, the occasion of his return home after a long absence are widely celebrated Indian festivals.

The story of Rama: the dutiful son who left his kingdom, Ayodhya, to fulfil a promise made by his father; of Rama the powerful warrior who battled with the mighty Ravana to retrieve his wife Sita; of Rama the noble king who put his people before his marriage; were known throughout the length and breadth of the country. It was the stuff of bedtime stories as well as philosophical discourses.

It had also been a fount of inspiration for poets and dramatists. The original Ramayana was believed to have been composed some time between 1500 and 200 BC by a robber turned sage Valmiki who was said to have been inspired by the god Brahma. Since then the saga had been written and rewritten innumerable times. According to the author, R. K. Narayan, who produced his own English version, *The* Ramayana *Retold*: 'India is a land of many languages, each predominant in a particular area and in each one of them a version of the Ramayana is available, original and brilliant and appealing to the millions of readers who know the language.' Kathakali dancers in the south routinely enacted the momentous war between Rama and Ravana. And a host of Ramlila troupes existed all over the country each performing its own idiosyncratic vision of the legend.

The television Ramayana however bore the unmistakeable stamp of Hindi cinema. Mythologicals though irregular were a familiar genre in Indian cinema and were characterised by a heavy reliance on trick photography, theatrics, garish colour and emotive music.

That all these elements were forcefully present in the small screen adaptation was not really surprising for its maker, Ramanand Sagar, was himself the epitome of the Hindi film producer. The short, bald producer, a Hindu emigre from Lahore who came to Bombay following Partition, started his career as a writer and went on to make a series of successful films.

His Ramayana, which he scripted and directed, had all the ingredients of a filmi production. It also reflected his north Indian origins. The sets and costumes clearly belonged to the north Indian tradition; the chief characters, apart from Ravana the king of Lanka in the south, were cast in the Aryan mould and spoke high flown Hindi which was the language of the Indo-Gangetic plains.

The televisation of the Ramayana evoked a storm of protest. The complaints stemmed from a concern that television was being used to propagate a certain ideological message. The belief was not without basis. Despite the partial commercialisation of the medium, Doordarshan authorities had continued to exercise powers of selection by insisting that serials should combine entertainment with a desirable message. Hence soaps such as *Hum Log* and *Buniyaad* were approved for promoting, among other things, a desirable idea of 'national integration'.

What was not really questioned was the idea of a nation that came through these and similar serials which was clearly north Indian and middle class, a startlingly narrow definition for a heterogeneous country such as India.

With the decision to telecast the Ramayana and consecutively, the other great Hindu epic, the Mahabharata, concern mounted that in secular India, where 15 per cent of the population consisted of non-Hindu religious groups, the state was also propagating the ideal of a Hindu Nation. Predictably, the apprehensions were voiced most forcefully by a vocal section of the minorities, particularly the Muslim community which comprised 12 per cent of the population, and in the South the intellectual elite was also appalled by Sagar's kitschy representation of the Indian classic.

The actual popularity of the Ramayana however, silenced its many critics. Within weeks, the serial had garnered one of the largest audiences in the history of television. And soon it was clear that its following, far from being solely Hindu, comprised people of various religious persuasions. According to an account by Mark Tully in his *No Full Stops in India,* fan letters poured in from Christians, Muslims, Sikhs, the very communities on whose behalf cudgels had been taken up against the serial. 'May our Lord Jesus and Mother Mary Bless you and keep you well,' wrote a Christian lady from the South to one of the characters. 'Your name will shine and shine like the morning star in the horizon,' gushed a Muslim in a letter to Ramanand Sagar.

So powerful was the impact of the serial that its cast of unknown actors not only achieved overnight celebrity status but the chief protagonists came to be venerated as gods. 'At functions really grown-up people come and touch your feet,' Deepika, the young actress playing Rama's wife Sita told Tully. The programme's popularity also enabled its maker, Ramanand Sagar to extend the serial way beyond its contracted period of 52 weeks and collect more money from his sponsors which included a toothpaste company, a noodle-manufacturer and a textiles producer.

****

By the middle of 1990, the much-sponsored, widely revered Ramayana had been laid to rest, extensions and all. The controversial Mahabharata too, had spent its thunder and the country had settled down to more prosaic forms of entertainment.

On Dussehra, the day marking the victory of good over evil, however, the city of Bombay prepared to receive another wannabe incarnation of God. This time the mode of conveyance was not the television set, but a Swaraj Mazda souped up to resemble a chariot. And the new, self-styled avatar of Rama was not an actor but a politician: L. K. Advani, president of the BJP.

For a week the bespectacled, balding 63-year-old leader had been traversing the country in his contraption. His aim was not to seek votes but gather support for the construction of a temple at the site of what he and other Hindu revivalists were claiming to be Rama's birthplace. His yellow *rath* with its air-conditioned cubicle and the BJP's lotus painted prominently on it had proved a suitable advertisement for his holy purpose; at various stops women rushed forward to perform the traditional *aarti*. On the road through villages, grown-ups and children chased after to touch the vehicle.

Residents of the country's most advanced city were understandably less awed by the pageantry; or at least not impressed enough to turn out on a holiday to welcome the 20th-century charioteer into their midst. The only people in evidence on Bombay's streets that Sunday morning were street urchins and the police. The *bandobast* was essential since the *Rath Yatra* had spawned communal disturbances between Hindus and Muslims elsewhere. Advani had no reason to carp about the absence of public response though since, a few kilometres away, waiting to welcome him was the Tiger of Bombay, Bal Thackeray himself.

Thackeray was a Bombay institution. The former cartoonist had first drawn attention to himself in 1966 with a strident call for protecting Maharashtrian interests in the cosmopolitan metropolis. In later years, however, Thackeray had widened his appeal by eschewing his 'sons of the soil' charter to cast himself anew as a saviour of the Hindus. His methods remained typically fascist (he professed open admiration for Hitler and the Nazis) though his targets changed: in the old days the enemy was the south Indian migrant, in the changed times it was the Muslim.

In his new avatar the Shiv Sena leader had much in common with the Hindu revivalist BJP and the two had entered into an alliance of sorts. The relationship however, was fraught with uncertainty. Thackeray's ego was not conducive to an amicable partnership. Moreover, sections of the BJP which had a strong support base in the urban middle class were uneasy about associating with a lumpen party like the Shiv Sena.

As Advani's *rath* approached, a cheer went up from the small cluster of people, mostly Shiv Sainiks, a few BJP supporters and the press, gathered outside Shiv Sena Bhavan. The scene—Advani standing tall on his gaudy chariot, the rabble in saffron headbands, the conch shells, the *trishuls*, the garlands and the vermilion marks on several foreheads—could well have been a still from Sagar's television epic. Thackeray greeted Advani warmly, and the reciprocal support expressed by the latter left little doubt as to the joint nature of their venture.

The convergence of religion and politics was not a new phenomenon on the subcontinent. Religion, in fact, had been responsible for splitting the Independence movement against the country's colonial rulers. The British created Pakistan to satisfy Muslim fundamentalists. Their Hindu counterparts though, had reason to be disappointed. Free India, under the influence of leaders such as Mahatma Gandhi and Jawaharlal Nehru chose to go secular and the scattered demand for a Hindu state was obscured by the development needs of the infant state.

In time, the fundamentalist lobby adapted to the new conditions. The Rashtriya Swayam Sevak Sangh, a pro-Hindu outfit, continued to impart Hindu values and physical training to willing youths but it was increasingly perceived as a social service corps rather than a religious one. Its political wing, the Jana Sangh, later renamed the BJP, became virtually indistinguishable from other political parties. In 1977 it joined the coalition of forces against the Congress. And after its 1984 debacle, when it won just two seats in parliament, it not only turned its attention to the hitherto neglected rural lobby but also adopted as its new mentor India's greatest secularist, Mahatma Gandhi.

Ironically, while the BJP was diluting its Hindu ideals, separatist movements in Punjab and Kashmir, led by Sikhs and Muslims, were whipping up resentment within the majority community in the country.

The Indira-led Congress had responded quickly to the new phenomenon. Indira and her ministers had flaunted their connections with temples and Hindu holy men. And Rajiv Gandhi's election campaign in 1984 pitted his party as a bulwark against Sikh fundamentalism.

Hardliners within the BJP, dismayed by the Congress's attempt at sweeping the rug from under their feet, demanded a return to the old ideals. As a political strategy, their demand appeared to make sense: the BJP's old Hindu urban middle-class constituency had grown in numbers and economic clout over the years and circumstances seemed to favour a chauvinistic appeal.

Accordingly, the BJP changed horses. The switch was made easier by the presence of a live and highly emotive issue that had already become the focal point of the Hindutva campaign: the dispute over the Babri Masjid.

The nondescript mosque in the northern state of Uttar Pradesh had been a bone of contention between Hindus and Muslims for over four decades. Certain Hindu groups claimed that the mosque actually stood on the ruins of a temple built to mark the birthplace of Lord Rama. Attempts by the Hindus to take over the structure included gimmicks such as installing a Rama idol in the shrine and proclaiming it to be a heavenly miracle. The issue however had lost steam in later years and few Indians were even aware of its existence. That is, till 1984, when various pro-Hindu organisations, spotting a magnificent opportunity to further their cause, mounted a crusade for the construction of a temple at the site of the mosque.

Their demand appeared to be reasonable: in real terms it meant that the Muslims would have to relinquish their claim over what was to them just another place of worship in acknowledgement of the extreme significance the site held for the Hindus.

The truth, however, was far more loaded. The Hindu revivalists believed that India should be restored to its original inhabitants, the Hindus, by undoing the consequences of historical events such as the Mughal invasion, British rule, and Partition. The destruction of the Babri Mosque was merely a step in the process. On the agenda was also the demolition of about 150 mosques that were believed to have replaced temples. Consequently, acceding to the demand raised for the Ram Janmabhoomi temple also implied the acceptance of the Hindu fundamentalists' central proposition soon to be known as Hindutva: that Hindus and Hindus alone constituted the Indian state.

Not only did the assumption have dangerous implications for non-Hindus; it also ran counter to the tenets of India's secular Constitution. The unexpected groundswell of support for the fundamentalist position, however, catapulted the issue to centre-stage. Over the next few years, the Babri Masjid/Ram Janmabhoomi dispute was to dominate Indian politics, bring down one national government and several state governments and spill blood across the land.

The reasons for the snowballing of Hindu fundamentalism through the 1980s were complex and several: the rise of extremist minority groups, the alienation experienced by the recently urbanised, newly prosperous Hindu middle class which left it vulnerable to the quasi-religious, jingoistic arguments put forth by the Hindu revivalists and so on. All these provided fertile soil for a carefully orchestrated propaganda campaign launched by the Hindutva brigade, the central feature of which was: an innovative and effective use of the media particularly, the audio-visual media.

The campaign, initiated by various like-minded organisations such as the VHP, the BJP, the Shiv Sena and so on was divided into three stages.

The first involved the creation of a Hindu consciousness. In a country where Hindus comprised 85 per cent of the population, this might have seemed like a superfluous endeavour. But, in truth, Indian Hindus were deeply divided by a host of considerations such as caste, language, regional affiliation and so on. Unlike Islam or Christianity, it was also an unorganised religion with a plethora of deities and no rallying institution like the mosque or the church. Hence the term 'Hindu' could be used to describe an Ayappa worshipper from Madras, a Durga devotee from Calcutta and a *Rambhakt* from Varanasi. Each could be equally religious and yet feel no sense of affinity with the other.

A factor that made a significant difference in this respect was the telecast of the Ramayana. By focusing on Rama, the serial provided a common point of reference for all Hindus. Moreover, the imagery in the serial—the apparel, the crowns, the *trishuls*, etc.—became a sort of visual shorthand that transcended regional and other barriers. So great was the impact of the Ramayana that it seemed almost credible that the state network had conspired with fundamentalists to project the idea of a Hindu nation.

The conspiracy theory though was never proved. Nor did it sit well with the network's telecast of other serials such as *Tamas*, a realistic account of the trauma of Partition which dealt evenly with Muslim and Hindu fundamentalism, or *The Sword of Tipu Sultan*, on the struggles of a Muslim ruler against the British.

The fact was that in the surcharged environment at the time, a programme—religious, historical or literary—that had anything to do with communal relations easily acquired labels such as 'pro-Hindu' or 'pro-Muslim'. And regardless of whether the effect was intentional or not, Hindu propagandists were quick to seize upon and appropriate the Ramayana and its baggage. This was done by flooding the market with lockets, stickers and display items based on Hindu religious symbols, many of which were part of the tableau of the Ramayana. Simultaneously, the Hindutva forces, in an effort to cement Hindu unity, launched a tirade against the largest minority community. In speeches and interviews, leaders heaped complaints about Muslims, many based on patently false claims. Hindu chauvinists maintained, for instance, that Muslims were reproducing at a rate that would soon enable them to outnumber the Hindu population. They also claimed that Muslim insurgents had destroyed nearly 40 temples in Kashmir (press investigations revealed this to be false).

The main point on the agenda though was the construction of the Ram Janmabhoomi temple. Or, more accurately, since one was not possible without the other, the demolition of the Babri Mosque. And one of the most effective methods used to drum up support on this issue was video.

Communications wizard, J. K. Jain, was the brain behind this part of the campaign.

Bhaye Prakat Kripala (The Appearance of the Merciful), the first in a series of highly watchable and potent cassettes, for instance, provided a 'historical' perspective (as seen by the *Hindutvawadis)* on the temple issue. This was as follows:

Once upon a time there was the sacred land of Bharat, its capital Ayodhya and its king, Rama.

To this lyrical place disaster came in the form of the evil Mughals who, led by their emperor, Babur, wrecked Hindu temples and targeted the holiest spot of all: the birthplace of Rama in Ayodhya. Local chieftains resisted. To no avail. The Mughals, ruthless and obdurate.

Then the heavenly miracle happened: Rama reappeared; not as a king, but as an adorable infant playing in an alcove of what was now the Babri Mosque.

Celestial lights beamed. The message was clear: Rama was beckoning faithful Hindus to fight and restore the glory of their ancient civilisation, symbolised by the Ram Janmabhoomi temple.

The story might seem to have emerged straight out of a comic book. But the manner of presentation: the use of maps, pictures of an advancing army, the sound of thundering hooves mixed with actual enactments and kitschy representations of the infant Rama somehow blurred the line between fact and reality.

Combining legend, fact and myth was typical of the methods used by the Hindu fundamentalists to evolve a new, more convenient version of events. In *Ajinkya,* a pseudo-documentary, the Shiv Sena used similar techniques of distortion: Indian history was compressed to include only an approved selection of events and figures which catapulted the Sena from the status of a parochial party into one of national and immense historical significance.

Pran Jaaye Par Vachchan Na Jaaye (A Promise Unto Death), another in Jain's series, was even more provocative. The subject in this film was the confrontation between Hindu chauvinists and the police in Ayodhya.

The incident had occurred in the winter of 1990, when thousands of Hindu volunteers congregated in Ayodhya for a proposed assault on the Babri Mosque. The attempt failed. A few fanatics managed to break through the cordons and plant a flag on the Mosque's dome. But security forces repelled the rest of the mob by opening fire. Twenty-six volunteers were killed, a remarkably low figure considering the numbers that had converged on the site.

In Jain's version though, the face-off assumed the proportions of a holy war.

The film began with shots of eager volunteers arriving in Ayodhya. Groups of strapping youths, middle-aged men, lonely pilgrims, variously attired and shouting slogans were shown streaming out of buses or arriving on foot. Wide-angle shots, close-ups and brief interviews established their missionary zeal. Then, as they gathered for the assault, came the moment of confrontation. The pious and good crusaders were beaten back. Hostile policemen with batons and firearms attacked them. People scattered, old men stumbled. Bodies fell.

Substantially, these were the facts. It was the treatment that made all the difference. If the contrast between the optimistic arrival and sad departure told the story of hope belied, the slow motion sequences, the emotive soundtrack and long shots of the mob being repulsed created the impression of large-scale bloodshed. Indeed, anyone watching the film could believe that thousands had been martyred that day.

Immediately after the incident, the Hindu propaganda machine had attempted to put out bloated figures of the number that had died in the firing. Press investigations revealed these claims to be unfounded. But the truth had little chance of surviving the whisper campaign that started up when the RSS disseminated Jain's stirring piece of propaganda throughout the country. The informal method of distribution and the anti-state nature of the content imbued the cassette with the attraction of the forbidden without any penal repercussions. The combination proved combustible. Jain claimed that after the 1991 elections, about 50 BJP members of parliament had credited their victories in part to the effect the cassette had on their constituents.

The last part of the *Hindutva* propaganda campaign involved translating the groundswell of sympathy into votes.

This required a change in strategy from confrontation to conciliation. BJP leaders, in particular, took pains to distance themselves from their earlier combative stances when required and to project themselves as responsible and mature representatives of society. One method of doing this was to bring out video cassettes recording their achievements for telecast by friendly cable television operators.

By the early 1990s, the concerted efforts of the *Hindutva* brigade had paid handsome dividends. The BJP had increased its tally in parliament from two seats in 1984 to 111 in 1991. It had also come to power for the first time in four states, all in the 'cowbelt': the Hindi speaking area in the north. One of these, Uttar Pradesh, the country's most populous state, which had given the country as many as six prime ministers was also home to the controversial Babri Mosque.

Resentment against the minorities, particularly the Muslims, had spread like wildfire within the majority community resulting in several incidents of sectarian violence. As many as 611 such incidents took place in 1988; many were in places with a history of communal harmony. And an awareness of the Mosque/temple issue had been successfully disseminated to the farthest corners of the land.

6 December 1992:

If the fate of a nation could be decided in a day, then this was one such day. From 3 December zealous Hindus had been trickling into the narrow serpentine lanes of Ayodhya apparently to participate in the *kar seva,* the construction of the Ram Janmabhoomi temple (since the Hindu lobby had repeatedly pressed for a temple on the very site of the Babri Mosque, the proposed *kar seva* was also a euphemism for the destruction of the Mosque). For many months now, their minds had been preoccupied with the overwhelming thought of Hindu supremacy. Several times their leaders had promised them that the realisation of the temple was imminent. Some of them had even travelled to Ayodhya earlier to contribute their labour only to be disappointed. But this time, they were determined to clear the looming obstruction in their path: the Babri Masjid. And nobody, not the judiciary, not the police nor any fickleness on the part of their leaders was going to stop them.

In Delhi the deliberations had gone on for days. The situation was a tricky one. The Congress government at the centre, in accordance with the secular principles enshrined in the Constitution, was committed to protecting the Mosque. The pro-Hindu BJP government in Uttar Pradesh which was also responsible for maintaining law and order in the state suffered from no such qualms.

The safest course for the centre seemed to be to dismiss the state government and take charge of Uttar Pradesh. Neither party was keen on the option. The BJP chief minister Kalyan Singh, loath to lose control of a key state, gave an assurance that the Babri Masjid would not be harmed. Prime Minister Narasimha Rao, on the other hand, concerned that dismissing the state government might be perceived as an authoritarian move and unwilling also to enter the messy confrontation on the ground, believed him. It proved to be a costly mistake.

By the 5th, signs of trouble were apparent. The *kar sevaks* who had gathered from distant corners of the country were in a belligerent mood. Media persons observed a group of swarthy *sevaks* conducting mock trials of a demolition. The crowd had swelled to nearly 200,000.

As the morning of the 6th dawned, daring *kar sevaks* took a dip in the freezing waters of the Sarayu river and joined their brethren spread out all around the disputed structure. Saffron was the colour of the moment and the sounds of *bhajans* and militant slogans rent the air. Media persons took up vantage positions. Armed constables and RSS volunteers, acting on behalf of the BJP government, were in place.

By 10 am sadhus, *mahants* and various leaders had arrived. The crowd of *kar sevaks* had swelled and some attempted to breach the cordon around the Mosque. By 11.35 am, the sadhus were scheduled to commence a puja ceremony at a safe distance from the structure to mark the symbolic *kar seva* that had been decided upon by the BJP leaders. But by then, events had taken a dramatic turn. Around 50 *kar sevaks* had slithered across the security wall at the rear of the structure.

A hail of stones aimed at the guards provided cover for more intruders to follow. A young *kar sevak* scaled the protective railing and reached the top of one of the domes of the Mosque. The brickbats grew heavier and the police abandoned their posts. This provided the opening for an all-out attack.

BJP leaders appealed for order but the crowd was in no mood to comply. In retrospect their appeals rang hollow for what followed appeared to be a brazenly premeditated invasion of the structure the BJP chief minister had sworn to protect.

Hundreds of *kar sevaks* armed with pickaxes, shovels and iron rods rushed towards the Mosque. Some skimmed to the top on a rope that had been anchored to the dome by a grappling hook. Others began to attack the base of the edifice.

Elsewhere, as if by prior arrangement, *kar sevaks* started attacking media representatives. The objective, which appeared to be to prevent journalists and photographers from recording the event, was carried out with acute brutality. Men and women were beaten up, cameras smashed, clothes ripped off and purses snatched. A few minutes before 2 pm, the first dome fell.

Mohamad Ali road, one of Bombay's arterial roads, snakes through the underside of the city. On one side are the docks, obscured from view by high walls and a series of shaky tenement blocks. Till recently the road skimmed past Bombay's wholesale markets stocking, among other things, timber, scrap, crockery, vegetables and grain. Many of these markets had been moved out to distant sites but the little lanes abutting the road still played host to traders dealing in an assorted range of basic goods.

The roughly 2.6 km area surrounding Mohamad Ali road, consisting of Dongri, Bhendi Bazar, Pydhonie and Umerkhadi, was certainly one of the more vibrant parts of the city where gaudy acrylic blobs, *zari* borders and plywood lengths mingled with the smell of kababs and freshly baked *nankhatai*. It was also home to a large section of the city's Muslims.

It was to this region in central Bombay that Muslim migrants, mainly job-seeking Pathans and poor Muslims from Uttar Pradesh and Rajasthan, had gravitated in the early part of the century. Many had found work at the docks, others had set up small shops. Later migrants settled further north and in the distant suburbs but residents of the area surrounding Mohamad Ali road continued to live and proliferate in its filthy and increasingly congested lanes.

It was in this direction that the Shiv Sena's Bal Thackeray would point to substantiate his view of Muslims as a lot of illiterate India-bashing fanatics. The stereotype was a combination of truth and myth. Discrimination and poverty had contributed as much as religious camaraderie and backwardness towards sustaining the ghetto. But such complex arguments did not cut ice with Thackeray's middle-class Hindu supporters. Fed on his anti-Muslim rhetoric, they came to view the typical central Bombay resident, more commonly known as 'the Bhendi Bazar Muslim', as a dangerous presence in their midst.

On 6 December, the area was tense. The rising tide of Hindu chauvinism had increased the Bhendi Bazar Muslims' sense of isolation and bred a new, more aggressive consensus. Events of the day would determine their future course. Initial reports of the attack on the Babri Masjid had already reached Bombay. Even Doordarshan, the government's staid television network had been forced to reveal the bare facts in its afternoon bulletin. Still, the outcome was uncertain. Most people were secure in the belief that the *kar sevaks* would be turned back before substantial damage was done. By the evening, anxious Muslims began to gather on the streets of Bhendi Bazaar talking and keeping an eye on the BBC's hourly bulletin.

In distant Ayodhya, the destruction continued. The local law enforcers had thrown up their hands. A 25,000 strong force from the central paramilitary units waited for orders. A part of the central battalion that belonged to the Rapid Action Force was summoned by the district magistrate soon after the assault began only to be turned back 2 km short of the site.

The reasons for the absence of an official response on the part of the centre were and remained unclear. Observers, later analysing the course of events, would disagree on whether the prime minister's decision to trust the BJP and his refusal to intervene with force was evidence of a miscalculation or an unspoken reluctance to displease the Hindu lobby.

By 5 pm, defenceless against the frenzied mob, the 400-year-old structure surrendered utterly and completely leaving a red cloud of dust over a heap of rubble.

By late evening the scenes of mayhem and destruction had been flashed into several million Indian homes by the BBC and CNN. And on the streets of central Bombay, violence erupted.

Two years earlier, when the VHP had mounted its first assault on the Babri Masjid, I was working at a daily newspaper. For months the Babri Masjid/Ram Janmabhoomi controversy had dominated not just the headlines but gossip in offices, restaurants and street corners. At our editorial meetings the liberal view, generally though unusually considering the prevailing outlook in the city, prevailed. Advani's *Rath Yatra* provoked some bitter fights but the day on which the *kar sevaks* gathered in Ayodhya with the intention of storming the structure, the mood in the office was sanguine. Perhaps no one believed the *kar sevaks* would go so far; perhaps faith in the state chief minister Mulayam Singh Yadav's determination to stop them was strong. Whatever the reason, we watched the teleprinter with curiosity rather than anxiety.

And the news was reassuring. For the majority of the senior staff, whose sympathies weighed clearly on the side of secularism, its faith in Yadav was justified: the *kar sevaks* had been stopped and no damage to the Mosque was reported.

Late in the evening, however, the photographer assigned to the occasion called to say he had pictures of a few *kar sevaks* planting a flag atop the domes. The information generated the usual excitement that accompanies a scoop and much attention was diverted to the logistics of transmission. But the next morning the photograph, prominently splashed across the front page evoked a near hysterical reaction in the office. An assistant editor burst out crying and for most of us, the visual, regardless of the more heartening news had a profoundly unsettling effect.

The power of the visual. This had long been the most potent argument against liberalisation of television in India. The country's founding fathers while giving the lowliest peasant the vote still thought it fit to withhold the truth from reaching him through the mass media.

Mrs Gandhi, of course, made no secret of her contempt for the idea but even her apparently more liberal son, Rajiv Gandhi, had once said in answer to a question on media autonomy that: 'India is not ready for it.'

Politicians were not alone in this respect. Many journalists, jurists and other members of the intellectual elite held similar views. Their gravest trepidation was that the occurrence of a clash anywhere in the vast and perennially conflict-ridden land when flashed on television would lead to an instant and uncontrollable countrywide reaction. In the December of 1992, thanks to satellite television, the doomsayers' worst fears were being played out on the streets of central Bombay.

Angry young men, women, children and even the aged were out stoning public buses and uprooting bus stops, fire hydrants and post boxes. The focus on these symbols of state authority was not accidental. 'If the Mosque had been demolished after a court order, things might have been different,' observed A. Siddiqui, leader of the Tanzeem Allaho Akbar, a local Muslim organisation, 'but when they actually *saw* people rushing towards the Mosque and the security forces doing nothing to stop them, they felt the state had really let them down.'

The police bore the brunt of the onslaught. Riots in central Bombay, were wont to follow a predictable pattern given the excitable nature of its residents and the predilection of the largely Hindu police force to use bullets rather than less harmful methods of mob control.

In this case, the local Commissioner of Police, perhaps sensing the gravity of the situation, apologised to the crowd on behalf of the government. To no avail: three of his men were killed and 17 injured as they tried to restrain the aggressors. The retaliation was typically heavy-handed. The violence also spread to other parts of the city. And as horror stories of stabbings and killings by fire multiplied, the army had to be called in to restore order in a city with a long and much envied record of communal harmony.

In defence of the media, it could, of course be said, that it merely precipitated the inevitable response; it did not actually cause it. This is no doubt true. Yet, in a country unused to free and immediate access to information the satellite television channels, in the highly volatile situation, made news as much as they reported it.

Reports of the demolition on CNN, for instance, provoked angry demonstrations in neighbouring Islamic countries sparking off fears of a reprisal against Hindus in those countries. In Bangladesh, the government blacked out CNN (customarily relayed on the state network) as a precautionary measure but had to restore it after viewers protested.

In India, viewership of the BBC, the foreign news and current affairs channel with the highest penetration, rose sharply during that period. Liberals, fence sitters and even many pro-*Hindutvawadis* were shocked by the spectacle that showed up on their television screens on 6 December. At least one BJP supporter I met the day after the demolition seemed abashed by the incident.

But not for long. When the BBC interviewed L. K. Advani, who was arrested along with his party colleagues, the BJP leader showed no sign of the remorse he was reported to have felt over the demolition. Nor did he apologise for his party's failure to protect the Mosque. Instead, the canny politician spewed fire and repeated the old charge about temples being destroyed in Kashmir, an act that served to boost the sagging morale of his supporters at a critical time.

Apart from inadvertently providing a platform for the BJP leader, the BBC goofed up in other ways as well. For several hours the correspondent on the spot referred to the demolitionists as 'Hindus' giving the impression that all Hindus were in favour of the demolition. A newsreader also asked a BBC stringer in Bombay to identify the community of the victims in the riots (a major departure from the code followed by the Indian media: even the free press usually refrained from identifying victims or rioters by community). The stringer claimed they were 'Hindu' when in fact they were Muslim. Such lapses were perhaps understandable for a network grappling with immensely sensitive issues in uncharted territory for the first time. Even so, the experience brought home, forcefully, the perils of untrammelled television.

It also revealed television's unique ability to lay bare the truth for all to see. Television coverage of the demolition provided proof that the *kar sevaks* had come equipped with the tools of wreckage giving the lie to the BJP claim that the demolition was not a pre-meditated act but the culmination of a spontaneous upsurge. Footage of the *kar sewaks* patiently clearing the rubble and laying the foundation for a temple also gave the impression that the centre was being soft on Hindu extremists even after the event. And BBC man Mark Tully's description of the central security forces shedding their footwear and paying obeisance at the makeshift Hindu shrine revealed the difficulties of upholding the secular ideal in a deeply religious nation.

But above all what the Ayodhya incident demonstrated was that technology had turned the debate over television autonomy into a non-issue. As scriptwriter-poet Javed Akhtar pointed out, 'Indians have got used to being protected from unpleasant facts, but in an age of satellite communication this is no longer possible.'

The impact of the demolition was felt all over the country. In Madhya Pradesh, Hindu extremists celebrated their triumph in Ayodhya by distributing sweets and bursting crackers; in Assam, Muslims went on a rampage. In Gujarat a Hindu mob attacked a group of intellectuals protesting against the demolition shouting: 'Where were you when Hindu temples were demolished in Kashmir?' Over 700 people were killed in the countrywide riots.

In Maharashtra, the toll had risen to 259. Mohamad Ali Road, when I visited it soon after the outbreak of violence, presented a picture of devastation. Twisted traffic signals, the remnants of a bus stop, gunny bags, even an old dressing table lay strewn on the road. The wholesale textile market was completely gutted. Black acrid smoke emerged from the linoleum shops in the adjacent lanes where rolls of rexine had been set afire. The JJ Hospital close by had recorded 94 casualties: 70 bullet injuries; 15 stab and glass wounds; 5 stone injuries; 4 miscellaneous.

It took nearly a fortnight for tempers to cool and calm to return to the beleaguered city.

It did not last.

On 6 January 1993, exactly a month after the demolition of the Babri Masjid, I was on the road headed north. It was late but there was a fair amount of traffic on the road. At Mahim, the point where Bombay city meets the suburbs, the line of cars came to an abrupt halt and began to reverse.

I followed them through a series of hastily improvised diversions that brought me to a bylane which was pitted with small fires. Behind me smoke hung thinly in the winter air and as I crunched over stone and glass, shadowy figures on either side of the street whispered and regarded each other with narrow, suspicious stares. The trouble had started again.

For the next few days anarchy reigned. No one knew quite what was happening and why. But rumours filled the air. Armed Hindu mobs were said to be roaming the streets looking for Muslim targets. The Islamic states in the Gulf were reported to have sent a shipment of deadly arsenal to their Muslim brethren in Bombay. Kashmiri militants were claimed to have been discovered in a Bombay mosque. One day the milk supply was alleged to have been poisoned; another day it was bread. Muslim nameplates vanished from buildings and doors and ordinary Hindus banded into vigilante groups to protect their families against anticipated Muslim assaults.

A cleaner at a suburban club informed me that Hindu women in a particular locality had been raped and butchered. Where did she learn that, I enquired. 'Television,' she bluffed. In the earlier round of rioting, similar gossip about Bal Thackeray's purported arrest had resulted in widespread unrest after it was falsely attributed to the BBC.

In the middle of the chaos, the city's cable operators struck work on a totally unrelated issue. A family in one of the distant suburbs, deprived of their daily diet of video films turned to the state network and became aware, for the first time, of the riots that had been raging in the city for a week. The strike ended almost immediately: the police commissioner had apparently requested operators to resume services to keep troublemakers off the streets.

It did not help, however, for the killing and wreckage continued amidst general confusion. However shocking the December riots had been, the provocation was clear and visible. But for the January riots there seemed to be no logical explanation. In Bombay, people of varying castes and communities had lived together harmoniously for years. Apart from any other reason the commercial drive of the city had ensured that disruptions and disasters, and the city had a fair share of those, were not allowed to linger.

Bal Thackeray, whose followers were at the forefront of the tumult, maintained that they were merely retaliating for the murder of two Hindu workers in central Bombay

and the burning of a Hindu family in Jogeshwari by Muslims. Indeed, his claim and the half-truths that reigned during the period had it that the two communities were at war in the city.

The facts, though, clearly pointed to the contrary. The first areas to be brought under control were the predominantly Muslim ones where curfew was imposed after a spate of stabbings—the nature of which suggested the involvement of professional killers—had taken several Hindu lives. But all over the city, including its outlying suburbs, a virtual pogrom had been launched against the minority community, the systematic implementation of which indicated that it had been some time in the planning.

Muslims were systematically ejected from their homes, their shops looted and possessions destroyed; in some areas the marauders had lists that enabled them to home in on their targets. Newspaper reports claimed that the ringleaders in Bombay also used video recordings of Muslim women being molested by Hindu fanatics in Gujarat to enthuse their followers.

Thousands of victims fled the city. Others huddled in makeshift refugee camps. And as the cloud of obfuscation and lies lifted, it seemed increasingly clear that the riots had little to do with religion. Religion, in fact, was merely an excuse to effect an economic takeover. The prize in many cases was Bombay's scarcest commodity: space. Slumdwellers in Dharavi, for instance, returned after fleeing their homes to find new locks on their doors. In Behrampada, violence was said to have been engineered in the hope of clearing the slum to make way for the expansion of the neighbouring Bandra-Kurla Complex.

Murder, theft and looting were committed on Bombay's streets during those dark days. But the fear, mistrust and fanaticism whipped up among the city's law-abiding citizens not only sanctioned these crimes but gave them the respectable cover of sectarian violence. The flames that spread over the city were meant not just to destroy but to lay the ground for a new way of life.

Three weeks later in distant Delhi, I found conversation turning inevitably to the bloody and violent madness that had seized the commercial capital. Delhi was said to be envious of its thriving western neighbour but the riots appeared to have evoked sadness rather than triumph. It was as if, with Bombay's descent into hell, an entire nation's dream of a jostling, harmonious mix of caste and community had died an instant death. And as the violence wound to a desultory end, the bewildered question of how something like this could have happened in Bombay was quickly replaced by a yearning that the city would regain its old, all-inclusive character.

My unfailingly pessimistic response to this was greeted with protest. No one, it seemed, wanted to believe that Bombay could change. The city was too vibrant, too ebullient; surely it would survive the blow.

Perhaps. As soon as peace returned, Bombayites set about recouping their losses. Traffic steadily increased and late-night revellers were back on the streets. Evidence of turbulence—a stray burnt out shell of a car, the shambles of a house—disappeared in a frenzy of cleaning and rebuilding. And frequently one heard the smug assertion that the city had regained normalcy.

Beneath the robust patina, however, portents were grim. Some of the most commonly heard grounds for the Hindu chauvinists' bias against the minority community were the latter's reluctance to join the mainstream, its adherence to archaic religious laws and mullahs and the propensity of its members to live in clusters. The Bombay riots underscored all these tendencies.

A stream of Muslims terrified by the violence unleashed on them during the riots began to flee to Muslim strong-holds while Hindus, fearing retaliation in predominantly Muslim areas, attempted to move out. The trend was not restricted to the lower classes. Even prosperous middle-class building societies with a majority Hindu occupancy informed potential flat sellers that Muslim buyers should be discouraged. If Bal Thackeray's intention as he stated emphatically in an interview was to 'teach the Muslims a lesson', then it was a lesson learnt well by all communities: that there is safety only among one's own.

The Muslims of Bombay had learnt other lessons as well. Visiting several Muslim areas of Bombay I met and saw women who had lost their husbands in the riots, men who had been arrested and beaten by the police, gutted houses surrounded by the charred remains of ordinary everyday objects—a plastic bucket, a child's spelling book, letters.... Yet, amidst all this tragedy I found little grief. An old woman whose husband had been shot by the police as he ascended the rickety stairs to his house exhibited a carefully preserved bullet; a fresh-faced adolescent took me on a tour of a building stormed by the police and pointed out smashed windows, bullet marks and blood stains with the assurance of a professional guide; a young woman standing amidst the debris of her burnt hut brandished ration cards and sale deeds while dispassionately recounting her losses.

In the aftermath of the first round of riots, I had found anger, hurt and a grim determination to teach the Congress (I) a lesson. The second time round there was just a cold-blooded obsession with dates and numbers, in short, facts and their dissemination. A shopkeeper in Bhendi Bazar said to me matter of factly: 'We are ready for revolution, call the BBC, call CNN, we will tell them.' A self-appointed leader claimed that atrocities committed by the police against Muslims had been recorded on video and cassettes sent out to the Gulf. 'These Hindu leaders don't realise,' he said, 'there is just one India and many Muslim countries.' His words came back chillingly to me in March when a series of bomb blasts, masterminded by Muslim underworld leaders, ripped through the city leaving destruction and death in its wake.

Two years later, the state elected a Shiv Sena-BJP government for the first time. Muslims were perceived to have played a major role in ensuring the Congress's defeat. In Bombay, the Congress (I) lost all but one seat.

In a sense I suppose, we had survived. In Delhi the number of armed guards politicians needed to secure themselves against the growing gulf between them and sections of the people they were supposed to represent had long been perceived as little more than a minor nuisance on busy roads. Similarly, in Bombay, we had become accustomed to the sight of guns and uniforms. Metal fabricators, particularly in the suburbs, were flooded with a sudden demand for collapsible gates and iron grills after the riots. And the new timber mart constructed on the site of one razed during the riots was reported to have one extra feature: a high *pucca* wall.

And life goes on. I remember the faces in the cars around me the night the January riots began: of a finely bedecked couple returning presumably from a wedding; a harried young man, probably a businessman or professional working late; a family with children out possibly for a late dinner. They were impassive, matter of fact, as if they had been driving through a strife-torn city all their lives.

They will survive, so, will the rest of us. We will put strong locks on our doors and grills on our balconies, we will learn to drive with an ear cocked for signs of disturbance and run home early at the slightest intimation of trouble. In short, we will survive by adapting and closing our eyes to the change that has taken place all around us.

EVERYTHING MUST GO

BY THE MID-1970S TELEVISION WAS no longer a marginal issue in India. The emphasis, from the government's point of view, had shifted from social welfare to propaganda, but the primary concern was expansion, not programming; hardware not software.

The situation continued into the next decade. The preoccupation with dissemination and numbers was not accompanied by a corresponding improvement in infrastructure or studio facilities. Consequently, even as large tracts of the country were being covered by television, only about a dozen stations were equipped to produce programmes locally; the rest were merely relaying centres for telecasting programmes uplinked from Delhi via INSAT 1B.

At the Doordarshan Kendra in Delhi, where software for the entire country's upliftment and entertainment was made, the conditions were primitive. No training had been provided to technical and programming staff to handle colour broadcasts. Teleprinters and gimmicks such as windows opening on screens had added a touch of professionalism to presentation but no attempt had been made to bring the equipment or staff in tune with the needs of a vastly expanded system.

A paper presented to the Information and Broadcasting ministry by senior Doordarshan staffer, Kamalini Dutt (In Search of A System, 1985) reflected a sense of despondency stemming from this lacuna. 'Failure to make the right initial choice in the light of clearly defined options and taking account of installation costs, the cost of equipment and production is the cause of television not coming up to expected standards,' the report claimed.

The government's approach to television content was equally skewed. In 1984, a working group on software headed by the distinguished economist, P. C. Joshi had submitted a detailed report propagating the concept of an 'Indian Personality' for Doordarshan. Over the next two years, Namedia, a media watch outfit, organised a series of seminars to discuss the concept further. Its report, presented in 1986, harked back to the network's original aims. 'In India,' it observed, 'the entertainment component, though essential for recreational purposes and mitigating the rigours of daily life was secondary to instruction, education and information and the tackling of larger issues like unity, integrity, socio-economic integration and secular justice.... It means a shift from a predominantly urban setting to a poor, unprivileged countryside setting.'

All these considerations notwithstanding, by the late 1980s, Doordarshan was determinedly set on a course where the stress was on entertainment and profit. And for its programming, the network relied less and less on its own personnel and infrastructure and more on independent producers from outside.

It could, of course, be said that that was what the viewers wanted. On the other hand it was also true that the situation had been arrived at by default. Despite the government's oft-stated rural dispensation as far as television was concerned, all the television stations had come up in cities and programming clearly reflected the biases of its urban creators.

Moreover, the majority of television sets were owned by the haves, where the demand was for entertainment rather than upliftment. So, even though television was firmly controlled by a democratically elected government, viewership and actual management of the medium was in the hands of the more privileged section of Indian society. In the circumstances, it was only to be expected that, at some point, the intentions of one would come into conflict with the needs and sentiments of the other.

One area in which a deadlock seemed ineluctable was news and current affairs. Regardless of the widespread and longstanding demand for autonomy, successive governments had been reluctant to relinquish control of the powerful medium. Even Rajiv Gandhi's experiment with autonomy proved to be short-lived.

In fact, the Rajiv Gandhi government's blatant use of television for propaganda in the latter half of his tenure as prime minister was a significant rallying point for Opposition leaders during the 1989 parliamentary elections. And when the National Front came to power after defeating Rajiv's Congress, a new television autonomy bill based on the abortive Prasar Bharati Bill of the Janata regime was formulated for introduction.

The bill did not have a smooth passage, however. For one, not everyone in the new government was keen on the idea of autonomy. Deputy Prime Minister Devi Lal, for instance, was decidedly against any move to dilute the government's hold over the medium. But more important than internal dissensions in the ministry was the very real confusion over the meaning of the term itself. What did autonomy constitute? Did it imply freedom from government control or a total surrender to market forces? Was total autonomy really desirable? Who was to decide how much of it was okay and how was it to be enforced? These and other questions came up time and again in the press and at seminars organised to discuss the bill.

And from the tenor of the debate, it was clear that when faced with the actual prospect of autonomy, even its most ardent supporters had second thoughts.

In March 1990, I attended one such seminar organised by the Indian Documentary Producers' Association in Bombay. The guest of honour was the Information and Broadcasting Minister, P. Upendra. And the list of speakers included art filmmaker Kumar Shahani, media expert P. Sainath, and Nani Palkhivala, an eminent jurist best known for his annual post-Budget ruminations that drew a football stadium-size audience every year.

A large part of the proceedings was dominated by complaints. Each of the several documentary and feature filmmakers present had a grouse against the network, most of which had to do with corruption and nepotism. The part liberalisation which enabled Doordarshan to source from private producers while still retaining control had been subverted by officials in charge of processing proposals, they alleged, with the result that bribes and contacts had become the criteria for selection rather than quality.

A couple of documentary producers railed against Doordarshan's propensity for blanking out specific programmes for political reasons and some time was spent on discussing how the proposed bill which recommended putting a semi-autonomous board in charge of the network could prevent such occurrences.

Much of this was old hat. Capriciousness and corruption were now endemic at Doordarshan (press reports alleged that even the *paanwallah* outside Mandi House was the producer, author and director of two serials and a telefilm). And intervention in television was hardly earth-shattering news.

What was new was the theoretical debate sparked off by the bill. And here, oddly, there was a certain degree of consensus among the assorted and disparate delegates. The move towards liberalisation found general approval and yet equally persuasively, speakers warned against the dangers of replacing political tyranny with the tyranny of market forces.

The privatisation of one channel is a dangerous area, claimed film critic Iqbal Masud, and should not even be considered for another 25 years. No priority should be given to market forces above form of programming, was Kumar Shahani's view. Even Nani Palkhivala, India's most prominent advocate of liberalisation, expressed reservations about freeing television of all controls in his speech.

If anyone saw the obvious dichotomy in demanding freedom and controls at the same time, no one mentioned it. Certainly, apprehensions concerning the social cost of privatising an influential medium in a country of great divisions of caste, class and religion were understandable. On the other hand, could such sharp contradictions find an amicable resolution?

At the end of the meeting, P. Upendra was handed two white doves to release as a mark of hope and goodwill. In their zeal, the organisers probably forgot that the meeting was taking place in a large, but closed hall. And the predictable happened. The birds soared high and free only to find themselves boxed in. Confused and frightened they flew around aimlessly watched by a houseful of disapproving delegates. It was symbolic of the day's discussion. And of the future of Indian television.

The Prasar Bharati Bill was eventually passed with a number of amendments but brought little change. Doordarshan continued to offer much the same fare; political meddling did not abate and producers still had much to gripe about. In the absence of any real motivation for change, the only course that could be taken was one of drift. And in the light of events that were to follow, indecisiveness regarding the mass media left the initiative in other, unknown hands.

***

Through the 1970s, India's biggest bogey was not Pakistan, not China, not its endemic poverty nor its truant rains but the Foreign Hand. Multipurpose, omniscient and all-powerful, the Foreign Hand was said to be responsible for almost anything that went wrong in the country. No one would specify what exactly the Foreign Hand was. In fact, its very potency lay in its mysteriousness. What was clear though was that it was Western, probably American, and its sole purpose was the downfall of the Indian civilisation.

In the 1990s the Foreign Hand seemed to have returned in the shape of Star TV. While the lacklustre CNN and even the far more pervasive cable TV had aroused little reaction from Indian viewers, the stepped up invasion from the skies evoked a response of panic proportions. 'The threat is to our national space, cultural values, communal harmony and international image,' warned former Information secretary S. S. Gill. 'History will not forgive them,' prophesised ex-Supreme Court judge, V. R. Krishna Iyer, for those who failed to stop the march of the new media.

These included, of course, the State. By law even a municipal corporation had the power to penalise cable TV operators or satellite dish owners. But, despite its habitual paranoia regarding the electronic media, the government had done nothing to check the proliferation of cable. Its response to satellite was equally passive.

According to *India Today,* dated 31 March 1992, an internal report of the Information & Broadcasting Ministry had predicted as early as February 1991 that 'programmes specifically targeted at Indian audiences are likely to be beamed from foreign satellites in the near future'. Special committees recommended counter moves such as delinking dish antennae from cable to limit viewership for satellite television, and setting up a private national channel. No action was taken on any of these suggestions. Mahesh Prasad, Secretary, Information & Broadcasting, dismissed satellite television as a 'nine-day wonder' and many in the government actually believed that the dish antennae sprouting all over the country were being installed to receive Doordarshan more clearly.

To some extent the belief that Star with its English-language programming would attract a negligible number of viewers was not wholly unrealistic. But in October 1992, Star TV decided to launch Zee, an indigenously produced channel in Hindi.

***

The story of Zee's beginnings goes something like this. Sometime in 1991, Star invited bids for a locally produced Hindi channel to be aired on the network. One day, Star's owner Li sat before the hefty pile of applications and picked one at random. The lucky winner was Subhash Chandra, trader, wheeler-dealer and small-time businessman with no previous experience of the media.

The story may be true or apocryphal, but the choice turned out to be a windfall for the Hong Kong-based network. For Chandra made up for his lack of knowhow with foresight and a considerable amount of business acumen. In 1992, Star offered him the channel for 5 million dollars and the 41-year-old Haryanvi along with an associate went about setting up a production outfit relying on a shoestring budget and an enthusiastic staff. The result—the first truly autonomous channel in an Indian language—was nothing like the country had ever seen before.

Zee had film-based competitions, trailers of the latest film songs, a magazine programme for women, model hunts, game shows, chat shows and soaps. But the difference was not just in the format but in the attitude that pervaded the new channel.

On Doordarshan, comperes were demure and aloof; on Zee they could be loud, sarcastic, friendly, crazy or even offensive. Controversial topics were taboo on Doordarshan; Zee's chat shows thrived on controversy. Doordarshan debated the state of the nation; Zee's *Aap Ki Adalat* was more likely to discuss Bal Thackeray's fondness for beer. The atmosphere in a Doordarshan studio was stiff and formal; on Zee's game shows contestants threw buckets of coloured water on each other. Doordarshan carried documentaries on rural development; Zee gave away gift hampers, air coolers and silk saris. Doordarshan presenters dressed decorously and spoke chaste Hindi; Zee hosts appeared in gaudy designer apparel and used the language of the streets.

In the space of a mere three months, Zee with its chatty and colourful programming had spawned a huge demand for cable connections (proving to be an effective vehicle for Star to piggyback on). 85,000 gushing letters poured daily into its office and its following extended even to countries such as Pakistan and Dubai that fell within the Star footprint. The programming on Zee was loud, often crass; its production values were tacky. The secret of its success was that it spoke directly to the burgeoning Indian middle class.

Unlike Doordarshan, Zee did not preach; nor did it attempt to address the aspirations of an entire nation. Its aim was clearly to entertain and the concerns it reflected were those of the relatively affluent urban class.

Doordarshan and I & B officials watched Zee's rising popularity with alarm. There was much to be concerned about. As Zee collected more viewers among the prosperous, advertisers began to divert their spending to the new channel. In December 1992, at a meeting between representatives of the Information & Broadcasting ministry and top advertising agencies, advertisers warned the bureaucrats that Doordarshan would lose out on revenue if it did not improve its programming. Viewers in the top income bracket were increasingly moving over to Star. In November 1993, a random survey on viewership of a recently concluded Hero Cup cricket tournament conducted by *The Afternoon Despatch & Courier* revealed that 95 per cent of people polled had watched the matches on Star in preference to Doordarshan.

Belatedly, the Information and Broadcasting ministry came up with the idea of revamping Doordarshan's second channel, viewed in the metros and a pale imitation of the first, by farming out time slots to private producers.

The idea by itself was not new. The Varadan Committee, set up to figure out ways to counter the satellite threat, had made a similar suggestion. In its report, however, the committee had also expressed the need to guard against 'the dangers of unrestrained commercialism which may follow the establishment of additional channels financed solely through advertising'.

Confronted with the ongoing dilemma of combining profit, autonomy and public good, the government established the Air Time Committee of India. By early 1993, the ATCI, which consisted of a group of seven eminent citizens, had drawn up a blueprint for the proposed Metro channel which, apart from describing a 66-hour weekly content mix, also laid down stringent guidelines for the selection of producers.

But suddenly, inexplicably and without waiting to consider the ATCI's recommendations, Doordarshan went ahead and launched its Metro channel. The initial package, a two-hour capsule of mainly film-based programmes hastily cobbled together by private producers, proved to be an instant hit with viewers (studies found that Metro viewership rose to 40 per cent while both Zee and cable television registered a decline).

Emboldened, Doordarshan announced the launch of four new channels, slots on which would be available on a first-come-first-serve basis. Producers took the announcement literally. Days before the scheduled date for applications, representatives of film companies, some had hired taxi drivers for the purpose, queued up outside the Doordarshan headquarters in Delhi like buyers at a milk booth.

The situation turned even more farcical when some companies started a parallel queue claiming theirs was the correct one. Members of both queues wound up in court and the ministry hastily changed the first-come-first-serve policy to one of random selection by a computer.

The ATCI report was thrown out of the window and the committee resigned in protest. P. S. Deodhar, chairman of the ATCI, was trenchant in his criticism of the new policy: 'It was devoid of professionalism and based on crass commercial considerations in disregard of the national interest,' he claimed.

Information and Broadcasting Minister K. P. Singh Deo, on the other hand, was sanguine. 'The new channels were introduced to attract more funds,' he said categorically, 'budgetary support has come down from 80 per cent to 20 per cent so I have to find the money to keep Doordarshan going.

Indian television had long been veering away from the purpose for which it had been introduced. But in the competitive atmosphere of 1993 the fig leaf of social concern was dropped, to the dismay of old school ideologues. Harish Khanna, former Director-General, Doordarshan (1987), reflected a widespread concern in intellectual circles when he maintained that: 'Indian television has come to reflect the ambivalence, the genteel hypocrisy of our system, which is supportive of inertia. It also reflects the political, moral and intellectual confusion into which we have landed, choosing the easy path of a loosely-structured evolution as against either a principle based revolution or a carefully conceived and sustained evolution along pre-determined lines.'

The phenomenon was not restricted to the state television network though. The arrival of new media technology had spawned a similar response in other areas as well. One of these was the monolithic film industry.

In the days before video and commercial television, the chief form of entertainment for the country's masses was the cinema. For decades, films, particularly Hindi films had determined the hairstyles, dress and fantasies of successive generations of youth. No medium could have been more unrealistic: Hindi cinema abounded with tales of separated twins, impossible villainy, prodigious valour, uncanny mishaps, fights, dances, songs, songs and more songs. And no medium could have been more idealistic. The country was struggling to uphold democracy and secularism in the face of starvation. But in the movies it happened so easily: good triumphed over evil, the poor man was vindicated, high caste married low caste and Hindus, Muslims and Christians lived harmoniously. India was a land of misery. But hope was just a cheap ticket away.

By the mid-1980s, much to the disgust of the movie moghuls, even the ticket was dispensed with. While they were spending millions to weave their celluloid dreams, video pirates and cable operators were gifting away their creations virtually for free. And there was little that they could do to stop them. The anti-piracy front and the legal battles fought by the industry had yielded nothing substantial. The pirates continued to supply illegal copies to the proliferating cable networks. And films began to flop. From a success rate of 70 per cent (the popularity of the Hindi cinema ensured that the majority of films managed to recover their cost and make at least a marginal profit through reruns; only 5 per cent of films actually lost money), the scales tilted to a failure rate of 85 per cent. Only five out of a hundred films were hits, and 10 recovered their money. The others bombed. And in the first three months of 1989, 20 cinema houses closed down all over the country.

Part of the problem lay with the industry itself. In the 1940s, when Indian cinema was still at a nascent stage, the industry was patterned loosely on the old Hollywood model. Artistes, musicians, scriptwriters and others were contracted to one or the other of a clutch of companies which made most of the films. In the early 1950s, the companies faded away and filmmaking became the realm of the independent producer who would raise funds from various sources and recover it by selling the rights of his film to distributors who in turn would make money from the exhibitors.

It was an extremely unprofessional set-up and a needlessly expensive one. The heavy reliance on individuals, particularly stars, and exorbitant interest rates charged by lenders (no bank or financial institution was willing to invest in films) upped the stakes considerably. But the popularity of the cinema and the consistently high returns ensured the survival of the industry and of the men and women who earned their living from it.

With the video and cable invasion, cinema houses were emptied of audiences and the whole precarious system came close to collapse. Exhibitors could no longer afford

129

to run theatres, distributors went bankrupt and traditional sources of finance dried up. Video piracy had transformed the business of cinema the world over; in India too, the situation called for adaptation and restructuring.

But the film industry did not see it that way. Instead of closing ranks, it frittered away time in power struggles. Instead of seeking solutions to suit the changed circumstances it cribbed about the high entertainment taxes levied by the government. Instead of coming to terms with the technology, it buried its head in the sand.

'Nature always breeds a solution,' claimed veteran distributor N. N. Sippy, when I interviewed him in 1989. Gulshan Rai, maker of ace hits such as *Johnny Mera Naam* indulged in a similar piece of escapism: 'The more you fall, the more you rise. Like in Hindi films, after every crisis, there must be a climax, and a happy ending.' Such unbounded optimism was possible for only one reason: an endless supply of money.

Since its inception, the film industry had attracted a stream of fly-by-night operators: fortune-seekers or rich men in search of one elusive hit or glamour. The emergence of a host of fan magazines had further amplified the attractions of the film world drawing suckers like bees to honey. Some of these were content to play a behind-the-scenes role and fund established filmmakers; others were looked down upon and usually ended up making the odd B or C grade film.

In the post-video scenario, however, they presented a significant source of finance for the cash-strapped industry. It was with this money that the industry continued to churn out as many films as before. In fact, the launch of new films registered a sharp increase in 1988.

New banners sprouted overnight; novices turned producers and the film trade magazines were flush with news of *mahurats*, the traditional ceremony conducted to mark the launch of a film.

Many of these never made it beyond the first reel and those that actually reached completion disappeared from the cinemas often within a week of their release. Failure did not prove a dampener though, for in the casino that the film industry had increasingly begun to resemble, the high rollers were wealthy and prominent members of Bombay's crime fraternity.

A weak link between filmdom and the underworld already existed. In the late 1970s the former had assiduously wooed ex-smuggler, Haji Mastaan (he eventually made a film starring his starlet wife). Other lesser known criminals had followed in his footsteps without leaving a mark. A decade later however gangsters had made major inroads into the film industry: they controlled the video business, sponsored films, coerced defaulters into paying up their dues and were generally respected figures of patronage. And since their foray into filmdom was occasioned by a desire to mingle with the glitterati, and not any commitment to filmmaking or for profit, producers and directors took full advantage by floating projects that were unlikely to ever see the light of day. Stars jacked up their prices and signed more films than they could reasonably expect to work on at a time, secure in the knowledge that half of them would never get beyond a few reels.

For the more professional filmmaker, however, the problem of dwindling audiences continued. And the manner in which the industry chose to tackle it was to intensify two selling ingredients in the movies: sex and violence.

In the early 1980s, Hindi cinema could be divided into distinct categories. There was the multi-starrer extravaganza, the tender middle-of-the-road film, the serious art film, the family melodrama and then there was the low-grade product characterised by its tackiness, a cast of unknowns and huge doses of titillation.

By the end of the decade, the middle-of-the-road and the art film had more or less disappeared. The dividing walls between the other categories too were fast vanishing. Bollywood's top star Amitabh Bachchan and several of his peers had gone into semi-retirement leaving the field open for a host of new faces. In fact, the number of star-aspirants zoomed dramatically. Unlike in the old days, stars no longer guaranteed the success of a film and producers found it more economical to use inexpensive newcomers. The other advantage of working with the NYTs or New Young Things as *India Today* dubbed them was that they lacked the inhibitions of their predecessors.

This had become an essential requirement in the rapidly emerging film scenario where plot and acting had been replaced by action and well-toned physiques. Films had become increasingly bawdy and violent. The censors, a scissor-happy breed used to snipping off even shots of a couple kissing, seemed to been paralysed by the torrent of rapes, assault, sexual innuendo, scantily-clad women and bloodshed. 'In the old days,' commented actor Shashi Kapoor, 'There was a class C film to satisfy the hunger of a particular kind of audience. Now A, B, C, D, they are all together.'

Exigent business reasons were quoted in support of the phenomenon. Filmmakers claimed that with video having deprived them of viewers from the middle and upper classes, which had earlier formed the bulk of the cinema-going audience, they were forced to cater to the more prurient tastes of the paying cine-goer who was typically lower class and male. Moreover, they argued, the consistent exposure to blue films and Hollywood movies on video had made Indians more blasé about sex and violence; In fact, Indian audiences now *expected* a higher degree of titillation from domestic cinema. Whatever the merits of the argument (there were no actual success stories to back up the theory) the strategy did have an unintended fallout.

Over 10 per cent of urban households had acquired a video player/recorder and 13 million viewers had access to cable television by the late 1980s. A study of cable households by the market research unit ADMAR revealed that most households viewed some kind of audio-visual medium for 6–8 hours a day.

And since the most popular fare on cable and video was Hindi films it was clear that a sizeable segment of the urban population was exposed to a strong dose of titillation, not in the dark alien surroundings of a cinema hall, but in the bright confines of a home every day.

Then in 1991, came Star TV with its bagful of cheap imports. The Indian middle class, ensconced in an almost Victorian code of morality was suddenly and unexpectedly exposed to the bizarre realities of third-rate American soaps, Phil Donahue-led talk shows with sex offenders, and the raunchy world of MTV.

Two of the more popular programmes of the time were *The Bold and the Beautiful* and *Santa Barbara*. By any standards the happenings in these never-ending sagas were extraordinary: elaborate conspiracies, characters returning from the dead, intricate love triangles, or quadrangles (one involved a young woman, her ex-lover, his father and her mother) and so on.

But from the point of view of sexual mores, just the sight of a couple French-kissing or in deshabillé was nothing short of a revolution. And though these indulgences were restricted, initially, to 3.5 million English-literate households, all that was soon to change. For by the early 1990s, emboldened by the launch of Zee and Doordarshan's Metro channel, a clutch of Indian entrepreneurs, including the enterprising J. K. Jain, had floated television channels by renting transponders on one of the many satellites available.

All at once, Indians had a host of television channels to choose from. But the striking aspect of the phenomenon was not quantitative, though the sudden flood was indeed overwhelming, but qualitative. In the general hurry to latch on to the hardware revolution, no one, it appeared, had given much thought to the question of software.

Doordarshan floated a Metro channel and then five language channels without preparation; Jain TV infiltrated cable networks with amazing speed, yet it had a mere handful of programmes to put out. ATN—one of the first of the privately-owned channels—ran an endless stream of film songs. The priority, in each case, with the exception perhaps of Zee, appeared to be to get on the air and deal with the question of content later.

'In India software is chasing hardware,' observed film director Shyam Benegal at a seminar, 'this is not normal.' At a party held to announce the launch of the *Business India* television network, Shekhar Kapur, a film director and one of the network's three chief guns, openly expressed his dismay at the excessive attention focused on hardware in preference to programming.

Expectedly, given such short-sightedness, the electronic media barons soon found themselves with a surfeit of air time and nothing to put on it. And the imperative to fill the gap set off the 'great software rush'. Overnight, about 500 studios sprang up in Delhi. In Bombay, home of the advertising and film industry, it seemed as if a new serial was being launched every day. 600 pilot episodes were said to be in circulation. And everyone had jumped onto the bandwagon, from the big names in Bollywood to a clutch of Johnny-come-latelies, which included shop owners, sundry exporters, real estate agents, newspaper hacks, housewives, transporters, etc. Film studios had been converted into production centres for television. And anyone who could act and many who couldn't were flitting from studio to studio and role to role in the race to fill the slot.

In October 1994, actor Mohan Gokhale confessed to acting in as many as 22 pilots during the previous six months. Producer and scriptwriter Karan Razdan found people willing to pay him double the market rate just to get their hands on a script.

As could be expected, the results were far from imaginative. Film-based programming continued to be the mainstay of every channel while the rest of the time was made up with tawdry imitations of American formats: chat shows, soaps, top-twenty shows, games and tele-shopping.

Title track. Two shadows dancing. It is a man and a woman. Their movements are jerky, like a bad imitation of a James Bond film opening. The music builds; they embrace frenziedly. Fade Out.

The lights come on to reveal a house. It belongs to a rich man. There is a street. A woman is crying. She is delivering a child, she needs help. Her husband begs the rich man for money. He refuses. The woman dies. The husband clutches the child and swears revenge.

Next scene. The rich man has a daughter. She is spoilt and in love with a vagrant. They drink. They kiss. He takes off her clothes. They make love. The girl laughs hysterically.

This was the world of *Yudh,* advertised as a blockbuster to end all blockbusters. The sets looked like they had been borrowed from *Santa Barbara,* the script sounded like a decimated version of *Dynasty.* But the actors were undeniably Indian and the language they spoke was Hindi.

Yudh did not live up to its promise of epic grandeur. But in the first few episodes itself, it managed to reveal how far the new channels were prepared to go in their desperation for audiences. For, like the film industry in the preceding decade, the foundling television industry had decided that the only way to beat the competition was to include huge doses of sensationalism and sex.

Partly this was a fallout from the film industry: film songs in Hindi and the southern languages that were flashed continuously on the various channels had become obsessively vulgar and filled with *double entendres* ('I am 18 and my blouse has become smaller', 'What lies behind the blouse?' etc.). But even original television programming had become a no-holds barred affair.

Zee was the first to set the trend. One of its top-rated shows was *Tara,* a soap that revolved around the trials of four girls who, by Indian standards sported extremely promiscuous lifestyles which included cigarettes, and affairs. Another programme, *Dillagi,* had a couple in a passionate clinch. Archana Puran Singh, the lively presenter of *Kya Scene Hai* wore body-hugging suits and miniskirts; Mohan Kapoor's idea of humour was asking a pretty participant on his show, *Saanp Seedi,* to be the mother of his children.

On El TV, a sari-clad compere asked men about the state of their libido. Jain TV went so far as to relay soft porn films on Saturday nights. And soon Doordarshan was also in competition with more 'bold' soaps, fashion shows and compilations of Hindi film songs complete with *entendres* and suggestive gyrations.

The indigenisation of the western format was extremely significant. As Rekha Nigam, creative chief with the ad agency Trikaya Grey and a mother of three observed: 'As far as Star was concerned it united most families in the feeling that what they were watching was not part of "our" culture. But with an Indian cast doing the same thing that gap disappeared. Also, television tends to legitimise things. No one can deny that the new Hindi film songs are extremely obscene, yet the fact that they are on television somehow conveys the impression that someone has deemed them okay for us to watch.'

The last, in actual fact, was far from the truth. Many of the songs in question had climbed the charts on the various channels three months before the censors had a chance to clear the films. Their ensuing popularity made it difficult for the authorities to take them off the screen.

Facts however had been rendered irrelevant. For the huge burst of permissiveness in the electronic media had not only transformed other media but had also brought about a sea change in lifestyles and attitudes.

'LML,' said girl to boy.

'GTH,' said boy to girl.

Capiche?

No?

Try again.

'Let's make love,' said girl to boy.

'Go To Hell,' said boy to girl.

Just a decade before, such an exchange between an unmarried couple on screen would have evoked cries of outrage and condemnation. The classic idea of romance as shown in the movies had more to do with covert glances, quickening heartbeats and moonlit duets. Pre-marital sex was a strict no-no; the kind of thing that brought illegitimate babies and social ostracism in its wake.

But that was in the past. The screen lovers in the 1990s were getting down to the nitty-gritty in an instant and to hell with the consequences.

The aggressor, increasingly, was the woman. The contemporary mini-skirted virago was no simpering doormat. She winked. She leered. She threatened. And if her brawny, woolly-headed male counterpart was too busy contemplating his biceps, she was off with a shrug of her delicate shoulder singing 'Sexy sexy sexy, *mujhe log bolein'* (Sexy sexy sexy, people call me).

In E. M. Forster's *Passage to India* a misspelt inscription read 'God Si Love'. In modern India the equivalent of love was another four-letter word: lust.

The evidence was all too visible. News-stands displayed a choice of lascivious publications. Topless starlets and scantily clad models peeked alluringly from magazine covers. Advertisements for products as diverse as condoms and coffee used lust to attract customers while *Stardust,* the country's most popular film magazine, ran a feature on 'The New Morality', illustrated with photographs of bare-chested hunks.

The bestselling books of pop fiction writer, Shobha De, were scattered with expletives and fornicating couples. A new show on radio FM discussed sexual queries sent in by listeners and a slew of television chat shows were blowing the lid off previously taboo subjects such as adultery and pre-marital sex.

Puritan India was shedding its inhibitions. And how!

In Bombay and Bangalore, for instance, a host of jazzy pubs had opened where fashionably-attired young people gathered to drink and listen to the latest MTV hits. Star Plus received letters from housewives asking for information about breast augmentation after a Donahue show had been aired on the subject; Bombay-based psychiatrist Rajish Parikh noticed a sharp increase in patients reporting symptoms of bulimia after a related talk show on Star Plus.

On the Hindi talk show on Zee, *Chakravyuh,* ordinary people participated actively on sexual stereotyping and obscenity; one woman made the startling (by Indian standards) disclosure on a show that she was in love with her cousin and had sought psychotherapeutic help to deal with her problem.

Prominent sexologist Prakash Kothari claimed that the widespread exposure to pornography on video had led to exaggerated sexual expectations and triggered off a licentious trend among the middle class. A magazine article on married couples seeking sex with other couples revealed that many of them had been inspired by watching blue films on video.

The clearest indications of change came from the inhabitants of filmdom. Partly because of their visibility and partly due to the fantasy element in their work which allowed them to get away with things ordinary mortals could not, stars had always been at the forefront of permissive trends. In the 1960s, actress Sharmila Tagore created a furore by wearing a bikini in a film; in the 1970s the romance between the statuesque Hema Malini and her married co-star Dharmendra provided grist for the gossip mills. And as late as the 1980s starlet Neena Gupta set tongues wagging by having a child outside marriage through her liaison with a West Indian cricketer.

By the 1990s film stars were bedding each other with gay abandon and admitting it so proudly that nothing they did, it seemed, could shock anymore. 'It's boring to be a virgin,' declared a young actress, 'It's my body and I can do what I like with it,' claimed another. Starlet Pooja Bedi posed nude for a condom ad; Pooja Bhatt shed her boyfriends as rapidly as she did her clothes. Actor Salman Khan was reportedly caught cheating on his fiancée who immediately did a tell-all interview with a film magazine.

In the space of a few years the scandalous had been converted into the routine. A wave of permissiveness was sweeping through the country and definitions of acceptable and unacceptable behaviour had undergone a dramatic transformation.

The substitution of outrage with tolerance ironically boosted the exploitation of sex for commercial purposes often in the most retrograde manner. For two decades *Debonair,* a semi-literary monthly men's magazine, was the only English language publication to carry pictures of semi-nude women. By 1994 the market had widened to include a choice of lascivious magazines such as *Fantasy, Chastity, Fun, Playways* and so on.

Newcomer Mamta Kulkarni posed topless on the cover of *Stardust. Movie* magazine carried a feature on macho men and their muscles. 'The feedback to the article was fabulous,' gushed editor Dinesh Raheja, 'women are finally asserting their voyeuristic rights.'

Voyeurism was the key word. The entertainment sections of newspapers were crowded with ads for plays with suggestive names: 'Carry on Pappa', 'Home Is Where The Trouser Is', 'Up Yours' and the like. The Sunday sections, Saturday sections and all the colour pages were choc-a-bloc with features on fashion. Flimsy creations were paraded by lissom models and intense-eyed young men at select parties, launches, even on airplanes and trains. At ₹10,000 to ₹100,000 a throw, designer wear was beyond the reach of 99 per cent of the Indian population. But that was beside the point. For the fashion show had become the new cabaret in town. The fact that titillation could sell in a repressed society was not exactly an earth-shaking revelation. The Hindi film industry had long perfected the technique of getting past the censors by putting its heroines in clinging, wet saris. What was new was the claim that it was a sign of professionalism ('We are performers,' claimed film actor Shakti Kapoor, 'we will drop our trousers if we are asked to'), of progress and of a new and welcome openness.

Girls and boys from privileged families trained long and hard to model the briefest of clothes with ludicrously high price tags and were much admired figures among the young. Pooja Bhatt's promiscuous lifestyle made her the most written about actress of her generation without the films to match. *Glad Rags*, a glossy fashion magazine garnered free publicity in the gossip columns by undressing nubile models and hosting a 'manhunt' for the best looking male. Shobha De became a national celebrity by attempting a rip-off of sleazy western potboilers.

The trend reached its apotheosis in *Nikki Tonight,* a chat show on Star Plus featuring Nikki Bedi, a blonde, blue-eyed Anglo-Indian woman about town and an assortment of Indian celebrities. Sex dominated the show (What do silicone breasts feel like? Do you discuss sex with your father? Do you use a condom? were some of the memorable questions).

Even by India's new permissive standards *Nikki Tonight* was appallingly risqué. But, silenced perhaps, by the forbiddingly glamorous packaging, the oodles of hype and the smug assumption that India was 'ready' for this, no one protested.

But then, the elegantly coiffed Bedi went too far.

One of her guests, Ashok Row Kavi, a controversial gay activist known for his penchant for the outrageous, made a bitchy reference to India's most revered figure, Mahatma Gandhi.

Bedi laughed.

And all hell broke loose.

LOVE FOR SALE

14 FEBRUARY 1995. SHOPS AND fast food joints in Mumbai city were festooned with banners wishing patrons a Happy Valentine's Day. Entire pages of dailies were filled with soppy prepaid messages from people with names like Nasir, Aswini, Raj, Auntie Chips, Stranger, jaan, Charlie and Bond. Radio FM played sentimental songs through the day. Confectioners churned out heart-shaped pastries. Restaurants hosted special candlelight dinners. Love, or some version of it, was most certainly in the air.

A traveller arriving in Mumbai on that particular day could have been forgiven for wondering, at least momentarily, if he had landed up in some western capital rather than a place with professedly ancient local traditions and deeply conservative norms regarding relations between the sexes.

The phenomenon was startlingly sudden even for us native Mumbai-dwellers. A friend whose mother had her birthday on the same day looked at the wilting flowers and soggy cake, the best that she had managed to procure amid the bedlam, and shook her head in bewilderment: 'I don't know what's come over everyone.'

The answer was really quite simple: India or at least its metropolitan cities had been initiated into the global brotherhood of Romance Inc., the most basic principle of which was that the demonstration of ardour was an expensive thing. Consider for instance some of the options that were dangled before Mumbai's amorous couples on V Day 1995. Endless love at *Sheetal Again,* a six-course Valentine dinner at *Cafe Royal;* Hugs n Misses at *Leo's Pub,* cost: ₹400–2000 for two. Feeling 'the experience' at Shopper's Stop, cost: no limit. Archie's card, the absolutely minimum requirement on the teenage circuit, cost: ₹10–35.

More money was spent on saying 'I love you' on that one day than had probably been spent over the previous 10 years. And the single factor responsible for turning an obscure foreign ritual into a momentous event at least as far the young, westernised Indian elite was concerned, was the media.

Weeks before the event, Star TV's various channels had been choc-a-bloc with ads, fillers and programmes on the theme, including random interviews with people on the streets of Hong Kong ('What do you expect to receive on Valentine's Day?: Flowers/candlelight dinner/diamond Ring'). Shops selling gift items announced competitions and prizes. Spurred by the apparent flurry, newspapers and magazines got into the act, carrying articles on the 'card craze' and the origins of St. Valentine's Day.

By the time the day rolled up the hype had snowballed enough to enter the consciousness of a vast number of Indians and sent a considerable number scurrying to the nearest card/flower/ cake/jewellery/soft toy/assorted gift shop, a simple case of love meeting commerce in perfect harmony.

Then again what was new? After all what was the Indian convention of 'arranged marriage' (where caste, religion, social status and money were the prime criteria) but a semi-business proposition; a trade-off between families where, in many cases, the prospective couple did not even set eyes on each other till the day of the wedding? True, some movement had occurred in the romance department over the last couple of decades or so. The increased opportunities for fraternisation between the sexes had thrown up trends such as teenage sex, office romances and intercommunal marriages, all duly covered by the local magazines. Couples holding hands and necking had become a familiar sight in the cities and even in cases where the search for a suitable partner had been initiated by the parents, children were being given a greater say in the selection leading to the curious phenomenon of 'love-cum-arranged' marriages where couples claimed to have fallen in love between the first meeting and the actual wedding.

On the other hand, marriage bureaus, agencies that provided lists of marriageable candidates and matrimonial columns, had mushroomed in recent years. A large number of the nubile men and women and even children I met all over the country expected to marry according to their parents' wishes. Two-thirds of 1,365 undergraduates in eight cities polled by Marg for *India Today* in 1994 claimed that they would settle for an arranged marriage. And 84 per cent of women and 80 per cent of men polled in Delhi by Current Opinion and Future Trends in 1994 claimed that an arranged marriage was fine by them.

A typical marriage bureau I visited in 1989 revealed how little had changed even in a progressive modern city like Mumbai. The bureau was located in the high-ceilinged drawing room of an apartment in an unpretentious Mumbai colony. When I entered, it was filled with about half-a-dozen middle-aged couples intently poring over long notebooks. Periodically one would pause to make a note or point out something to his or her partner. The process seemed laborious but despite the heap of notebooks there was no idling or complaint. The mood was one of intense concentration.

Vimal Phadke who ran the bureau was a small, birdlike woman, a contemporary version of the village matchmaker who relied on the grapevine and her reputation for new business. In the high caste Maharashtrian circles where she practised, she was known to be eminently reliable: in two decades she had joined together over 5,000 couples in matrimony. Her stock in trade were her notebooks containing names and information on prospective grooms and brides neatly divided by caste with special ones for the most prized catch of all: America-settled boys/girls.

Her clients came from all over. Manohar Athavle had come from the neighbouring city of Pune to find a husband for his cost accountant daughter. 'She would like to marry an MBA,' he said, 'but would settle for a chartered accountant plus cost accountant.' The reasons behind the explicit requirements were clear: 'A girl wants someone with better height, better education and better status,' he explained, 'It must be higher, but not equal.' Bombay-based S. D. Kulkarni was also seeking a groom for his young daughter. 'It is usually the girl's parents who have problems,' he complained. 'Boys can wait till they are in their thirties but once a girl is in her twenties you have to find her a husband.' Kulkarni did not see an alternative to the arranged marriage system. 'Boys like to fool around, but when it comes to marriage they want an arranged match,' he said decidedly.

Clearly then, notwithstanding other changes, marriage in modern India was far more likely to be prearranged and fixed according to cold practical considerations rather than the abstract and allegedly western concept of love. The hoopla over Valentine's Day was of marginal significance and no more indicative of a social revolution than the plush five-star hotels which had replaced drawing rooms as favoured venues for Marwari families to discuss alliances.

What both phenomena did however indicate was the increasingly crucial role played by money in matters of love and matrimony.

The first signs had appeared in a rather macabre way in the late 1970s when feminists noticed that a mysteriously large number of women were dying in domestic fires. Investigations revealed that the deaths were not accidental; many of the women had been murdered by greedy husbands and in-laws for bringing insufficient dowry—the sum of money, gifts and/or jewellery demanded by the groom and supplied by the bride's family.

In 1983, as many as 690 such deaths had been recorded in the country's capital, Delhi, and in 1987, 1,786 dowry deaths had been registered all over the country. The figures spoke volumes about the status of women in

India; it also revealed how urbanisation, consumerism and mechanisation—usually considered indicators of progress—had led to the spread of a pernicious practice earlier restricted to a few communities and areas in the country.

Following revelations of bride burning, social activists mounted a campaign against dowry. Their efforts resulted in new legislation and increased public awareness. None of this, however, succeeded in reversing the trend which had acquired a sort of unspoken legitimacy in society with civil servants drawing the highest lots in the dowry stakes and one-third of undergraduates interviewed in the *India Today-MARG* survey saying yes to dowry. There was no protest even from the section most affected: parents of marriageable daughters. The reason as S. D. Kulkarni, who was groom-hunting at Vimal Phadke's, put it was: 'It is the only opportunity for the middle class to demand and get.'

By the late 1980s it was clear that avaricious tendencies were no longer restricted to grooms. Consumerism, fuelled by the media, had raised women's material expectations from marriage.

One afternoon in late 1994, I visited the head office of the marriage bureau, Swayamvaralaya. The office was housed in a low-lying structure off the railway tracks in the middle of a busy bazaar in the West Mambalam area of Madras. It consisted of a large airy room with a partition. On one side middle-aged couples peered through files while a young girl conducted the bureau's new side business: stock brokerage.

On the other side V. Mahadevan, Manager, Swayam-varalaya, sat in an alcove watched over by a row of calendar icons. On his desk, squeezed between a flowered tablecloth and a glass top were pictures of assorted awards received by the agency.

The pictures testified to the agency's growth from a small, low-key operation to its current eminence as one of the most prominent marriage bureaus in South India with branches in Mylapore, Maleshwaram, Gandhinagar and representatives in Delhi. All data, Mahadevan pointed out proudly, was now computerised. Candidates could avail of the agency's services by coughing up ₹900–₹2000 (concessional rate for the handicapped being ₹350) and filling up a form stating name/age/occupation/district/family size/caste/subsect/horoscope.

Matters had slowed down a bit in recent times, with couples insisting on a greater say but Swayamvaralaya still managed to settle about 2–3 matches a day. And dowry, though driven underground by the flood of anti-dowry messages in the media, was still an omnipresent factor. 'These days people do not ask for cash but "things" like a scooter, a Godrej storewell, jewellery, a refrigerator,' said Mahadevan, outlining trends in the contemporary arranged marriage set-up, 'boys also want employed wives because it is difficult to survive on one salary.'

'The important thing,' he stressed 'is that ambitions have increased. There are no limits. Even boys earning a thousand want their wives to work so that they can get a fridge, a two-wheeler, a three-bedroom house, and so on. Everyone wants a TV, not just any TV, but a colour TV. Earlier girls were happy with 4–5 saris, now they want one for every day of the month. This status business has come in only over the last few years. Even children are sent to fancy private schools.'

The aspiration for unaffordable lifestyles, according to marriage counsellors, was becoming a prime cause of marital break-ups. (According to some social workers, as many as 30 per cent of Indian marriages were expected to end in divorce. Though this was merely a projection, figures of cases registered in family courts all over the country showed a remarkable rise. In Lucknow, the number had risen from 74 in 1978 to 738 in 1990. In Kerala, the number was said to have multiplied by 350 per cent. And in Delhi, five district judges were required to handle divorce matters while in the past only one judge, working part time, was considered sufficient.)

It would have been simplistic, of course, to attribute the growing divorce rate to a single factor. The urban woman's increasingly expressed needs for companionship and freedom and the inability or reluctance of men and their families to cope with these were significant factors. Women's strides towards self-reliance had also gone a long way in creating social acceptance of divorce.

At the Madras Family Court, set up to handle marital problems speedily and at low cost to litigants, I saw a stream of mainly lower-class women patiently waiting for a decree of separation. 'Divorce is no longer taboo,' explained A. C. Srinivasan, a counsellor at the Madras Family Court. 'Many women are now educated and employed, they are less willing to tolerate things like alcoholism, violence and bigamy. In the old days the parents would have urged them to reconcile but now they are more likely to say, you are earning enough, do whatever you want.'

In Gondal, a small town in the conservative heartland of Gujarat, a young man informed me that his sister, had ended a bad marriage. 'She earns enough to support herself, so the family thought "to hell with the husband!"' he said, with a casualness that would have been unthinkable less than a decade ago.

In a western culture where the cult of individualism was better developed, the connection between material aspiration and divorce would perhaps be difficult to comprehend. But in India, marriage, particularly for women, was and continued to be a repository of a myriad expectations. And if it had worked consistently in the past it was because expectations were low and the level of acceptance extremely high. In the reverse situation dissatisfaction appeared to be inevitable.

The area where this was acutely felt was in the realm of, for want of a more representative word, passion.

Love, desire, romance, these may have played a marginal role in the lives of most Indians. But they were not alien concepts. Far from it. Krishna, one of the most revered deities in the Hindu pantheon, was said to have had worked his seductive charms on thousands of women. The *Kamasutra*, probably the world's best-known erotic work was written in India. Temples in Khajurao and elsewhere were adorned with carvings of men, women and even animals making love. And the most popular theme in Indian cinema since the 1930s was the triumph of love.

Films in every language were replete with young lovers cavorting, singing, sighing and aching with desire. In fact, for a society that scorned passion in real life, Indians were unduly obsessed with its cinematic representation. Or perhaps the movies were the reservoir into which the middle class channelled its aspirations in that direction. For, however much they might have admired and emulated its intense-eyed heroes and voluptuous heroines, an overwhelming majority of ordinary Indians submitted to the custom of arranged marriage and its clutch of attendant responsibilities that seemed to leave little or no room for romance. Nor was there evidence to suggest that this was a violently unhappy state of affairs. For the large part people muted their expectations to meet reality. They saw no reason to question the status quo and actually considered this form of passivity to be a virtue.

Later, this was no longer true. Between 1991 and 1992 I edited a monthly men's magazine, *Debonair*. One of the most popular features of the magazine was a two-page agony column for which we received a heap of letters every month. A considerable number of these, which came from both men and women described fantasies or actual instances of pre-marital sex, incest, homosexuality and adultery which, to me, suggested that beneath the patina of a highly moralistic society was a tumult of real or imagined promiscuity.

Perhaps it had always been so. Perhaps the frigid and dutiful façade of the Indian middle class had always concealed and probably even encouraged a host of secret passions. This was of course entirely possible. What was new in contemporary India was that these unspoken desires were suddenly coming out into the open. Physical incompatibility, thwarted sexuality and romantic disappointment were no longer being perceived as facts to be lived with but as Problems. And the complaints were being aired most decidedly by the gender that had been more docile and compliant in the past: women.

Psychiatrists and sexologists reported a sudden and sharp increase in their female clientele; the general complaint being: 'I don't get any satisfaction.' If the phenomenon was, at one level, further evidence of the urban Indian woman's growing assertiveness, it was also a reflection of the heightened expectations created by the media.

Kothari, India's best-known sexologist for one, told me that he blamed pornographic video films, widely circulated in India, for creating discontentment and feelings of inadequacy in marriage. More and more married couples, he claimed, were coming to him with complaints of monotony, mismatched desires, guilty fantasies about committing adultery, and fervent appeals for multiple orgasms. Many admitted to using blue films to enhance pleasure. And there were cases where men complained that their wives, having seen a mammoth-sized penis on videotape, were increasingly dissatisfied with the capacities and sizes of their more average husbands.

D. Narayana Reddy, a Madras-based sexologist, widened the influence to include the media in general: magazines, films and the emphasis on youth, physical attraction and virility placed by advertising on video and television.

One of Reddy's clients, a 26-year-old woman, for instance, agitatedly confided that she was contemplating divorcing her husband on the grounds that he never held her 'hand when they went on walks' and that he omitted to say 'I miss you' when he called from his tours. 'There is a popular ad for coffee in south India where the husband comes home from work dressed in a suit; his wife, dripping with jewellery, serves him coffee. Miraculously revived the couple takes off for a romantic walk on the beach. It seemed to me that this is the kind of scenario she and many others are hankering after,' Reddy claimed.

The connection was admittedly conjectural but there was reason to believe that fanciful notions of love and romance were rapidly gaining ground in the 1990s, particularly among the younger generation. Counsellors in city colleges expressed amazement at the adult terms ('affair', 'divorce', 'adultery', etc.) used by the young to describe teenage turmoil. One girl in a fashionable south Bombay college for example wept for days because her boyfriend had 'deserted' her. On probing, the college counsellor discovered he had merely gone abroad for three months. In another case, a teenager threatened to commit suicide after her boyfriend left her. Her complaint: 'he used my body and took my CDs.'

Ironically the proclivity towards exaggeration was accompanied by a rise in permissiveness on the campus. From being a no-no, sex had become an increasingly casual affair at least, among the fashionable young elite. It was not unusual for teenagers to notch up sexual conquests. Or for a group of girls to have 'fun' by scanning pubs and discos for men to have short term sexual liasons with. Or for both girls and boys to have two partners simultaneously (one-third of the teenagers interviewed in the *India Today-MARG* youth survey claimed they would not mind having a fling while going steady).

But perhaps the two trends were not as contradictory as they seemed. For both represented a preference for drama and excitement, basically, a heightened state of being rather than commitment. I found the divide most vividly illustrated by the reaction of students in a girls' college in Gondal to *Darr,* a successful Hindi film released in 1993.

The film had two male protagonists: One, a psychopath who spent many hours locked up in his room talking to his deceased mother; and the other, an officer of the Indian navy renowned for taking on a gang of terrorists on the high seas. Both men, played by equally well-known actors, were in love with the same girl, a role essayed by Juhi Chawla, a popular actress.

Their styles of loving though, were vastly different. The psychopath, played by Shahrukh Khan, was relentless and obsessive in his pursuit, shadowing Chawla, threatening her over the phone, spraying her walls with blood and generally reducing her to a nervous wreck. The sailor, played by he-man Sunny Deol, on the other hand, was warm, supportive and brave; in the end he managed to identify and kill her manic suitor.

In an impromptu discussion about the film, the students, all girls in their late teens, were united in their support for the claims of the psychopath over the sailor, 'That,' they sighed, 'was true love.'

LET'S PLAY LIFE

THE LARGER-THAN-LIFE HOARDINGS HAD BEEN up for a while, advertising the spectacle of the season: The WMWF show at the Sardar Vallabbhai Patel stadium. The previous year, the World Wrestling Federation had caused a sensation by bringing Prime Sports stars Hulk Hogan, Yokozuna and Kamala to Bombay. Every kid-about-town was there wearing his favourite on his chest and screaming from his shaky chair-top perch.

The line-up for 1994 was tame in comparison. None of the TV biggies: The Hitman, The Undertaker (he of the rotating eyeballs fame) were there. The expensive seats were mostly unfilled. The ₹500 tickets seemed to have been distributed among the friends and families of the sponsors.

On the other hand, the trickle-down theory clearly worked as far as addictions went. The cheap stands were packed and juvenile representatives of the lower economic classes were crowded around the ticket window. Gambling on gaudy pictures of wrestlers (sold at ₹4 a sheet) was a big sport in Bombay's slum world and its young denizens had turned up in force for some live action.

Pravin and his three friends who had travelled by bus from a nearby hutment colony were cockily contemplating a break-in. Abdul, alone and with far less initiative, was hoping for a free ticket to magically fall into his lap.

Inside, the show was just beginning. The lights had been dimmed, the music turned up and the master of ceremonies made a flamboyant appearance to weak claps from the crowd. A couple of kids clambered up on chairs to mimic the host's exaggerated gestures.

Act One: Amity knows no barriers

A burst of music. Two men in long hair, painted injuries and eye patch, skulking around the ring. Excitement builds. Children flail their arms in frenzied ritual.

The Warrior (in a hoarse whisper): 'In Ludhi-yana, the Demolition tried to destroy me. But Tiger Jeet Singh Junior and Senior came to my rescue.'

Tiger Jeet Singh Junior (a shout): 'Warrior! Me and my dad were happy to be there for you.'

Warm recognition of Indian hospitality spreads through the stadium confusing the many who have come to witness hate not love.

Act Two: David Vs Goliath

The Contestants. The Iran Sheikh, massive, white, bald. Enters slapping huge, bare paunch. Cowboy Bob, puny but dandy in poncho and cowboy hat. Enters to the strain of a country tune.

Action. The Sheikh bullies, Bob whines. The Sheikh bullies, Bob whines. The crowd losing patience yells to the Cowboy: 'Fight!' '*Khatam kar do*' and warns: '*Pachchas rupiya diya hain*'.

Bob taps the Sheikh. Sheikh falls. Women titter. The Cowboy leaps on the Sheikh and stamps on him. The audience sighs.

Akshay and friends in the front row are not impressed. 'They are just fooling around. See the pillows on the side, they are so soft. Only on TV it looks real.'

Act Three: Come on girls

Ms Fuji does not like the Hollywood Blonde. 'She's pulling my hair,' cries Fuji. 'Look at her!' cries Fuji.

A group of kids race around their seats.

'Why aren't you watching?' I ask them.

'We're watching,' they chorus.

'What do you do when the wrestlers get hurt?'

'We laugh.'

'Do you think this is all true?'

They all laugh.

Except for Rohan. 'It's all true,' he says plaintively, 'It is true.'

***

In the early 1980s when television was synonymous with Doordarshan, a study in Delhi and Madras had revealed that while television occupied a significant chunk of the leisure time of young people, it had a marginal effect on study, play and hobbies, mainly due to selective and spasmodic viewing.

A decade later, with the proliferation of cable and satellite television, however, the scenario underwent a complete transformation. A survey by the State Council of Educational Research and Training in Calcutta discovered that 75 per cent of schoolchildren were glued to their television sets for 3–4 hours a day, often missing play and household chores to do so. Few of them evinced an interest in travel, sports, cultural or educational programmes. Most admitted to spending their time on films and serials.

It was with reason then that one of urban India's most pressing concerns in the early 1990s revolved around the impact of television on children.

In 1994, Dr N. Bhaskar Rao, convenor of the Union Communications ministry's Social Audit Panel announced plans to set up a Social Audit Panel for the mass media with eminent citizens and teachers who were alarmed by their loss of control over students.

The announcement reflected a widespread concern.

It was top of the mind for most of the adults I interviewed. Even people I met socially, regardless of profession or calling, dropped all other forms of identification at the mention of television and became, for the moment, just apprehensive parents of television-viewing children. One man admitted sadly to disposing of his television set after noticing the violent reactions televised wrestling bouts seemed to spark off in his infant son. Others talked worriedly about the influence of the explicit sexual content of many of the programmes.

What I found remarkable was that while each and every parent I met was inordinately concerned about the effects of television on the younger generation, no one, it seemed, had given even a fleeting thought to how it had affected his or her own life.

One Monday morning the art teacher at the Sardar Patel Vidyalaya, a school patronised mainly by the salaried middle class in Delhi, described the various ways in which a family could spend Sundays and asked her class of 8-year-olds to illustrate what they considered the happiest time in the lives of their families.

Thirty-four of the forty students drew near-identical pictures of a small nuclear family clustered around a television set. In each one, the people were represented by faceless, anonymous backs; the focus was unwaveringly on the idiot box.

Shaken by the incident, Vibha Parthasarathi, principal of the school commissioned a study on the impact of television on her students. The study, conducted in 1991–92 focused on the effects of satellite television on senior students (Class 9–12) and its findings, accompanied by first-hand observations made by teachers and the astute principal yielded interesting insights into the phenomenon.

Older students, in the critical final years, expressed worries about the negative impact on their studies. For many of them, living in cramped Delhi Development Authority flats with parents and one or two elderly relatives, the issue was one of juggling the needs of the entire household (the television set, in 64 per cent of the cases surveyed was in the shared area of the flat; an additional 6 per cent had sets in their own rooms; and 41 per cent of the total sample also had at least one elderly relative at home). They could not have turned the set off, even if they wanted to, and often ended up reading in poor light with a perpetual drone in their ears.

Among the younger students, teachers found a rise in the incidence of incomplete homework, poor development of handwriting and spelling skills and an inability to complete tasks such as covering books and handling craftwork projects, all of which required some assistance from parents.

Among pre-schoolers, teachers also noticed a uniform and unprecedented rush for the toilet in the mornings accompanied by the opening of lunch boxes as early as the second period of the day. Questioning revealed the facts behind the pattern: parents tended to stay up late watching television, overslept and consequently had less time to take the child through the routine morning chores of toilet and breakfast.

The abdication of parental responsibilities then, was clearly one of the most crucial and certainly the least recognized aspect of the impact of television on children.

The direct effects of television on kids were a bit less tangible and dispersed. Teachers found students, for instance, strangely reluctant to linger on at picnics or to attend overnight sports camps because that would have meant missing out on their favourite TV shows.

Another noticeable trend concerned the tendency to praise the foreign and denigrate the Indian. At the same time an informal discussion with senior students revealed that many of them were faking comprehension and in actual fact did not understand parts or entire episodes of the western shows they professed to enjoy. 'This is worrying because it indicates that dishonesty is necessary to win acceptance,' claimed Parthasarathi. A significant if somewhat tangential example being children getting parents to sign unpleasant remarks while they (the parents) were engrossed in a television programme.

I found many of these trends reflected in group discussions I had with middle-class children in Bombay and Madras. In Bombay the group ranging between the ages 6 and 12 was overwhelmingly male. And the favourite programme of these pre-adolescent boys was (hold your breath!) *Baywatch* on Star Plus, a programme better known to cater to the lascivious tastes of older men. In fact, so fascinated were they by the show that 8-year-old Jai grew increasingly restive during the interview as its time approached and only settled down when the older boys assured him that he could watch a rerun later that evening.

But rather than a single programme it was television in general that seemed to have captivated their minds so completely that all life seemed to revolve around it. When I asked the group to describe the things that made them angry, for instance, the answer was: 'if someone calls when I'm watching something good on TV; the other day my mother brought some people into the room when I was watching a movie on cable, it made me so angry.'

In Madras, I had found my young interviewees sprawled on the floor playing cards. 'The power has gone off,' the father of one volunteered brightly, 'otherwise these kids wouldn't have been playing, they would have been watching television.'

Increasingly, it seemed to me that if, despite their undeniable concern, parents felt unable to stem the influence of television on their children it was because they were equally in its thrall.

This was not a widely shared perception. Most parents I met tended to talk of their children in terms that would suggest that the younger generation occupied another orbit almost and were driven by forces beyond their, that is, the parents', control. The stock phrases were indicative:

'I hardly watch television but my children.... You know today's children, they just don't listen' or 'I tell my kids not to watch television but it is difficult to stop them when their friends are watching'.

Facts indicated, however, that children, far from being different, were increasingly reflecting, in perhaps a more acute manner, the changing values, habits and attitudes of their parents. Not just with television but in every other way. And the most fundamental of these changes had to do with the growing significance of the young in Indian society.

Traditionally in India, youth had not counted for much. The greatest veneration and respect was reserved for those who had earned it with years. Wisdom, it was believed, came with age. It was the old that laid down the laws and it was the duty of the young to obey.

In modern times, however, attitudes had begun to shift. One indication was the rising amount of money spent on children. In 1995 under-14-year-olds were estimated to consume about a fifth of all consumer goods produced in the country. Children were believed to eat ₹200 crore worth of ice-cream every year, motivate the purchase of 600,000 colour TVs and sustain up to 70 per cent of the health foods industry.

Moreover, kids were playing an increasingly important role in decisions regarding household buys. So much so that 40 per cent of corporate ad spend was directed at targeting children and, in 1994, a whole advertising fair was organised to explore methods of grabbing the attention of children. 'If the consumer is king,' said a marketing executive to *Sunday* magazine, 'the child is emperor.'

There were various sociological factors responsible for the emerging significance of the child, such as modernisation and the breakdown of the joint family system which restricted the size of families and allowed parents to lavish more resources on their offspring. Material aspirations also formed a significant aspect of the phenomenon.

Murli Desai, a sociologist at the Tata Institute of Social Sciences in Mumbai, hazarded a theory that linked the shifting focus from the old to the young with changing notions of social approval. 'In today's world it is wealth rather than moral virtue that wins approval,' she observed. 'Looking after the old isn't glamorous while children on the other hand can advertise your wealth by what they wear, what they eat, where they study and what they buy. They are visible status-adders, hence the high spending.'

This explained to some extent the sprouting of old people's homes—previously, putting the aged in such places would have invited extreme social censure—in the cities and the simultaneous boom in childrens' products.

Proclaiming status, however, was just one aspect of the phenomenon. For many middle-class parents, particularly those from lower income backgrounds, children were sometimes a means of assuring themselves that they had arrived. If such parents went a bit overboard with expensive toys, games and other luxuries it was often because: 'We want our children to have everything that we could not have.' Women, more so than men, seemed to vest their sense of fulfilment almost totally in their children.

The rise in material provisions however, was also accompanied by greater parental expectations. Expectations that put untold pressure on kids to perform and resulted in a stampede at institutions of higher education in a country where half the population continued to be illiterate. Magazines reported an emerging trend of child depression and youth suicides. Many of the respondents in the Sardar Patel Vidyalaya study claimed to be depressed when they could not 'achieve' or when they had to 'give up'. At the National Institute of Mental Health and Neuro Sciences in Bangalore, there was an increase in parents bringing in children for consultations with what child psychologist Shekhar Sheshadri described as 'sub-threshold' problems, i.e., problems that did not amount to disorders. Common complaints were introversion, low motivation or lack of achievement.

Significantly, the term 'achievement' had come to acquire a uniform definition, the measures of which could be described as money, marks and popularity. In some ways, the scenario was pretty much akin to the past, to the time of large, sprawling families where each child was just a number, another mouth to feed. Expectations might have touched the skies but there was as little room for individuality, as little space for nurturing individual talents and weaknesses as in the days gone by.

The difference was in the *appearance* of things.

In contemporary India, choices for the young appeared to have multiplied. The media explosion for one, had brought home a wealth of information and broadened their worldview. Study and career options had expanded. In the late 1980s, Delhi University, for instance, introduced a range of new courses ranging from bio-chemistry and microbiology to electronics and applied psychology;

and a host of private institutes had sprung up offering training in computers, graphics, catering and electronics.

Students in the 1990s were not only more adultlike and more likely to know what they wanted to become, they also had a whole lot more to choose from: till the 1980s the most desirable careers could be said to lie in the civil service, the public sector and traditional professions such as engineering, medicine, law or accounting. Just a few years later, however, a multitude of exciting opportunities had opened up: advertising, business management, architecture, interior design, photography, fashion, to name just a few.

Ironically, the more varied the world seemed to become, the more singular was the motivation driving the young. In 1983, students responding to a survey by the Foundation for Organisational Research rated 'opportunity to use my special abilities and aptitudes' highest among factors governing their choice of a job; 'chance to earn a lot of money' got the lowest rating. In 1994, the priorities were reversed. Moneymaking had made it to the top of the list while special abilities sank to the bottom (Number 9 for men and 10 for women out of a scale of 10).

Similarly, the 'opportunity to be creative and original' slipped from its high perch between 1983 and 1994 while 'work that involves variety' moved up the list. Clearly, creativity and self-actualisation were passé. What the 1990s kid was seeking was exciting ways to make money. In the face of such pragmatism, rebellion, idealism, romanticism—characteristic qualities of youth in the past—seemed irrelevant.

To this extent, the urban Indian youth was echoing a worldwide trend. A 1994 report on teenagers by the Research International Observer based on group discussions with 13–18-year-olds in 27 countries claimed that 'conformism is the order of the day rather than rebellion which requires boldness and strong self-motivation, sadly lacking in many.'

Better information had not resulted in an enhanced ability to deal with problems and the contemporary generation's resolution of external conflicts was found to be in avoidance. 'Rather than try to change a flawed system, they resist engaging with it,' the report claimed, suggesting that this implied a retreat from the immediate surroundings, in which differences with other groups could be magnified.

Evidence of these trends could be found in urban India. The 1994 *India Today* survey on teenagers noted a loss of support for broad-based political causes and the emergence of casteist groups, the latter owing their origins both to an upsurge of chauvinism as well as to a need to network.

In 1989, while interviewing college students for a piece on youth trends, I found expressions of complete bewilderment when I mentioned the word 'ideology'. On campuses where less than two decades before students had been getting high on Marx and marijuana, I found a crowd of youngsters straight out of a bubble gum commercial, all with part-time employment and a 'natural' aversion to communism ('See, morally it's true, you must share. But practically you wouldn't like to share something you worked so hard for'). A teachers' strike that year had evoked no response from the Students' Union Council in one of Bombay's most prestigious colleges: a handful of students when they tried to protest were mocked by their peers.

It was not as if the modern urban youth did not care at all. But increasingly his or her concerns were either targeted against a hate group: in 1990, urban students led a countrywide agitation against the government's decision to hike reservations in government offices for the lower castes; or reflected the pre-occupations of another and more affluent state: the average urban collegian for instance, was more likely to see the environment issue in terms of littering on the beach than forest depredation.

Youth programmes on satellite television with their western orientation widened the gulf between the urban elite and their surroundings even further. At a college festival in a fashionable Bombay college on Independence Day in 1994, for example, Star TV's popular VJ Ruby, wandered through the crowds with a microphone discussing 'issues facing the country'. Her choice of 'issues': drugs and condoms. On the latter, the chatty VJ nodded approvingly as 16- and 17-year-olds with veteran-like panache expounded on the subject of condoms in the age of AIDS (a 'good thing' since everyone could have safe sex).

Nothing wrong with that of course. Except that the interpretation of 'safe sex' in India till recently had been something quite different. For decades condoms had been probably *the* most publicised item in the government's family planning campaign. And in a country fast galloping to the world's most populous nation status, a view that linked a contraceptive to AIDS alone could not but seem a highly skewed perception of reality. Other instances of the alienating and desensitising effects of television abounded. A friend living in Dhule, a medium-sized town in Maharashtra, told me that one of her daughter's favourite games was to enact an American prime-time-style murder by burying her doll in the park and then imitating the siren of a police vehicle.

In the corridors of a progressive school in Delhi, two groups of senior students pelted each other with fresh vegetables in what appeared to be a pre-planned fight. The teachers who had prided themselves on the school's ethnicity and sensitivity to the have-nots were horrified. 'After all our lectures on not wasting food, we were shocked,' said one, 'but when we talked to the students we realised that they were quite unmindful of the implications. They were merely imitating a television game show. It was their idea of fun.'

Ideas of 'fun', 'good', 'bad', 'right', 'wrong' seemed to take on an increasingly pliable shape. And in a world without moral consequences, pragmatism was the new god. The trend was clearly reflected in the heroes of the times. Harshad Mehta, prime accused in a multi-billion securities scandal, was a much-admired figure. Market researcher Meena Kaushik claimed from interviews with youngsters that popular contemporary role models tended to be heroic without being all good. In my discussion with upper class children in Bombay, the mantle of most admired soap character fell surprisingly on the manipulative and aggressive matriarch of the Forrester family in *The Bold and the Beautiful*. The reason: 'She is smart, she doesn't trust anybody.'

THE BACKLASH

I MET SWAMI AGNIVESH IN late 1994 in his office which consisted of a couple of gloomy rooms on the hindside of a ramshackle mansion that housed the offices of the Janata Dal in New Delhi. A board outside read: 'Bonded Labour Liberation Front', which was the name of the non-governmental organisation headed by the Swami. Three months earlier, Agnivesh had also become All India General Secretary of the Arya Sabha, a newly floated political party that had an ideological affinity with the Arya Samaj. Agnivesh had long been a part of the Hindu revivalist Arya Samaj which, he was at some pains to prove, was *not* a sectarian organisation ('our first donation came from a Muslim and many of our office bearers were Sikhs').

Despite his record of serious activism (his office was littered with posters against bonded labour and depredations against local fishermen) and impressive appearance—hypnotic eyes, crisp orange turban and matching robes—Swami Agnivesh had long been regarded as a maverick, a colourful and slightly comic figure tilting at windmills.

His most recent claim to fame was a much-publicised stand against Michael Jackson's proposed visit to India as part of his *Dangerous* tour in 1992.

Agnivesh's eyes glinted wickedly when I mentioned it. 'Michael Jackson was scheduled to perform here at Jawaharlal Nehru Stadium. Tickets were between ₹500 and ₹2000. Pepsi was the sponsor; some of the money was supposed to go to charity while the rest he would take away,' he recounted.

'The TV channels were carrying clips on him for two months before he came. The *Times of India* introduced a Michael Jackson lookalike contest. Overnight MJ prototypes were emerging....We thought things were moving fast. This man was not only going to dance but he was going to destroy our civilisation.'

So Agnivesh and other 'socio-cultural activists' formed the Bharatiya Sanskriti Manch with the sole purpose of stopping the Jackson concert. Fate however deprived Agnivesh and his followers of a confrontation. Days before he was expected in India a case of child molestation was filed against Jackson causing him to· cut short his visit and return home. 'His *dangerous* tour fell through,' Agnivesh observed, laughing.

He laughed often, I noticed, as if the world for all its grimness was a vastly amusing place. It was an endearing quality and it made one suspect that he did not always mean what he said.

This, of course, was far from the truth. His penchant for self-deprecation notwithstanding, Swami Agnivesh had strong views on what was wrong around him. And his latest preoccupation was the cultural invasion by the electronic media and its ramifications which included western influences such as a Michael Jackson concert.

What was so harmful about a concert, I asked him. Many would think his opposition smacked of overreaction. He did not agree. 'If we had let him (Jackson) come it would have been a symbolic establishment of new values,' he explained earnestly, 'there is so much sex and violence on television, particularly cable television. And all these glamourous foreign serials are going to lead to alienation and new tensions such as divorce in our society.'

The western emphasis on individuality and selfhood were some of the values feared by Agnivesh. 'The family and community living are the pillars of Indian society,' he claimed passionately, 'We do not need the western concept of social security, we always had it. In my native village, for instance, no one was allowed to sell a cow or milk. Whenever there was a surplus it had to be distributed among the needy. That spirit of sharing will go.'

These fears led Agnivesh to launch a crusade against the electronic media. In August 1993, he took out a procession to the Doordarshan headquarters at Mandi House. In December he demonstrated outside All India Radio headquarters, Akashwani Bhawan. Some months later he met with principals of about 60 schools in New Delhi to prepare a memorandum against Doordarshan. In March 1994 he led yet another procession to Mandi House. And later in the year he planned to launch a concerted drive in the rural districts of the north against liquor, lotteries and the media.

The combination was a clear reflection of Agnivesh's view that the 'consumerist culture' popularised by the media was injecting new vices into Indian society.

'It is not as if we did not have vices before. The difference was that they did not have social sanction. Boozing, gambling and smoking were considered evils. People did give bribes but there was a shame and fear associated with the act that has disappeared.'

'People made money then too but they were not worshipped. Respect was reserved for *tyaagis* and *tapasvis*- the ascetics. Those values have disappeared after industrialisation. Congressmen used to wear khadi, today they lay flowers on Mahatma Gandhi's grave in three-piece suits. And television is abetting the degeneration of values.'

'It reminds me,' he said reflectively, 'of my childhood in Chattisgarh, where no one drank anything but milk by the bucket. Then the shopkeepers came with gramophones and free tea. That was it—we were hooked.'

Swami Agnivesh fingered his beads and turned philosophical: Why are we here on this earth? I don't believe the West has an answer. It has 20 per cent of the world's people and they are consuming 80 per cent of its resources. We, on the other hand, have a more holistic vision that includes nature, animals.... We treat life as a means to an end and not an end in itself as they do. The communication revolution presented us with an opportunity to voice some answers from our culture but we are squandering it away. Today even if Gandhi were alive, he would have a tough time getting his message across.'

***

One summer evening in 1995, Tushar Gandhi settled down for a period of relaxation before the idiot box. The movie he had switched on did not seem appealing so he flipped channels and chanced upon *Nikki Tonight,* just, as it happened, in time to hear India's gay crusader, Ashok Row Kavi, mutter an obscenity about his great grandfather, Mahatma Gandhi.

The next day almost all the papers carried news of the ₹500 million suit Tushar Gandhi planned to slap against Nikki Bedi, TV 18, producers of the show and Star Plus. The offence was not merely personal. Hundreds of outraged Indians had called up Row Kavi and the channel to express their anger over the denigration of the Mahatma. The controversy rippled through the press and even reached Parliament where the home minister promised to consider enacting a law to rein in satellite broadcasters. The channel which had continued airing further editions of *Nikki Tonight* apologized for the lapse and then, overwhelmed by the reaction, scrapped the show.

India, as Star Plus realised to its discomfiture, is a land of holy cows. No other place in the world is mined so thick with potential grievances and no other people in the globe nurse their thin skins so avidly.

India was one of the first and the only non-Islamic nation to ban Salman Rushdie's *Satanic Verses*. During the Gulf war it refused to take a clear, unequivocal stand for or against Saddam Hussein even though thousands of Indians suffered losses in Kuwait. Several lives were lost in Maharashtra over the renaming of a university. In Calcutta the mere suggestion of a romance involving Netaji Subhash Chandra Bose evoked a storm of protest. In Gujarat, devotees of the saint, Baba Jalaram, were so miffed by a villain's use of the phrase *'Jai Baba Jalram'* that they forced the actor playing the role to visit the Baba's village, Virpur, to render an apology.

The *Nikki Tonight* controversy had been preceded by a countrywide conflict over the screening of the film *Bombay*, a love story set against the backdrop of a communal riot. Soon after, Bal Thackeray made the headlines by refusing to permit a memorial to his old adversary, the recently deceased former prime minister Morarji Desai, to come up in Maharashtra.

In the circumstances, the *Nikki Tonight* imbroglio had all the makings of a major confrontation. Postcolonial India was sensitive to perceived slights from foreigners. By airing an insult to the Mahatma, the foreign-owned TV network, Nikki Bedi with her British accent and Row Kavi with his unorthodox lifestyle had wandered into exceedingly dangerous territory.

Too dangerous, felt some liberal observers who without defending the trashy nature of the programme or the Gandhi comment believed that the affair was setting an unwelcome precedent and, in the absence of a regulatory board, was paving the way for political interference in the electronic media.

The argument was not without merit. Though the administration had done nothing to halt the burgeoning growth of the private media, it still retained its prerogative to interfere in the affairs of Doordarshan. The state-owned network had undergone a tremendous change between 1992 and 1995. It had introduced new shows, started a movie channel and even co-opted privately produced video newsmagazines such as *Newstrack* and *Eyewitness*.

Where legislation had failed, competition had succeeded. Doordarshan was more autonomous in 1995 than it had ever been. Yet, for all its newly acquired gloss and freedom, it was still under supervision. The government could and would yank a politically inconvenient interview off air or stall a daily news-oriented breakfast show. In the absence of any laws protecting their rights there was no guarantee that this principle would not be extended to foreign broadcasters as well.

To focus solely on the freedom of expression argument however was to ignore the genuine sentiments of a vast number of Indian viewers.

By the early 1990s, concern had mounted over the growing vulgarity in both the private and the government-controlled media. The fears expressed by Swami Agnivesh, far from being the preoccupations of a hypersensitive minority, reflected the feelings of an increasing number of ordinary, middle-class people all over the country.

Everywhere: in the press, at private dinner parties and at public debates, one heard the angry assertion that television was destroying 'our Indian culture'. Groups of parents, educationists and concerned citizens in various cities were preparing campaigns, signing petitions and staging street plays against the phenomenon. The Delhi-based Jagriti Mahila Samiti filed a petition in the High Court against the excessive display of sex and violence on television.

An angry band of activists descended upon starlet Mamta Kulkarni's house with a set of clothes after she posed topless on the cover of *Stardust*. A similar group forced Zee TV's obstreperous Mohan Kapoor to apologise for his risqué remarks on air.

Women politicians presented a memorandum to the president on the issue; elected representatives debated the increase of sex and violence on television and cable in Parliament and even the prime minister expressed his concern at public meetings. In one middle-class colony in Mumbai, feelings ran so high that over 300 families disposed of their television sets, many by the dramatic method of tipping them out of the window.

The backlash was not in the least unexpected, the surprising thing was that it was so long in the coming. For over a decade the electronic media had been expanding and proliferating on the instincts of a small band of software producers, advertisers and entrepreneurs. The content was mainly entertainment and the motive overwhelmingly commercial. Yet in all this there was little room for critical feedback or audience response.

In a new medium a certain amount of trial and error is to be expected. But in the situation that obtained at the time, the needs and preferences of viewers appeared to be of minimal consideration.

The film industry for one, having rightfully prided itself on its familiarity with the public pulse for decades, seemed to have lost its magic touch and appeared to be blind to the fact as it churned out one box office disaster after another.

As for the new television producers the plethora of channels ensured that any kind of software—good, bad or indifferent—could find a time slot. With about 30 channels of free entertainment on the air in 1995 the race was on to fill time rather than ensure quality. As a result, programmers ended up imitating each other, borrowing from the clueless film industry or adding huge doses of sensationalism.

A survey of soaps across channels (including Doordarshan) in 1995 would have revealed sordid sagas of illegitimate children, adultery and revenge. In television women smoked freely and were bold and outspoken about their sexual preferences; men, when they were not busy disposing of rivals, were asking guests to have a drink (a convenient method of getting around regulations that forbade the advertising of alcohol on Indian television).

Greedy capitalists set fire to slums and hacked helpless people to death in film clips while the person on the street and the expert of the moment debated issues such as orgasm, promiscuity and drugs. Melodrama, body exposure in the garb of fashion and violence had become staple fare on Indian television.

The same, arguably, was true of television in many parts of the world. But in India the phenomenon created a problem; a typically Indian problem that derived from the country's own peculiar social traditions and explained, in part, the bitterness of the reaction evoked by the medium.

For a clear understanding of the phenomenon, one had to take into account the manner in which television was viewed in India. Television watching in India was almost uniformly a communal affair. A very small number of homes had more than one television set. In cities where nuclear families were on the rise, television was likely to be watched by five or six people (potentially the father, mother, two children, an elderly relative and the domestic help) at the same time. Elsewhere, where joint families were the norm, the number could be higher. In small town *chawls* and villages, entire neighbourhoods would cluster round a set.

The reason for this was not merely economic. In India the individual had always been overshadowed by the group, whether it was the extended family or the community. Accordingly, most activities, from celebrations to domestic pursuits, revolved around the family leaving little room for privacy or individual enhancement.

In such a rigid, family-oriented scenario, the scope for change would appear to have been very limited. And to a certain extent, it was. The young were expected to obey their elders, women were expected to be subservient to men. The old was revered and the new looked upon with suspicion. Yet, even given these factors, the Indian social structure was not as intransigent to change as it would seem.

In fact, the middle class in particular, had long evolved an ingenious method of incorporating external influences without upsetting the status quo.

The method consisted of anticipating signs of rebellion and deflecting them to a safe place. In practical terms this meant, for instance, children from strictly vegetarian households eating meat in a restaurant; young men drinking and smoking with friends outside but never at home; married women in *purdah* packing pant suits and skirts for holidays at hill stations.

In the past, when attitudes among the old were set and inflexible, this entailed a considerable amount of deception. But with time and exposure, views broadened and there was an acceptance, tacit at least, of acts outside the house. So, women, for example, could flash photographs of themselves in modern attire on holiday even if custom still dictated a constricting dress code at home.

The result was admittedly schizophrenic with two sets of values operating for the home and outside. But it was a system that allowed the adoption of western decadent habits without taking the halo off or interrupting the solidity, or so it seemed, of Indian tradition.

The same principle allowed the film industry to get away with a relatively large amount of permissiveness. The cinema was entertainment *out* of the house; the movies were fantasy and stars distant, unattainable creatures who lived in a remote self-contained world which had its own norms. Characters in films often went against social conventions, but within certain limits it was all right since none of it was real.

Television changed all that. It flashed the values of a small westernised elite and the sort of vulgarity that Indians, usually men, were used to enjoying on the sly, into drawing rooms occupied by *families*. By bringing the forbidden into the home it made a mockery of the old custom-preserving technique and, most significantly, it embarrassed its viewers.

In studies, both men and women confessed to being embarrassed by each others' presence during obscene scenes in a film on cable. One woman I interviewed said she walked out of the room each time a love scene came on in case her mother-in-law disapproved.

People tried various ways of coping. One was to treat television as fantasy, as something that was 'not for us' and hence not to be analysed, aspired to or applied in any way to their lives. So women in traditional middle class households could extol the aggressive go-getting qualities of a female character in *Santa Barbara* to a PhD student researching a thesis on television, even if their lives reflected the opposite. Similarly, in Madras and Gondal I found viewers hooked onto big city soaps with no apparent signs of rejection or aspiration based on the same logic.

But treating a medium in the home as an alien entity like the cinema was not always possible, particularly in the presence of children.

A study by the Delhi-based Media Advocacy Group found that children operated the set everywhere. Apart from the afternoons when the housewife had some power over programme selection, it was children and, to some extent the male head in the evenings, who decided what was to be viewed. Two sets of children I interviewed in Bombay and Madras were intimately familiar with television schedules and claimed that they fought if necessary and usually got their way on programme selection.

The lack of gradation, according to sociologist D. L. Sheth, was one of the chief problems with television in India. Children below 18 constituted 45 per cent of the population. Yet children-specific programming formed a miniscule percentage of the total broadcast time. And in any case the communal nature of television viewing meant that everyone watched everything regardless of its suitability. In some households, parents tried to deal with 'the problem' by practising crude forms of censorship. 'I have devised my own way of diverting the attention of my five-year-old daughter when (steamy) scenes are on,' claimed housewife Merlyn Desouza in an article on soaps in *Midday* in September 1992.

Most methods however failed in the face of peer pressure. Scores of parents including Bangalore-based journalist and media analyst Ammu Joseph, who banned their children from watching inappropriate shows, found that they got the latest juicy details from their friends anyway.

As market researcher Meena Kaushik discovered from group discussions she conducted: 'there is a general sense of powerlessness all over the country over what kids are exposed to.'

The Indian viewer was mad. Mad enough to stick his head out of the window and scream, just like the deranged television newsman in the 1970s Sidney Lumet film *Network* had advised ('Stick your head out of the window,' he said, 'and scream "I'm mad as hell and I'm not going to take it anymore"').

A sense of powerlessness was, however, just one aspect of the backlash against the media. In part the violent response was also evoked by another potent but unheralded agent of social transformation: the urban, middle class, working woman.

***

In India, as in most parts of the world, women had always occupied a secondary position to men. The birth of a girl child was widely regarded as a curse. In matters of health and education, daughters were neglected in favour of sons. A woman's existence, in fact, revolved around marriage, procreation and domestic responsibility. In rural India it was not unusual for women to help their menfolk in the fields, but her contribution did not bring her additional gains.

By the 1940s, spurred by social reform, a few women had thrown off the veil and begun to acquire degrees, notch up achievements in diverse fields and participate in political and social movements. Post-Independence the trend grew. According to N. Desai and S. Anantram's *Review of Studies on Middle Class Women's Entry into the World of Work*, the 1950s saw a sudden increase of women white collar jobs such as nursing and teaching with women's magazines avidly debating issues such as 'should women go out to work?' and 'when should mothers start work?'

By the 1970s, with the expansion of the public and tertiary sectors, opportunities for the small but steadily growing number of educated women increased. By the early 1980s in all the major cities of India, women had become a familiar sight in colleges, buses, trains and offices.

Attitudes towards the schooling and employment of women also underwent a dramatic transformation. Marriage was still considered *de rigueur* for all women but education and a job far from being obstacles had become stepping stones for a better match. Increasingly, men were looking for employed wives. And in matrimonial columns women proudly advertised their educational qualifications and employed status; jobs in the public sector were particularly prized for their access to cheap housing loans.

The motivating factor behind the changing attitudes to women working was economic. In the difficult 1970s the middle class realised the value of a second income. The consumer revolution of the next decade created new demands, further boosting the value of a double income and relaxing taboos against working women (data released by the National Readership Survey in 1995 revealed that the chief wage earner in one out of every 20 urban households was a woman).

Employment, in turn became a catalyst for other changes. A survey by the market research agency Pathfinders in 1990 found that women tended increasingly to be educated rather than homebound and more aware of their social responsibilities. Half of the working women interviewed had married and borne children relatively late. Nearly all could read English and 50 per cent were graduates.

The advertising industry was quick to spot the trend. And by the 1990s more and more ads even in male-oriented product categories such as scooters, computers and holiday packages were speaking to women. The reason, according to Amitav Mitra, Delhi branch manager of Everest Advertising, was that 'in most buying decisions it is no longer just the man's opinion that counts.'

A significant factor in catapulting women into the spotlight of the marketing effort was television. The traditional avenue for advertising, the print media, had a higher reach among men than women. But surveys revealed that the latter were more avid viewers of television. Television had another unique advantage: it was able to enter homes and reach potential consumers in small towns and villages where women's movements were still restricted. In such places, women rarely left their immediate surroundings; the shopping was done by men at the marketplace which left women grossly underexposed to products. Television changed all that and women showed an increasing awareness.

'The big difference,' claimed Meena Kaushik, 'is that women now know exactly what they want. Their demands are not vague. Even if it is a basic object such as a mattress they know exactly which one they want.'

Activated by the growing demand, the distribution networks expanded beyond the cities fuelling consumption. Demand for women-specific products such as kitchen appliances and cosmetics also zoomed. Old attitudes that dictated fresh meals and time-consuming methods of cooking died a sudden death. Beauty parlours sprang up in small towns and villages where the use of make-up, particularly for unmarried girls, had long been considered a sign of promiscuity. Advertising executive Rekha Nigam while doing a detailed study of Hindi magazines in the early 1990s was struck by the overwhelming curiosity and eagerness for tips on enhancing physical appearance. By 1992 there were approximately 15 million working women in India. And the change had percolated down to the next generation. In late 1994, I interviewed female college students from conservative backgrounds in Bombay and Madras and found that though their views on matters such as arranged marriage were unchanged, there was a new and unanimous determination to work.

Economic self-reliance was a consistently mentioned priority. Another interesting fact that emerged was that while socialising was restricted to the family and late nights absolutely taboo, exceptions were readily made for a late evening tuition or an extra study course revealing how much emphasis was placed, even by the older generation, on education.

The change was reflected in advertisements as well. The traditional image of housewife as doormat persisted. But increasingly there were other role models: Lalitaji in the Surf detergent ads who was vehement about her choice; the 'Rin manager'; the job seeker in the Ponds talcum powder ad; the young girl stating categorically *'Humko Binnie's mangta'* and so on. The most dramatic change was in the manner in which the younger generation was projected. In earlier times advertisements reflected the excessive preoccupation of Indian families with sons. But increasingly the focus was on the girl child. Not only were female pre-adolescents selling products from soft drink concentrates to washing machines but mothers were shown to be mixing milk-foods and snacks for daughters, a marked difference. The television commercial for Ariel detergent where a lower middle-class mother lovingly washes the stains off her daughter's uniform to make her presentable at her upwardly mobile school reflected accurately the growing trend of ambitions being vested in daughters as well as sons.

The birth of a vibrant feminist movement in the late 1970s—a host of non-governmental organisations focusing on women's issues had come up between 1975 and 1985 following the declaration of the International Women's Year—also aided the process of emancipation.

Many of these feminist groups consisted of urban middle class women who successfully pushed for a range of pro-women laws, established institutions to provide legal and material support to destitute women and watchdog committees for monitoring phenomena such as the representation of women in the media and so on. One of the consequences of the movement was also a deluge of 'women-oriented' serials on Doordarshan between 1982 and 1987.

The serials encompassed a variety of genres: soap, sitcom, docu-drama, self-help and so on. *Adhikaar* for instance, dealt with the legal rights of Indian women. *Kashmakash* was based on short stories by women writers. *Stri* drew portraits of 'extraordinary' women while *Airhostess* explored the lives of single working women. The intention, to present a positive image of women, was clearly a laudable one. Filmmaker Deepa Dhanraj in *Whose News? The Media and Women's issues* (SAGE Publications, 1994) noted that, 'given the scarcity of non-fiction programmes centred around women, practically any images are to be celebrated'.

In implementation however Doordarshan did not quite live up to its promise. Analysing the 'pro-women' programming of the time, Dhanraj concluded that the attempt had misfired on several counts which included oversimplification of the causes of women's oppression; structuring serials with a view to male gratification; and suggesting solutions that often ended up reinforcing rather than changing the status quo.

The medium also put out contradictory messages. Programmes such as *Adhikaar* on women's legal rights and *Aur Bhi Hain Raahein* on career options for women were telecast cheek-by-jowl with advertisements in which glamorous models played out the traditional roles of wife, mother and sex object. In Ramayana, the highest rated serial at a time when Doordarshan was trying to encourage liberal attitudes towards women's emancipation, the main female character was Sita—a woman who unquestioningly joined her husband, Rama, in exile, was kidnapped by Ravana provoking a war between the two kings, and was eventually dumped by her husband when his citizens cast aspersions on her chastity.

The proliferation of cable also meant a wider dissemination of such reactionary messages. As former Doordarshan Director-General Shiv Sharma admitted ruefully, 'You make a concerted move to talk about the emancipation of women but with one retrograde Bombay film the effort could be wiped out.'

By the early 1990s Doordarshan's fervent efforts at positive discrimination in favour of women had abated. But with the expansion of channels and a relaxation of bureaucratic control over the state-owned network the portrayal and representation of women on television became an even more controversial affair.

A study of television programming in various languages throughout the country by the Delhi-based Media Advocacy

Group in March 1993 revealed that most serial plots revolved around men while women were cast in stereotyped roles of the cementer or destroyer of families with 'bad' women or independent, progressive women reverting to being doormats or shadows in the end. Marriage too being shown to be of overwhelming importance for women was an attitude that contrasted strongly with frequent spots on Doordarshan which portrayed women in traditionally male professions such as the police force and the army.

Even foreign soaps such as *The Bold and the Beautiful* and *Santa Barbara* propagated the stereotype: men were providers and driven by ambition; women, even if they worked, were nurturers and dominated by their emotions.

Some change was evident inasmuch as women did sometimes hold managerial positions particularly in companies owned by deceased fathers or husbands. And the letters received by *Humraahi,* a serial propagating women's equality, indicated a growing support for independent women who could speak out against male tyranny and some impatience with the doormat stereotype.

A second study by the Media Advocacy Group in May 1994 on the representation of women in news and current affairs programmes also revealed a definite bias. The findings showed that panelists selected for discussions on 'hard' subjects such as politics or foreign affairs were almost always men; women, when they were included at all, were usually chosen to discuss 'soft' topics such as education or women's welfare. Female representation in interviews with 'common' people on issues such as the annual budget too tended to be low.

Women rarely made it to the list of newsmakers unless the story revolved around scandal or show business. And interviews with successful women—which ranged from dissident Bangladeshi writer Taslima Nasreen to Bombay mayor Nirmala Prabhavalkar—were often trivialised by an excessive interest in their physical appearance or personal lives.

By 1994, Hindi films and the burgeoning number of soaps on television however showed a startling though not necessarily positive change in the depiction of women. Gone were the long-suffering wives and oppressed victims. In their place was a new breed of young, self-sufficient, aggressive and manipulative 'hussies' who smoked and drank and manifested all the habits of the archetypal vamp without the shame or the punishment that they were usually accompanied by.

There was some element, however slight, of truth in the new trend. By the 1980s, women in Hindi films like women in real life were less likely to be papa's pampered daughters or selfless housewives than journalists, airhostesses and businesswomen. Even the man-chasing, big screen heroine of the 1990s reflected a new-found boldness among young upper middle-class women.

The Machiavellian, booze-swilling nymphomaniac that was fast becoming staple fare of TV soap life however was far more of a myth, born of the collective despera-tion of greedy assembly line soap producers than reality. Yet, bizarre as in many ways it was, the world of soaps was inducing a widespread change in middle-class atti-tudes, much to the relief of the younger generation of women who suddenly found age-old shackles disappear-ing overnight. A twenty-something garment fabricator in Bombay, for instance, held television entirely respon-sible for the fact that her conservative Muslim mother no longer pressurised her to leave her job and get married. Teenagers in small towns like Indore found themselves in a position to flaunt the latest bold fashions without running up against parental disapproval. Sexologists, psychiatrists and marriage counsellors also testified to a sharp rise in awareness and acknowledgement of sexual desire among women.

Clearly, the urban middle class woman had come a long way. But so much change in so little time could not but provoke a reaction.

***

In the last weeks of 1988, a small item appeared in the Delhi newspapers announcing the formation of an organisation called the *Akhil Bharatiya Patni Atyachar Virodhi Morcha* (All India Front Against Atrocities committed by Wives). The title was self-explanatory though the report said little, apart from identifying the founder and honorary secretary general of the Front as one R. P. Chugh, a local lawyer.

The organisation's unconventional agenda (at a time when Delhi was sprouting organisations aimed at protecting *women* against atrocities by men) however, had aroused my curiosity and I decided to find out more about it.

I was not the only one. R. P. Chugh, who turned out to be a short, stout man in his late thirties with sparse wire-coiled hair, had already received callers from a couple of international publications in his 'office', a rather grand term for a table, a broken chair and a board that said 'R.P. Chugh: Advocate(s), High Court(s) Supreme Court' in the open ground around Delhi's Tees Hazari Court.

I started by asking him about the reasons that led to his forming an organisation with the unusual aim of protecting men from women.

Chugh turned misty-eyed and his voice quivered as he said: 'Marriage'. The hapless lawyer, it appeared, had had two unhappy brushes with the institution, both of which apparently convinced him that the 'very character of woman was bad'.

Saddened by the realisation, Chugh would probably have lived out the rest of his life in silent solitude. But that was not to be. Filled with revulsion for the female sex, Chugh read with horror of the advances made by women's groups and viewed with equal terror the plethora of feminist programmes on television. He came to the conclusion that he had to do something to halt the Long March of the Indian Woman before (and he shuddered at the thought): 'We have films with titles like *Main Chup Nahin Rahungi.*'

I had set out to meet Chugh expecting a crank and a publicity seeker. And indeed so far the nondescript lawyer fitted the bill. What I had not been prepared for were the respectful glances on the faces of his colleagues as he accompanied me to the gate. I stopped for a chat and found many of them actually shared Chugh's view that 'women were stepping out of line'. 'Women should stay within their religious practice,' said Sikandar Ali, a middle-aged, soft-spoken man, 'young people are trying to ape the West; all that won't work here.' Amidst murmurs of agreement he concluded: 'Our support is with Mr Chugh.'

If these were the beliefs held by representatives of one of the most educated sections of Indian society, it was a fair indication how a considerable number of the male population felt.

Indeed, if the late 1980s-early 1990s at one level seemed to herald a phase of tremendous achievement for Indian women, it also offered evidence of growing resentment among men.

Crimes against women doubled between the 1980s and the 1990s. In 1994 a record 82,818 crimes were registered against women and the records showed that a woman was raped every 47 minutes and one abducted every 44 minutes. According to Jean D'Cunha, professor of sociology at St Xavier's College Bombay, 'conflict of outlook' between the sexes was a major cause. 'When a woman stands up to a man, he cannot tolerate it and interprets it as an affront to his pride'.

The same year, a sordid scandal broke out in Jalgaon, a town in Maharashtra. Newspaper reports revealed that local politicians aided by hoodlums and the police had lured as many as 500 women into a prostitution racket by raping and later blackmailing them. Encounters with the victims had also been videotaped and distributed as blue films all over the country.

The electronic media also abetted the rising anti-women trend. The lewd songs flashed incessantly on television became a handy weapon in the roadside Romeo's arsenal. Cases of 'eve-teasing' registered a sharp rise and a number of women claimed to feel helpless with even children singing innuendo-laden songs such as *Tu cheez badi hain mast mast* and *Choli ke peeche kya hai?*

Direct attacks on women were perhaps difficult to condone. But what was more insidious and hence, more publicly acceptable, was the argument that equated women or a certain kind of womanly behaviour with 'Indian culture' and held that any diversion from this definition constituted, not an act of personal liberty, but an infringement of that sacrosanct culture.

This, in fact, was a vital assumption underlying the backlash against the media.

The indications were many. In the middle of a Jain TV discussion on the corrupting influence of pubs on the young, a middle-aged man pronounced that no one would allow his son to marry a girl who went 'regularly' to pubs because it was against 'our Indian culture'. Policemen raiding a swinging nightclub in suburban Mumbai slapped a starlet when she tried to protest about the treatment meted out to the patrons. Anjali Kapur, a Delhi High Court lawyer and part-time model, invited self-righteous criticism and threats of disbarment from her male colleagues when she posed semi-nude on the cover of a girlie magazine; even though she stuck to her belief that she had a right to do whatever she wished with her body, the controversy turned hot enough to send her into hiding.

In 1995 Madhu Sapre and Millind Soman, two Mumbai models who happened to be affianced to each other, raised a storm by posing in the buff for a shoe ad. One of the criticisms voiced against Soman was: 'How could he let his wife-to-be pose in the nude?'

In fact, all the so-called moral controversies in the early 1990s revolved around women. Not just any women but self-reliant, independent women. Between 1992 and 1994, at least two godmen were accused of abusing their hallowed positions to rape and exploit female devotees. The stories came and went without raising a whimper. On the other hand, reams of newsprint and time at public fora were focused on Mamta Kulkarni (actress), Pooja Bhatt (actress), Anjali Kapur (lawyer) and Madhu Sapre (model). Their crime: they took their clothes off for the media. Even Soman, who posed alongside Sapre in the controversial Tuff shoes ad was criticised less for what he did and more for 'allowing' his fiancée to do the same.

D. L. Sheth, a sociologist I met at the Delhi-based Centre for the Study of Developing Societies ventured the theory that what frightened the Indian middle class most about television was sex. I believe it was not just sex—the Hindi film industry would have shut down years ago for its huge quantities of titillation if that had been the case— but the possibility of *women* seeking sexual gratification that appeared to be so threatening to the Indian male and to the large numbers of middle-class women still firmly rooted in the old patriarchal structure.

As long as women were restricted, controlled or even exploited by the old, inequitable power structure, things were fine. But the forces of modernisation and powerful media such as television appeared to have given rise to a new breed of women: women who ran their own lives, women who made their own decisions even if it was about whether to strip or not to strip, and women who (horror of horrors!) probably went 'regularly to the pubs'.

It was fear of losing control that drove men to hit back with threats of abandonment, rape, violence and more commonly, exhortations of morality couched in the all-inclusive notion, 'Our Indian Culture'.

In the 1990 Pathfinders study on working women for instance, interviewees expressed joy at the latitude and confidence their work gave them to 'mix freely with men, go home late and expound new ideas'. But talking to sexologists and, marriage counsellors in various cities, I found that these very things relished by working women were a primary cause of marital disagreements. 'Husbands are changing but at a slower pace than women. Men and laws are finding it difficult to adapt to the changed woman,' said a divorce lawyer at Bombay High Court.

Brinda Karat, general secretary of the All India Democratic Women's Association, claimed that the electronic media had boosted cases of domestic violence by 'allowing violence to enter people's lives in a more socially acceptable way: a slap or a kick is now more likely to be seen as a routine manner of expression rather than a disturbance as it might have been earlier.'

Often the resistance put up by men to the emancipation of women, particularly in groups which had just begun to enjoy the fruits of social mobility, was a reflection of the gap between traditional and modern notions of progress. Sociologist Murli Desai, for instance, found that her low-caste male students reacted violently when she talked about ways of putting gender equality into practice such as sharing housework. 'They feel they have progressed up the social ladder and now we are asking them to go back to the kitchen,' she explained. 'Their sense of getting ahead does not mean equality for all but individual elevation which implies the need for someone (to be) inferior who will look up to them.'

Clearly then, the burst of liberalisation in various areas, particularly the electronic media, had resulted in a confusing set of circumstances for women. On the one hand, the urban Indian woman was likely to be better educated, more independent and assertive than her predecessor. On the other hand, it was these very indicators of progress that made her vulnerable to reprisals from men. Her new-found freedom, though certainly welcome, was a precarious one. For before she could begin to explore her options, to appreciate and enjoy the fruits of liberation there was the threat of subversion.

INDIANS IN BLUE JEANS

FIRST THERE WERE THE PROMOS: the dark, jowly and very Indian cowboy, Quick Gun Murugan, riding into town, ordering a masala *dosa* and fobbing off women with the charming excuse: 'The room in my heart is already rented. House Full!' An old couple rambling on about a new show and its effects on the digestive system.

Sari-clad housewives screaming 'Red Hot Chilli Peppers'.

Postmen demanding a dinner date with Ms Bjork.

Then there were the comperes:

Javed Jaffrey moulding himself to a range of stereotypes, the crystal gazing Future Furtado, the foppish Queenie Singh and the oily Abdul Cutpiece. Lanky and flirtatious Ruby jumping into a swimming pool with the villanous Gulshan Grover.

And then there were the shows:

'First Day First Show', 'Timex Timepass', 'Videocon Flashback', 'The Great Indian Manovaigyanik Show'.

This was the world of Channel V, the new-look music channel that in 1994 had replaced MTV on the Star network.

Predictions at the time of its launch were pessimistic. Observers felt that MTV's young following, disappointed by the disappearance of their favourite channel, was not likely to take kindly to a substitute.

They were proved wrong. Within months, the new channel had become the hot topic of conversation at cocktail parties and in college canteens. Columnists and newspaper articles raved about it. The old chortled over its promos and even children were lisping the punchlines.

The sudden adulation was hardly surprising. For Channel V was different from anything that had gone before. Neither was it a foreign channel with concessional local programming, nor was it a 'me too' version of MTV in the vernacular. It was wild, whacky, funny and irreverent. But all of it was Indian. The symbols it used, the references it made were all part of the urban Indian landscape and though it used all the technological wizardry of the advanced world to dress up its humour, the effects were best comprehended by the folks back home.

On second thoughts. Wild? Funny? Irreverent? Could these terms possibly apply to the prissy Indian?

For years, the West had characterised Indians as a dull, humourless lot, given to sentimental outbursts as in E. M. Forster's *Passage To India* or grim formalese as in the books of V. S. Naipaul. The Indian penchant for launching protests and evoking the censorship law at the slightest provocation had done nothing to disprove this characterisation.

And yet here was a channel with spoofs, talk of bowel movements and jokes about communities! Could the earlier perception have been wrong or was the huffy Indian finally begining to laugh at himself?

A little bit of both.

To begin with, the description of Indians as a dour lot though seemingly justified was not entirely correct.

Indians did have a sense of humour. In small towns, in villages, wherever people lived in large sprawling families or in tightly knit communities one could hear the sound of shared song and laughter. It was evident in ribald folk songs, in teasing rituals, in vernacular literature and in everyday conversation. This typically Indian sense of humour had neither British sophistication nor the gregariousness of the Americans. It was more akin to the gurgle of good-humoured banter and its comic effect lay in puncturing pretensions.

Such humour, however, required a rather high degree of security and comfort with oneself. And it was at the edges, where people had begun to doubt their way of life and aspire to a lifestyle they suspected was superior to their own but one that they were not at all comfortable with, that their self-assurance had got frayed. And humour had been replaced by a grim conformism, grimmer for being that much more difficult for its practitioner.

And a major source of insecurity in India, was language or, more precisely, the English language. Years after the British left the country, the English factor had continued to colonise and divide Indians into superior and inferior groups. In simple terms, those who spoke English were the elite and those who didn't, the non-elite. This unspo-ken division was responsible for the widespread middle class awe of 'convent schools' (English-medium schools set up by missionaries), the bureaucrat's love for wordy regulations and the dead, dull language used by judges, academicians and writers. It was the language of imitation, not invention.

But by the 1980s, signs of change were evident. Though India, by Asian standards had lagged in providing basic education on a mass level, the literacy rate in urban India had risen sharply. Schools and colleges reported a high number of first-generation learners and increasingly, in these institutions of education, the medium of instruction was English. In response to a widespread demand, a host of privately run English-speaking courses had also emerged.

A decade later, the preference for English over the vernacular had percolated from the upper classes in the past right down to pavement dwellers (In the 1995 hit film *Rangeela,* a roadside Lothario proposing marriage included the bait: 'our children will study in an English medium school'). The movement extended even to small towns and villages.

And to this expanding group of upwardly mobile, newly prosperous and often newly educated Indians, familiarity had bred, if not contempt, at least a degree of chutzpah.

This was evident in the growing signs of linguistic irreverence: in jokes (the Ajit jokes, the *Gujju* jokes and so on) that derived their punch from the deliberate manner in which they distorted the hallowed English language and in the growth of a new teenage vocabulary that freely mixed the English with the vernacular.

Kids talked of *pataoing, maroing* and *lagaoing.* Bharat Dabholkar, a Bombay-based adman, scripted a string of successful revues mixing English words with Indian accents. Zee TV spawned a new lingua franca— Hinglish, an arbitrary mixture of Hindi and English. Pious Doordarshan acquired a hip acronym, DD, and television shows sported whacky names such as *Jungli Toofan Tyre Puncture.* If Indian-born writers as diverse as Salman Rushdie with magical realism in *Midnight's*

Children and Vikram Seth with a novel in verse about life in San Francisco were introducing new forms to the West, English was undergoing a range of mutations back home. The new urban patois was significant for it symbolised the user's own conquest of the English language and all that it had stood for: wealth, breeding, progress, exclusivity.

Apart from education and economic progress, television had played a potent role in the transformation. Television in fact had acted as an influential leveller in modern India.

To understand its impact on the subtler forms of social disparity one had to look back to a time when information about international news and events was restricted to the English reading elite who, through relatives abroad, also had access to the latest global fads in fashion, music and so on. The rest of us had to look to the local cinema for pointers on fashion and lifestyle. And given the mindset which treated anything foreign as superior and more progressive than the ethnic, the westernised elite were automatically elevated to a higher position on the social scale.

The proliferation of the electronic media changed all that. Television broke through class barriers by making the same information available to all; it also diminished the gap between India and the world. Suddenly, the latest international news could be watched simultaneously by the gem trader in Jaipur as well as the cigar smoking executive in Bombay; both manager and waiters in a restaurant could stay up nights following World Cup football matches live; the teenager from Bhatinda was privy to the same fashion trends as her counterpart in Bangalore; and the sound of Michael Jackson's latest release could be heard in New York and New Delhi at one and the same time.

Loss of privilege implied loss of snobbery.

Channel V's unusual programming strategy was both an indication and a reassertion of this new-found egalitarianism. By placing Hindi and Tamil songs next to western rock; by mixing the typically Indian with a propah English accent; by elevating Bombay street lingo to the status of hip show titles, the channel had, in the words of its creative director, Shashank Ghosh 'expanded the meaning of "cool"'.

And in doing so it had reflected the crazy brew of influences that characterised a whole generation of young Indians both in front of and behind the TV screen.

Thirty-three-year-old Shashank Ghosh, one of the brains behind Channel V, was himself a typical example of the multicultural polyglot. A Bengali born in Delhi, Ghosh had studied at an airforce school, spent a year 'smoking dope and travelling on a friend's broken motorbike' followed by a management degree acquired in the semi-rural environs of Jodhpur and an advertising stint in Hong Kong, before joining Channel V.

There were others like him. Rock Machine, a band of earnest and talented young men in blue jeans, was India's best known rock band in the 1980s. A few years later, Indian instruments such as the *tabla* and the *dholki* had been added to the band's repertoire; t-shirts had been replaced by ethnic style jackets and the new look, new sound band, now renamed Indus Creed, bore little resemblance to the wannabe rockers of yore. Uday Benegal, the band's lead singer whose past included both schooling at the alternative Rishi Valley school and listening to his brother's *Who* records described himself simply as: 'a confused, anglicised Indian'.

The difference was that, increasingly, Benegal, Ghosh and others did not feel the need to apologise or conform to either of their apparently contradictory halves. And this newly visible rise in self-esteem was apparent in various fields such as literature and cinema.

A host of new writers had made an appearance in the 1990s handling language with a skill and dexterity rarely visible before. Prominent among these was Upamanyu Chatterjee whose first book vividly described the cultural contradictions in India through the story of a young westernised man addicted to dope and Marcus Aurelius on his first posting as a bureaucrat in small town India.

In cinema, an increased collaboration between the film industries of the West and the South had given greater exposure to the talents of, for instance, Mani Ratnam (director), A.R. Rahman (music composer), and the gyrating sensation, Prabhudeva. A new generation of trained directors brought up on videos and commercials had also imparted a sheen and faster pace to the scene. The top grossers in 1995, *Hum Aapke Hain Kaun* and *Dilwale Dulhaniya Le Jaayenge,* each sporting a gossamer thin storyline and a typically Indian weakness for a surfeit of songs, differed dramatically from the past in a certain lightness of touch and an absence of melodrama and self-righteousness. Though there was nothing memorable about these films, in their own marshmallow soft way they celebrated the joy of living; a far cry from the conventional high action-low comedy-cheap passion mix, though movies of this ilk continued to be made.

Partly the difference was made possible by a change in the audience. Yash Chopra, the veteran director and maker of films such as *Kabhi Kabhi,* believed that exposure to western soaps on television had helped Indian viewers learn to appreciate shades of grey where earlier they had looked for certainties in black and white.

A Media Advocacy Group study of viewers in Delhi also found a demand among the upper class for single-theme films as distinct from the hold-all formula films routinely churned out by Bollywood.

These various cultural trends indicated that from the gaudy, confused, contrite middle-class cauldron had emerged a new kind of Indian. It was an Indian who carried less baggage than his predecessors: he could speak the English but bend it his own way; she could be part of the couple in a cigarette ad laughing over a book of Polish dirty jokes. It was an Indian that was not at ease totally either with the East or the West but could live with such contradictions and, while laughing at them, could dismiss the white bogeyman with words made memorable by Channel V's flamboyant Quick Gun Murugan: 'Mind It, we are like this only'.

But would the new Indian survive the changes taking place around him?

＊

Shivaji Nagar is a warren of streets adjoining a thriving vegetable market in the heart of Bangalore. The residents of Shivaji Nagar are lower middle class. The men are mostly blue collar workers employed by companies such as HMT, and the Indian Tobacco Company while the women do a variety of odd jobs such as packing *agarbattis* into cases, tailoring, making candles and so on. Household income is, on an average, between ₹1000 and 1,500 per month.

I was taken there one afternoon in July 1994, by a helpful auto-rickshaw driver in pursuit of authentic local spices. There were several shops, lined up in a quiet street with sacks of rice and red chillies that used to be a characteristic feature of *bania* shops in the past. In each of them, the spices I was looking for were displayed, not loose as I had expected, but in shiny foil packets stamped with a brand name. Alongside there were packets of detergent, instant coffee, several varieties of tea, a whole range of soaps, including dainty three-bar packs of the upmarket Le Sancy, vermicelli, macaroni, soya nuggets and, all varieties and sizes of noodles.

I stared in surprise at the range of items and brands on sale, many of which seemed clearly out of sync with the generally shabby look of the place. The shopkeeper asked if he could help. I pointed at the noodles and asked him who purchased them.

'Oh everyone here eats noodles,' he said. 'After the Maggi ads on television, they have become a common thing.'

'What about the soaps, isn't Le Sancy an expensive brand,' I asked.

'So what,' he scoffed, 'there is a latheworker in this lane who buys three bars of Le Sancy every month. And now the Dove soap ads have begun to appear on television. It costs 30 rupees a piece but we have already started getting enquiries.'

Our conversation had generated some interest in the street. And soon, I was surrounded by several shopkeepers all eager to air their comments on purchasing trends in the locality. The shops had been in existence for half a century and most of the current owners being second or third generation inheritors were familiar with the history of the neighbourhood.

And according to them, television had transformed the place. 'Every house in the area has cable TV,' they claimed, pointing at the wires that hung limply from balconies. 'They have Star TV, Zee TV, Sun TV, Udaya TV. Films are very popular. Right now, the street is deserted because everybody is watching the afternoon film.'

From the shopkeepers I learnt that the Muslim women of the neighbourhood had dropped the *burqa* in favour of a more cosmopolitan garb; that the cosmetics and kitchen implements bought by the residents would put many 'high class' homes to shame; that just 10 years ago, the shops stocked just half the items currently available but so much had changed: now everything was instant and people were in a hurry to spend.

'They come to my shop and point, when I tell them the price, they say "who asked the price just give me a kilo," claimed Raj Shekhar, a stocky voluble grocer, 'If they make ₹1000, they will buy ₹2000 worth. Which is why the pawnbrokers at the end of the lane are doing good business.'

***

In 1985, a shift in state policy and the commercialisation of television had stirred the materialistic urges of a guilt-burdened middle class. Ten years later these urges had snowballed into a complete pre-occupation with money, facilitating an even more dramatic shift.

As with the previous metamorphosis, this one too was preceded by an accident. In 1984, Indira Gandhi was assassinated, paving the way for her son, Rajiv Gandhi. In 1991, Rajiv was killed by a bomb explosion, an event that led to the emergence of P. V. Narasimha Rao as prime minister. Seventy years old and in bad health, Rao did not seem like the best choice for the onerous task. But as it happened, the new prime minister startled everybody not only by staging a physical recovery but by pushing through an economic reforms package that sought to bring about more far reaching and permanent changes than anything that had gone before.

In essence, what Rao's new industrial policy did was to boost growth by deregulating almost all industries. It reduced the role of the state by setting the stage for disinvestment in various public sector units. And most important, it reversed the old, isolationist policy by removing the barriers to foreign investment (in the past multinationals were barred from holding a majority stake in Indian companies).

Just a few years before, such sweeping changes regardless of the country's empty coffers—foreign reserves had dipped to alarmingly low levels and the country was on the verge of defaulting on its loan repayments in 1991—would have aroused an outcry of protest.

But attitudes had changed so completely in modern India that Rao's fiscal measures won the acceptance not only of the middle class and the media but also of diverse and traditionally inimical entities such as Laloo Prasad Yadav, the rustic chief minister of Bihar, the populist chief minister of Andhra Pradesh, N. T. Rama Rao and West Bengal's communist leader, Jyoti Basu.

Even the BJP, the Congress party's most bitter rival, after making suitably disapproving noises about the government's new policy, admitted that in the event of their coming to power, the clock would not be turned back.

The West, for its part, was slow to respond to India's open door policy. Given India's tenuous commitment to liberalisation in the past, the hesitation was understandable. Additionally, there was the problem of exposure. While China and other successful recipients of foreign investment in south east Asia, received considerable play in the western media, India continued to be perceived by many as a country of snake charmers and wild elephants.

All this changed in 1993 when Australian media baron, Rupert Murdoch bought a 64 per cent interest in Star TV for $500 million; the British magazine, *The Economist* observed: 'Twenty years of fast growth and the prospect of another decade of the same have created a large Asian middle class. Murdoch is a risk taker, following instinct as much as reason into the world's greatest emerging market for media and for consumer goods. Others will surely follow.'

Murdoch's reputation for sniffing out good business opportunities focused attention on Asia's potential as a market; it also drove home, to a mindset that was used to seeing Asia in terms of south east Asia, the realisation that a large part of this market resided in India.

Though unacknowledged, satellite television played a significant role in changing perceptions of India at a crucial time. It was Star TV's success (largely unexpected: 20 weeks after the BBC launched its Asian service on Star TV, Christopher Irwin, chief of BBC World Service television, admitted that the Indian viewership had exceeded expectations that he would have entertained only in his 'wildest dreams') that forced people to acknowledge that India had a large, westernised, consuming class. It also brought others in its wake.

CNN began to work seriously at developing India as a market; MTV broke away from Star to launch an independent channel. Other international media companies such as Sony, the educational and anthropology channel, Discovery, and the sports-based ESPN began to make a beeline for the country.

Heightened interest in India as a market for media software inevitably affected India's coverage in the western media.

In early 1992, CNN opened a bureau in Delhi and introduced various Asia-oriented programmes; large chunks of these dealt with India. Said Ashis Ray, CNN's bureau chief in Delhi: 'We've expanded our bureau, we aim to put out a story on India almost every day on CNN International.'

More media houses, particularly television networks, set up base in New Delhi. Reuters expanded its network, and agencies such as Associated Press and Agence France Presse opened offices in Bombay. Foreign Correspondents used to seeing India as a passing phase began to dig in their heels. Some actually saw enough potential in the region to return as freelancers and stringers for various publications. 'India,' claimed Hamish McDonald, an Australian journalist who chucked up his job with the *Far Eastern Economic Review* to stay on in India as a freelancer, 'is a place from where great business stories emanate today.'

By 1995, the new economic policies had transformed the Indian marketplace. Advertisements for Cartier watches, Puegeot cars, Gilbey's Old Gold, Pierre Cardin suits and Adidas shoes dotted the landscape. At trade fairs, international hot shots such as Gianfranco Ferre, BMW, IBM, Kenwood and others appealed to the global aspirations of the upmarket Indian male while previously forbidden goodies such as Stroh's beer, Revlon lipsticks and Coke bottles appeared on Indian shelves.

The invasion of foreign goods had scratched a competitive streak among local manufacturers throwing up a whole new range of consumer items. At the high end of the price spectrum were suit lengths that cost ₹75,000, 14-carat gold frame sunglasses for ₹200,000, jewellery watches for ₹50,000, television sets for ₹100,000 and cars priced between ₹400,000 and ₹2 million. At the lower end were expensive trifles such as puff pastry biscuits, cosmetics, hair rejuvenators, Scotch and canned drinks.

In addition, everything (including many pre-existing brands) went premium: sanitary napkins sprouted wings; ordinary white toothpaste appeared in varied colours and textures; soft drinks emerged in new containers; lotions, potions, soaps and shampoos acquired costly fragrances; and Lakme, the country's leading beauty products manufacturer launched an entire range of high-priced cosmetics. Everything, including basic products such as lubricants, phones and fans, promised a new, qualitative difference at a new exalted price. The focus, whether by virtue of the product, packaging innovations or advertising strategy, was on the premium market, the 'upmarket' segment of Indian society.

In Delhi seven English-language newspapers screamed for attention in a billboard war sparked off by the new upstart that was threatening to take away the 'upmarket' reader's custom. 'Stamp around all night at the Oasis in Woodland shoes' ordered the 'leather that weathers' presumably again to upmarket denizens of nightclubs. And Doordarshan, yes Doordarshan took a decidedly unsocialistic swipe at its competitors by describing its new baby, Channel 3, as the channel that 'lists the top ten companies not the top ten hits'. Even an enterprising sweet and savouries shop owner in Delhi came out with nitrogen sealed, three layered foil laminated polypacks of Indian snacks commonly sold loose, by weight, in every bazaar in the country. His aim: 'to get into top-end brand marketing'.

But was India's top-end really large enough to sustain this onslaught of 'premium' goods?

Statistics suggested otherwise.

In its 1993 survey of Asia, *The Economist,* while assessing consumer trends for the region, predicted that by the year 2000 the continent (excluding the ex-Soviet Union) would have 1 billion consumers. Of these, the magazine claimed, the 'super haves', i.e., households with a high earning capacity of over $30,000 would number roughly 15 million (the figures excluded Japan). The 'have somes', i.e., households with an annual income of $18,000 and a more typically middle-class taste for houses, cars and durables would have increased to 75 million. The bulk of the consumers, 150 million households, would be the 'near haves' who would, characteristically, be consumers of products such as shampoo and entertain middle-class aspirations. The new Asian consumer, the magazine also predicted, was likely to be cost-conscious and looking for good value rather than a fancy brand.

Wealth distribution patterns in India appeared to be in consonance with the trends outlined by the magazine. Figures released by the National Council of Applied Economic Research (NCAER) in 1993 revealed that only a miniscule segment of the population (3.6 million households) were in the top income bracket of ₹78,000 a year and above.

On the other hand, the middle-income group of ₹36,000–78,000 contained a hefty 20 million households. And the ₹18,000–36,000 grossers, the 'near haves' numbered as many as 39.5 million households. Expectedly, the mass of the country's population (58 per cent) was in the gloom below ₹18,000 but even in this category a certain amount of consumption was visible: this class owned 36 million bicycles.

In the late 1980s when the first signs of the Indian middle class's growing prosperity appeared, the media, both domestic and foreign, had talked ecstatically about the emergence of 150–200 million new consumers. The figures were not exaggerated. But if one actually looked at what the numbers represented, then it would have been clear that only a small segment of the consuming class could be described as high spenders.

The vast majority of consumers were small-time shoppers. And it was among these teeming millions, many of whom still cleaned their teeth with twigs and used the same multipurpose bar of soap to bathe, wash clothes and clean the family buffalo, that the big markets lay. Indeed, the most successful consumer revolutions at the time had been led by a reasonably priced detergent powder and small affordable sachets of shampoo.

And yet, in the frenzied early half of the 1990s the Indian market was inundated *not* with reasonably-priced products of mass usage but with high priced, luxury items ranging from chocolates to cars (each level saw the entry of items that could be classified as luxury items in their own price category).

The phenomenon seemed to lend itself to only two interpretations: One was that a majority of manufacturers and advertisers were blind to the realities of the market (a distinct possibility since many of the new products were fated for an ignominious exit).

The other explanation possible was that the effects were intended to percolate as aspirations down to the non-premium market.

This however was easier said than done. Apart from the question of affordability, anyone seeking to conquer the

Indian market with a high-priced, westernised, luxury product had a few difficult obstacles to surmount. The first related to need. In India the crying need was for ice boxes and rugged transport vehicles not four-door fridges and Puegeots.

The second related to demand. Many of the products pouring into the market were clearly unsuited to Indian lifestyles. A personalised phone for teenagers (like the 'Rap phone' introduced in 1994–95) or a brand of cornflakes would seem to be of little relevance in a place where the emphasis was on the family and not the individual, and where people preferred their breakfast to be warm, soft and savoury rather than cold, dry and crunchy.

From the marketer's standpoint the only way to make consumers part with more than they could reasonably afford was to make them feel they *needed* or *desired* certain kinds of products.

Accordingly advertising budgets, particularly for non-essential fripperies such as cigarettes and soft drinks, zoomed. The Indian Tobacco Company spent a whopping ₹700 million on sponsoring the World Cup cricket tournament in 1996. Coca Cola paid ₹130 million to be designated the official drink for the event. Even OshKosh B'Gosh Inc, upmarket retailers of children's clothes with a potentially limited clientele, entered the Indian market with an advertising budget of ₹15 million for a single year. Full-page advertisements in daily newspapers and expensive multimedia campaigns became commonplace and roadside kiosks, awnings of shops, streetside walls, and every inch of available public space were plastered with brand names.

The most popular medium for advertising, not surprisingly, was television. Popular television programmes were soon swamped with advertisements for a range of consumer goods. The air was thick with advertising jargon such as 'niche marketing' that is, placing the ad in a position where it was likely to be seen mainly by its potential market. Such a strategy would ensure that an advertisement for an expensive car, for instance, was inserted in a programme with a select upper class audience rather than a lower middle class one. In actual fact however, advertisements for 'upmarket' products were everywhere. Even top-rated television programmes such as *Superhit Muqabla* and *Junoon* carried ads for, among other things, Coke and Thums Up cans, Revlon cosmetics, Johnsons's baby oil and soap, the new Puegeot 309—all luxuries for a bulk of the viewership.

The images and lifestyles portrayed in these and other advertisements were markedly western and elitist. This, by itself, was not a new trend. The Bombay advertising industry, peopled by members of the most westernised section of Indian society, had always derived inspiration abroad. And the avalanche of premium goods in the 1990s understandably necessitated an avalanche of premium advertising.

What gave this factor added potency was the relative novelty of television advertising in India. In the mid-1980s, when blocks of commercials made an appearance on state television, viewers would watch them as they would a separate programme. Ten years down the road, the fascination continued. Understandably, for commercials were not only more lavishly mounted and better produced than the programmes they accompanied but they depicted an exceedingly glamorous and alien world; a world where people lived in gracious homes and drank tea out of silver cups; where men wore suits and drove fast cars; where women were wooed with diamond bracelets; where youngsters dressed in jeans and miniskirts and spent their time in exotic pursuits such as surfing and bungee jumping.

Advertising was however just one method and not an entirely satisfactory one of achieving the desired end: changing the mindset of the consumer. The advertiser had to look for other, more effective means.

The existence of a free and thriving press amid a sea of illiteracy is one of India's many anomalies. Even more curious is the existence of a vocal and extremely influential English press. For a couple of decades following Independence however, the print media was somewhat stodgy and marked by its strong emphasis on politics. The front pages of newspapers were covered with political speeches (reported verbatim) and inside, eminent lead writers commented ponderously on the state of the nation. Other areas of life, art, culture, social trends and so on, were sidelined by the overwhelming preoccupation with politics. Moreover, events took firm precedence over personalities.

By the early 1980s however, a sweeping transformation had taken place. The market was swamped with a series of glossy magazines. Newspapers sported smart, new layouts and bold headlines. The change was evident in the content as well. Politics was still important but far more space was being awarded to other subjects: films, sports, social issues and crime. The writing was sharper and increasingly focused on people rather than events.

The press had also gained in influence. For a people who were fast losing faith in the political process and the tardy judicial system, the press had emerged as a bastion of hope. A new breed of investigative journalists were exposing corruption, kickbacks and shady deals in high places. Supreme Court judges were converting press reports into writ petitions and activists in a whole host of fields such as women's rights and labour were using the print media to challenge inequitable traditions. It was an exciting time for journalism.

But it was not to last. For the success of the press was paving the way for its own downfall. By the late 1980s, the daunting position of the press had begun to attract a new kind of proprietor: the industrialist, the builder, the politician, and the trader. In all fairness, this was not entirely a new phenomenon; many of the newspapers were owned by businessmen and politicians. But never before had they come in such numbers with promises of unlimited budgets and fat salaries for journalists.

The result was that all at once, there were too many publications chasing the same limited pool of readers and advertisers. And with the emergence of far more papers than the market could support, the press was forced to adopt populist methods. In short, journalists began to write about things that would sell.

The transformation of the journalist into a salesman was best demonstrated by events at Bennett Coleman & Co., publishers of some of the country's leading newspapers and magazines including the doughty *Times of India*.

For years, these periodicals had shaped the views of the Indian middle class and articulated the same to the politicians of the day. Editors of the various publications at Bennett Coleman were highly regarded public figures. Indeed, the editor of the *Times* was said to be one of the most powerful persons in the country.

In the mid-1980s however, under the stewardship of Samir Jain, a young scion of the Jain family which owned the company, the venerable institution underwent a complete overhaul: unprofitable magazines were shut down, innovative pricing strategies were introduced and advertising rates hiked to increase profit. And the marketing sections at the company's various offices redesigned to resemble plush lobbies of luxury hotels. The changes were not merely financial or cosmetic. They were accompanied by a deliberate undermining of the position of the editor.

At the *Times,* for example, a former cigarette company executive was designated managing editor. When the actual editor went on leave, his place was filled by an executive and finally, the post was scrapped altogether. At the *Times's* sister publication, *The Economic Times,* editorial control was in the hands of a company director. Jain also appointed brand managers to each publication who would vet editorial decisions and, if the need arose, lop off sections, alter the product mix and so on.

So blatant was Jain's disregard for the editorial function and his total preoccupation with money that Nicholas Coleridge in his book on newspaper barons, *The Paper Tigers* was moved to observe: 'Of all the newspaper owners in the world, I met no one so single-mindedly wedded to marketing as Samir Jain.'

To anyone wedded to the (increasingly old-fashioned) idea that newspapers existed to bare the truth, to analyse events from the standpoint of the public good, Coleridge's assessment would have appeared as gross condemnation.

But, as it happened, by the early 1990s, the role of the journalist had moved so far from its original purpose that there was actually growing acceptance of the notion that newspapers and magazines existed to make money not news; to advertise rather than inform; to sell rather than analyse. These were perfect circumstances for a takeover by the marketing industry.

Corruption in the press was by no means a new phenomenon. Journalists had always been susceptible to inducements from a host of sources. And as the print media grew in influence so had the efforts of politicians, businessmen and others to use it to their own ends. The difference was that in the past, attempts to subvert the press were condemned. *The Indian Express's* blatant support for textile tycoon Nusli Wadia or the *Times's* editor, Girilal Jain's links with Wadia's rival, Dhirubhai Ambani for instance, were frowned upon by journalists and readers.

But in the modern scenario the process of subversion was so relentless and often so insidious that it was no longer perceived as being improper or unethical. Business journalists, who could make or break a company's fortunes, were wooed with stocks and expensive freebies such as mobile telephones. Others were plied with gifts, invitations to parties and junkets, most of which were thinly disguised inducements to gain publicity (negative coverage implied being struck off the guest list). Advertisers of consumer products routinely struck deals with publications where ads were offered in return for plugs in the editorial sections.

None of this was considered wrong. Senior staffers at prominent publications flaunted the invitations and expensive gifts they received from corporate houses and the country's international carrier, Air India, announced publicly that it was setting aside free tickets for journalists to get favourable publicity. Twice, marketing executives approached me to write articles indirectly connected with products launched by their companies (example: the importance of eating fresh food, from a company that had just launched a freshness preserving gizmo) which, they informed me blithely and with absolutely no trace of irony, would then be planted in suitable publications.

With success, and the emergence of the electronic media, the attempts at subversion became even more blatant and unabashed. The high-profile chairman of the ₹30 billion United Breweries Group, Vijay Mallya, while commenting on his plans to enter the newspaper and television business, boasted that he was doing so to further his business prospects. Paul Hanneman, Vice-president, Asia/Pacific of the film company, 20th Century Fox, claimed proudly that Fox films were being avidly promoted by Star TV.

The absence of any laws on cross-ownership of the media, of course, meant that newspapers such as *The Times of India* and *Mid-day* could and did rent time slots on radio stations (and wrote about them) and media baron Rupert Murdoch could use his television network, Star TV, to launch a media blitzkrieg for films produced by his film company, 20th Century Fox.

The once sacrosanct boundary between the editorial and advertising sections of the media had been obscured. Everything was up for grabs.

For the marketing industry the increased pliability of the media was a significant and welcome development. There was a flip side to it though. For as the number of suitors expanded, marketers had to hike their budgets and think up new, more innovative methods of grabbing the attention of the increasingly fickle journalist.

Some of these were in the area of what in marketing jargon would be known as creating 'brand awareness' and 'image building'.

Hence, cornflakes giant Kellogs took to sponsoring a health show on radio FM called 'Breakfast with Kellogs' sparking off associations (in the minds of listeners and the press) between breakfast, Kelloggs and health. Similarly, shoe manufacturer Reebok planned a chain of fitness centres in the country. Flamboyant liquor manufacturer, Vijay Mallya, not only promoted high profile events such as the annual Derby in various cities but turned himself into an advertisement for his product. 'They (the media),' he admitted in an interview, 'talk about my cars, they talk about my horses, which suits me sometimes because of the lifestyle imagery our brands are creating.'

The method that was becoming more common however was the lavish launch. By the 1990s, there were parties to launch all kinds of goods and all kinds of entities (the portly entrepreneur, the high fashion designer, the multinational, the socialite). Competition spurred a hunt for exotic locations, bizarre themes and, most crucial, an ever-expanding list of celebrity-invitees.

In the old days when radio and cinema were the only popular forms of communication, celebrities were few and far between. By the 1990s, television and a personality-adulating press had conferred stardom on a range of new types: pop singers, pulp writers, pouting models, posturing designers, television actors, veejays, newsreaders and so on. The criteria for fame had changed. Talent was no longer essential. Packaging was everything.

And being a celebrity was profitable. Billboards were plastered with well-known faces. Sachin Tendulkar and Mohammad Azharuddin, the country's best known sportsmen signed hugely lucrative deals to endorse products. Amitabh Bachchan took a break from acting and launched a company to market his fame. Lesser known mortals too were making hay from their 15 minutes in the sun: the going rate for cutting a ribbon or merely appearing at a social event, even for a minor actor, was in the vicinity of a few thousands.

And fittingly, in response to the demands of the market, a clutch of professional event managers had emerged who would, on request, organise the event, make arrangements for travel, etc., contact sponsors, invite the publicists and even supply the requisite celebrities.

In September 1994 one such agency invited me to accompany a group of Bombay's Most Wanted to Delhi for the inauguration of what purported to be Asia's largest discotheque.

Bombay airport, on the sultry morning of our departure, was filled with faces, some distinctly recognisable, some vaguely remembered. There were musicians galore: three long-haired rockers, a veteran balladeer, a crooner-turned Hindi pop diva and a transcontinental rapper accompanied by a flunkey with neatly segregated identities ('My name is Vicky,' he told me, 'national name Vicky; international name Vick').

Scattered around were hungover, unshaven male models, representatives of the bicep-straining-through-sleeve school of actors, their fluffy wives, one out-of-work actress and a bevy of Kate Moss lookalikes.

At the airport in Delhi a fleet of white Contessas was waiting to transport us to a nearby five-star hotel. At the reception bedlam reigned. Guests crowded round the counter complaining about their rooms (a significant indicator of position on the pecking order); demanding keys, a car ('to go shopping'), a driver ('the same who drove us from the airport') . Hotel employees added to the confusion by hovering around trying to be photographed with anyone at all who would oblige.

By evening another planeload of celebs had descended upon the hotel. For the morning arrivals, the partying had begun with bottles of Scotch and Riviera opening in various rooms and distress calls regarding dress and makeup decisions going back and forth. A few hours later The Travelling Bombay Circus was on the road.

Meanwhile....

At Fireball, the spanking new disco on the highway snaking out of Delhi, the excitement had been building. Hundreds of local invitees paced the vast lawns outside. A long, never-ending line of people waited to join the thousands that appeared to be pounding the walls of the Cecil B. De Mille-like interior. All of Delhi and its cousins from neighbouring Haryana appeared to be in on this exclusive bash. Bombay's beautiful people, when they finally arrived, had to be led in through a back entrance.

Inside, a mass of bodies was churning up the dance floor, others were pressed against the walls, the various stairways, the gallery and every available space. Young boys with innovative gelled hairstyles and worldly-wise eyes set up a raucously alcoholic chatter; young girls in gowns, bell bottoms and other MTV-inspired attire darted around excitedly and groups of hefty Sardarjis made their way heavily through the crush.

Members of Bombay's glittering firmament skulked in the shadows, unnoticed. A couple of much-written about beauties, sinuously clad in figure-hugging minis, on encountering probing hands and catcalls, turned tail and made off for another discotheque in the city.

Suddenly, a scuffle broke out, not just any scuffle but a Delhi-type scuffle involving important people and relatives of Very Important people. The police swung their way through the melee. The party was almost over. The press and television cameras took due note of the phenomenon: a new discotheque had opened and Bombay's best-known had been there for the occasion. And that, after all, was all that mattered.

***

The concerted efforts of the marketing industry resulted, predictably, in an amplification of western and urban elitist values and preoccupations. If television had aided in the creation of a new, more self-assertive Indian; it was also, in turn, making him a stranger in his own land.

Television and the local press featured the O. J. Simpson trial in all its minute detail, regardless of the fact that no one in India was likely to have even heard of the football star before his fall from glory. The tribulations of the British royal family were awarded saturation coverage as was every trifling Hollywood event. Anorexic models displayed outfits totally unsuited to Indian wallets and Indian mores. Advertisements encouraged Indian girls to acquire their own blonde, blue-eyed Barbie dolls. At a time when even foreign channels were getting wise to the fact that India offered a limited market for purely western programming, the Indian media was increasing its western content. Large chunks of airtime on All India Radio's newly floated FM channel was given over to western pop and Doordarshan's Metro channel supplied a few hours of MTV every day.

The bias was also reflected in other ways. A veejay, for instance, blithely informed viewers that the sitar was an Indian version of a guitar and an advertisement for a department store urged readers to: 'Wear something really strange. A *salwar kameez'*. For a country with a rich musical heritage and one in which a huge majority of women dressed in a *salwar kameez,* such statements could be said to constitute a rather insulting distortion of reality. Yet, there was no protest. The hype machine had worked so effectively that many of these distortions had actually been internalised by many Indians.

In the circumstances then, the New Indian seemed to have little chance of surviving. For the unabashed glamourisation of a minority lifestyle was directed at creating another kind of Indian, an insecure and confused Indian. The kind who, for instance, would sustain and add to the garish mongrel architecture that was increasingly seen on the outskirts of big cities and in small towns. The kind who would fit an air conditioner in his bedroom even though he would much rather have slept out in the open under the stars. The kind who would instal a western-style commode in his bathroom and then perch on it Indian style for his daily ablutions. The kind, in short, who would have forgotten how to laugh at himself.

THE AGE OF INFOTAINMENT

THE POLISH LEADER, LECH WALESA, when asked what caused communism's stunning collapse in eastern Europe is believed to have pointed to a nearby television set and said, 'It all came from there.'

He was not exaggerating. In June 1989, searing CNN reports from Beijing's Tiannanmen Square stopped the Polish communist government from rescinding an election that brought Walesa's party, Solidarity, to the brink of power. The Polish election was scheduled to take place a day or two after the occurrence of the Chinese massacre. According to Richard Baum, a University of California at Los Angeles (UCLA) specialist in Chinese politics, 'Members of the Workers party central committee (in Poland) said, "We will have another Tiannanmen on our hands if we cancel with all the foreign media present".' And they decided not to cancel.

Indeed, the emergence and proliferation of cable and satellite technology were sending shock waves round the world. Through the 1980s, European policymakers in Brussels deliberated on measures to counteract what they perceived to be a potential deluge of cheap American media programming; in Islamic countries such as Saudi Arabia, Muslim zealots aimed stones at satellite dishes. In Kuwait, pamphlets warned against the dangers of western programming and in countries such as China and Malayasia, the unlicensed ownership of satellite dishes was actually banned.

In India, the arrival of satellite television had sparked off widespread anxieties regarding the invasion of alien cultural values and a threat to the country's sovereignty. By 1994, these fears had been replaced by new ones. And this time the threat came not from outside but from within the country.

Few regions in the world are as diverse as India. In 1897 Mark Twain described it as 'the country of a hundred nations and a hundred tongues, of a thousand religions and two million gods'. The problem of containing these disparate elements within a single unit has been perhaps the most crucial challenge for postcolonial India.

Policymakers in the early days following Independence attempted to tackle the thorny issue in various ways: Hindi was adopted as the national language with the expectation that it would serve as a link between various linguistic groups in the country; in the federal structure described by the Constitution, powers were strategically divided to ensure a strong centre. Both measures had a mixed impact.

The imposition of Hindi was strongly resisted by the south, particularly the state of Tamil Nadu, where a protracted agitation forced the central government to moderate its stand. And the provision for a strong centre resulted, over the years, in an accretion of power in the northern cow belt, comprising the states of Uttar Pradesh, Madhya Pradesh, Rajasthan and Bihar causing resentment and alienation among Delhi's more distant neighbours.

A significant medium of hope in this regard was television. In 1969, Vikram Sarabhai had identified 'national integration' as one of the key roles television could play in India. The methods used may not have been quite what he had in mind, but the goal was reflected both in the subsequent expansion of the national network and in its content. Doordarshan consistently hammered the message of a united India in serials, spots and in specially commissioned, imaginative short films. In its effort to achieve integration, the television network also replicated the federal balance with an emphatic Delhi orientation in its programming, again to disgruntled reactions from far flung states.

By the 1980s it was clear that the integration moves, rather than succeeding, seemed to have spread diss-affection. India's unity lay potentially in tatters with secessionist movements being waged in Punjab, Kashmir and the Northeast.

By the beginning of the following decade, a technology-driven factor had come into play: local television channels.

The trend began with cable television. In the early days only an adventurous few dared to enter the trade for fear that municipal authorities would activate the regulations providing for government monopoly of the airwaves to drive them out of business. But with the sprouting of foreign satellite channels and the authorities' continued reluctance to come down on cable operations, cable networks mushroomed and proliferated all over the country.

Under the government's customarily watchful eye, entire neighbourhoods were connected and the local operator in each area became a figure as familiar and essential as the postman or the milkman. In Bombay's Chembur area, the local cable kingpin expanded his services to include lotto games, music on request and advertisements for shops and restaurants.

In Delhi's Vasant Kunj colony, J. S. Kohli, popularly known as 'Star uncle' by the neighbourhood kids, made programmes on community activities, flashed birthday greetings and public service messages, often at the request of official agencies such as the police, through his cable network. In fact, on one occasion when the taps in the colony ran dry, residents phoned Kohli to complain.

Elsewhere, enterprising cable operators videotaped local or controversial news events such as irate commuters storming a railway station in Bombay or the sensational press conference where the rogue stockbroker Harshad Mehta named the prime minister as the recipient of a ₹10 million bribe. All these developments were harbingers of the more professionally-run local and community channels that were to come into existence on television and FM radio a few years later and revealed a deeply felt need for area-specific, home-grown information versus Doordarshan's all-inclusive, national character.

By the early 1990s however, another trend had begun to emerge: television channels in regional languages. In the southern state of Kerala, a Moscow-based Indian promoter, Raji Menon, launched Asianet, an ambitious project with channels in three southern languages, Malayalam, Tamil and Telegu and a cabling operation that involved stringing cables along electric poles in collaboration with the state's industrial development corporation and its electricity board. In Madras, there was Sun TV in Tamil and in Karnataka, Udaya TV. In October 1993, Doordarshan itself launched four regional language channels with plans to expand the number to 15 over the next two years.

Suddenly, it seemed the old wisdom of one channel, one language, one centre was being overturned, by accident or design, to cater to the many. The phenomenon also reflected the political reality of the times: a weak government at the centre and strong regional parties in the states.

Media observers however, saw in the phenomenon the seeds of fragmentation. Certainly, there was cause for concern. Globally, countries were being remapped. In certain cases barriers had come down but in many more ethnic identities were being reasserted at the cost of the whole. By the early 1990s the USSR was a faded dream; Yugoslavia was being torn apart by its fractious communities; in Canada, French-speaking Qubeckers lost, but just by a whisker, their demand for a separate state; and in Turkey, Iraq and Pakistan ethnic minorities were screaming for attention. The big was giving way to the small. Would India, with its disparate parts survive? And what role would the electronic media play in the process?

In July 1994 I went south to seek some answers.

Madras, the capital of Tamil Nadu, struck me as a city of jumbled impact. There were remnants of colonial history, a fort, ornate buildings and quaint street names; the market areas: Parry's (pronounced 'Paris' by the locals), Mambalam, T. Nagar where shiny, multi-layered frocks jostled with MTR's packaged masalas; a long clear stretch of beach and silent houses on leafy streets. Women in graceful Kanjeevarams on afternoons met to sample the hundred flavours of ice cream at Dasaprakash and long queues of would-be migrants formed daily outside the American Consulate.

But at heart the city was obdurate. Young women talked not unhappily, of living out their parents' lives. Young men cut short mention of aspiration with a curt 'that is not for us'. Duty hung heavy. So did archaic notions of custom, tradition and obedience.

It was with reason that advertisers rated Madras low in receptivity to new products, for any unfamiliar element, be it a bride or a washing machine, was resisted till its necessity could no longer be denied. Which is not to say that the average Tamilian had a longer and wiser vision for change. Far from it, for the air was thick with brittle flashpoints: strikes and sudden agitations that brought the higgeldy-piggeldy city to a halt and moved on with no lasting effect.

An eternal flashpoint, not surprisingly, was Doordarshan. It was to be expected that the network's blatant unity propaganda would be received with some scepticism in the southern city, but meeting people from various walks of life I found it was perceived as an instrument of subjugation in more ways than one. The litany of grievances was long and varied: the inauguration of a new studio for Doordarshan's second channel had involved only Congress (I) MPs even though Tamil Nadu was ruled by a regional party, the AIDMK; all the toppers in the recent school board examinations had been interviewed except for the student who topped the Tamil paper; reception of the national channel in Madras was technically poor; the classical was given preference to the folk, so on and so forth.

Ironically where the government's ham-handed attempts at foisting 'national integration' through television had failed, the entertainment industry had succeeded with consummate ease.

As I checked into a hotel room, overhung with the sickly-sweet smell of incense, an eager attendant rushed to switch on the television set. 'Which channel do you want, Doordarshan, Sun, Asianet, or ...' he offered with a flourish, 'your Zee?'

Zee TV, or 'Zhee' as many of the locals called it, I discovered, was a tremendously popular channel in Madras notwithstanding its use of Hindi and its definite orientation towards the north and the west. Cable operators reported a widespread demand for it and many middle-class housewives watched it avidly for information about new household products and north Indian recipes.

A report by the advertising agency Trikaya Grey on television viewership trends in August 1993 maintained that Doordarshan's entertainment savvy Metro channel had also garnered a wide following in Madras (32.3 television rating points compared to 13.2 in Bombay and 8.7 in Delhi). And one of the most watched programmes in the city at the time was a soap on Doordarshan itself: *Junoon,* a regular big city soap with glamorous women, family travails, evil gangsters et al. The serial was first aired in Hindi but later dubbed in Tamil for its south Indian viewers. The translation was so poor that it became the subject of cartoons and angry letters to the newspapers. Despite the furore over this, the touchiest of issues, *Junoon* went on to become a top-rated programme. People in Madras rushed home to watch the weekly episode and conversation on public buses and on college campuses the next morning centred around little else.

In general, a thawing of the old anti-north sentiment was visible. At Naidu Hall, a large department store in T. Nagar, a busy shopping area, women were scouting around for bargains. The *pavadai thavani,* the traditional half sari, was nowhere in evidence. Everyone was dressed in a full-length sari or the north Indian *salwar kameez.* In the old days, observed G. Venugopal, partner, Naidu Hall, fashions were 'born in Bombay, travelled to Delhi and buried in Madras'. But now, he claimed proudly, Bombay's latest was in Madras a week later.

A few metres away, Mansukh's was doing brisk business in *chapati bhaji, bhel puri* and other typically north-west Indian dishes. The proprietors, a family that owned a chain of sweetmeat shops in the city, had opened the snack-joint a year ago in response to a noticeable change in public tastes. The barriers were coming down. But the phenomenon had been preceeded by a dramatic change in mindset.

Of all India's diverse peoples, the Tamilian, apart from a markedly high intellect, was known for his spartan lifestyle and staunch resistance to change. Affluence did not necessarily imply an opulent lifestyle. The *dhoti-clad* Tamilian in the second-class train compartment, the story went, could well be a millionaire.

That, however, was in the past. The proclivity towards acquisition and conspicuous consumption evident all over the country had hit the traditionally austere and hidebound Tamilian as well, proving that greed could be an effective unifier. The most visible indication was the wave of speculation sweeping through the city.

The stockmarket, I was told, was booming. A variety of shopkeepers, including, I found, a marriage bureau, had set up a side business in share brokerage. The term 'sensex', an acronym for the sensitive index measuring volatility in the stock market, had entered the middle-class lexicon and several finance-related publications had sprung up to service this new fascination.

The other trade flourishing in Madras concurrently was in lottery tickets. Lottery sales had become a ₹5 billion business and even other states had taken to pumping their lottery tickets into Tamil Nadu. The new gambling mania was evident in other ways as well. A local jewellery shop had introduced a scheme whereby people were invited to participate in a lucky draw by putting in a sum of money every month; losers could take home a piece of jewellery equivalent to their contributions through the year. The scheme was a runaway success.

'The Madrasi loves getting something for nothing,' observed Janaki Venkataraman, ex-editor of a city magazine, 'and that is what all these schemes seem to promise.'

One person who seemed to have understood this and exploited it to the hilt was Kalanidhi Maran, Managing Director of Sun TV. In 1994, despite fierce competition (Asianet, introduction of Tamil prime time segments on Jain TV and Zee, and the launch of new enterprises such as Raj TV and *JJ* TV), Sun TV had established itself as the leading channel in Tamil Nadu with a presence even in remote parts of the state: Vadigapati, a village of 50 houses near Salem had acquired a satellite dish to catch the channel.

The channel's success was largely due to a formula that stressed entertainment over politics. In fact, Sun TV closely resembled Zee TV in its middle-class audience and its clutch of game shows with lucrative prizes for the lucky winners.

Most of Sun TV's game shows had the good-humoured, nudge-nudge quality of adult games. The most popular show when I visited Madras was *Jodi Purottam,* an exercise to assess compatibility between married couples. Another programme had mothers pitted against their daughters-in law. For other shows, dumpy housewives cheerfully donned animal masks while on Pongal, the major south Indian festival, Sun TV enabled viewers, through satellite link-ups, to flash greetings to friends and relatives in various parts of the globe. The attraction was most definitely commercial: many of the shows offered a range of expensive goodies ranging from gold jewellery to household goods and cars.

But they also satisfied and enhanced the average person's thirst for involvement and participation. Sun TV was flooded with applications from people seeking their 15 minutes of fame on television. And an executive with a market research firm in Bangalore told me that acquaintances in Madras had sought him out in the hope that he had friends at Sun TV and could get them featured on *Jodi Purottam.*

Apart from the game shows, films were the most popular form of entertainment. The Tamil Nadu film industry made over a hundred films a year and for the avid filmgoing public the electronic media had provided a hugely expanded range of options. Each of the satellite channels had a heavy quota of film-based programming and showed at least two films a week with a daily fare of three available on cable. And according to both market research and cable operators the overwhelming demand was for more and more 'cinema'.

The Tamilian obsession with cinema was not a new phenomenon and had, in fact, long been an object of fascination for the outsider. India, on the whole, was a film crazy nation, but in Tamil Nadu the dividing line between reel and real life was more conspicuously obscured: people 'break'danced in the streets, brides were transported to weddings in gilded floats and temples were dedicated to film stars. The police chief in the early 1990s, a flamboyant daredevil figure with a luxuriant moustache, was immortalised in a film by a character said to be based on him. Posters, photographs and giant cut-outs of the chief minister, a voluptuous former screen siren, dominated the landscape. Her chief opponent was yet another film star: a swarthy bus conductor-turned-actor famed for his action sequences and his real-life Robin Hood-like reputation.

Rulers were treated like demi-gods. When MGR, an immensely popular actor who went on to become Tamil Nadu's most charismatic chief minister, died, fervent fans actually killed themselves in grief. Jayalalitha, his on-and off-screen consort, who came to power in 1991, became an object of equal reverence. Her followers wrote paeans in her praise calling her, among other things, 'goddess', 'mother' and 'legendary vision of Tamil Nadu'. On her 46th birthday, villagers in Madurai named 46 infants after her while others including a minister displayed their allegience in more extreme ways such as tattooing her name on their bodies and rolling down a city street covered only in leaves. Similar instances of sycophancy abounded and caused much amusement outside the state.

Up close however, the implications were hardly funny. In fact, the fairy town façade concealed much that was ugly and sinister.

At the home of a friend, local journalists described the oppressive conditions in which they functioned. The chief minister with characteristic haughtiness ignored the press. Ministers and bureaucrats were too much in awe of her to give interviews. The lack of communication did not stop the chief minister's aides from coming down on critical reporters. Such was the shadow of fear that journalists in the state did not dare to meet or discuss politics in public—a scenario unheard of in any other part of the country.

They had ample reason, for criticism of the ruling party, real or implied, invited dangerous consequences. Chandralekha, a bureaucrat who questioned the chief minister's actions was attacked with acid. K. M.Vijayan, a lawyer who petitioned the Supreme Court on the government's reservation policy, was accosted by *goondas* who broke his limbs confining him to bed for three months. A High Court judge who was hearing a controversial case involving the state government was sought to be intimidated in a more indirect way: his son-in-law was arrested on trumped up charges of dealing in narcotics.

The police force too enjoyed untrammelled powers which they used freely not just against civil libertarians and political activists inimical to the chief minister but also against common people. At the hotel I was staying in, the manager informed me that his staff had to leave work early at nights to avoid harassment from the cops.

At the head of this state of terror, Jayalalitha, like a latter-day banana republic ruler, presided over lavish displays of pomp and splendour. Her party spent an estimated ₹500 million on a rally to celebrate the completion of a year in office; an ambitious undertaking, the World Tamil Conference, was organised in the holy city of Thanjavur at a cost of ₹800 million. For the wedding of her foster son in 1995, Jayalalitha decorated a 50-acre area with palm leaf *pandals* and plaster of paris palaces. Arches and lights brightened the route to be taken by the groom and 10 dining halls were erected to feed the 200,000 guests invited. Schools around the area were shut for a week for security reasons and state services deployed to make it the event of a lifetime. All this even as allegations of corruption and tax evasion against her and her associates were rife.

I had gone to Madras to see if the new local television channels thrown up by the march of satellite technology were encouraging fissiparous tendencies. What I found was that far from fuelling a movement they were helping to entrench and sustain a need for mindless escapism, the result of which was a stupor, deep and widespread. It confronted you in the sullen set of faces that you met, in the sad, unfinished look on cafés, department stores and other centres of modern indulgence, in the manner in which people squatted at bus stops, on roads, behind reception counters at hotels, and most vividly, in the willingness of a people to gift an entire state to the fantasy saviour of the moment.

Madras though, was no exception. It was more a reflection of the trends shaping the country.

***

In the 1970s, the urban middle class's chief complaint against television had had less to do with television and more to do with the state's monopoly over the medium. The restricted flow of information and Doordarshan's preoccupation with the government in power had provoked angry editorials and heated after dinner discussions. People had grown accustomed to taking the 'news' on television with a liberal pinch of salt or turning the set off in disgust.

Over the next two decades much had changed. The emergence of video enabled politicians, journalists and activists to air views inimical to the government on an audio-visual medium. The video magazine, despite its restricted reach, was an innovative method of bypassing the controlled mass medium and conveying stories with startling visuals to the people.

With the arrival of satellite television, the situation was transformed beyond recognition. While the BBC and CNN brought news about India and the world to Indian audiences, competition itself forced Doordarshan to drop its blinkers: outsiders were invited to handle news and discussions (highly protected areas in the past); privately produced newsmagazines were incorporated into the government channel; and Doordarshan even entered into a tie-up with CNN, whereby the American broadcaster was allowed to transmit on one of its channels.

Amazingly, none of these developments appeared to have influenced debate at the conceptual level. In late 1994, I attended a high-profile seminar at Delhi's FICCI auditorium where participants, *India Today* publisher

Aroon Purie, television journalist Manoj Raghuvanshi and the BJP affiliated lawyer Arun Jaitley, berated the government, represented unwittingly by Doordarshan's Urmila Gupta, for its continued monopoly over Doordarshan. The discussion ended with a call for a show of hands over the following options: Should the government retain a monopoly over the electronic media?/Should it be totally privatised?/Is it okay for the government to own one channel and let someone else run it?

I found this debate and others which, whatever the subject, tended invariably to turn into slanging matches between private producers, media activists and others against Doordarshan, strangely anachronistic.

Granted that the future of Doordarshan, which continued to be the channel with the widest reach, was a subject of widespread concern. Granted also that private media houses had a legitimate grouse against the government in that only Doordarshan was allowed direct uplinking facilities from India which gave it an enormous edge in covering news and live sports events in the country. (In March 1995, the Supreme Court directed the government to end its monopoly in this respect.)

But neither of these were as significant as they were made out to be for in the changed scenario of the 1990s the government had been rendered irrelevant. With the opening up of the skies, Doordarshan had become just one of many players. *Anyone* could start a channel and anyone could decide what its content should be.

But in their obsession with Doordarshan what most people seemed to ignore was the cold hard fact that liberalisation of the electronic media had not resulted in a proportionately increased flow of information.

This simple fact was a matter of immense significance. For after all, what is the longstanding and deeply felt need for autonomy but a need for credible news, for the free expression of views, for the truth about what was happening in the country?

Television's power to deliver on all these was not in doubt. In the 1980s, Nalini Singh's programme on booth capturing, for instance, had brought home unpleasant realities about the electoral process to a protected city audience. The video magazine *Newstrack's* report on teenagers protesting against the government's decision to implement the recommendations of the Mandal commission, despite its appallingly blatant bias, showed the police in a bad light and created a surge of sympathy for the students. Similarly, television visuals at the time of the demolition in Ayodhya provoked riots many miles away.

But what all these instances did was to illustrate vividly how trivialised television had become by the mid-1990s.

By early 1995 there were about 30 autonomous channels on the air. Yet a cross-section of programming across channels would have revealed an assortment of films, film-based programmes, sports events, chat shows, soaps and game shows. Four channels showed films through the day. One channel played film songs round the clock. Apart from CNN and BBC there was a near absence of news, documentaries or news-oriented programming on the private channels.

And this had nothing at all to do with the complaints routinely aired against the government. True, private broadcasters did have to tread warily in the absence of a definite state policy on satellite television. Yet that did not stop them from transmitting huge doses of sex and violence, widely decried by politicians and the public, on their channels. Again, the ban on uplinking from India was not conducive to quick news transmissions. Yet periodically, broadcasters found ways to get around the obstacle. BBC and CNN carried regular news capsules on India and for the state assembly elections in 1994 Jain TV put together a reasonably gripping election package by stationing a crew in a remote earth station outside Moscow and uplinking from there.

The truth was that in their desperation to attract a slice of the limited advertising pie, television programmers were not overly preoccupied with performing a social function. Their overwhelming concern was to put together a package that would sell. In practice, this meant a total capitulation to the marketer.

In a variety of ways, the marketer had come to play a powerful role in shaping television content. The first indication of the shape of things to come had been provided by video. As the sale of VCRs and VCPs rose, manufacturers, particularly those banned on the state media, had rushed to take advantage of the new medium.

Soon, as much as one-third of the screen was covered with advertisements. And often, in the middle of a tense scene in a film, a pair of briefs or an insecticide would move out of its ad space and hover round a character's nostril thoroughly ruining the moment. With the sprouting of television channels, the sponsor became omnipresent. Names of advertisers appeared in the backdrop, in the script and even the titles of many shows.

But, intrusive though it may have been, the advertiser's presence in these cases was, at least, identifiable. What was more dangerous was his influence behind the scenes.

To garner sponsors, channels had to provide evidence of an audience for their shows. The higher the ratings the more ads a programme could collect. But in the absence of adequate audience-measuring devices, reliable numbers were hard to come by and both programmers and the market tended to rely more on instinct which, in this case, was to play safe. In other words, this meant imitating tried and tested formulas rather than striking innovative paths. Hence the rash of top 20 programmes, film-based shows and melodramatic soaps which made each channel indistinguishable from its neighbour. Even Channel V, after its refreshingly original start had settled down to tediously replicating its own formula.

If mediocrity was one consequence of television's submission to the marketer, another was an exaggerated emphasis on entertainment. 'Anything serious does not sell' was a much-repeated axiom in the television business. True or false—the presence of a thriving news industry for decades had to indicate an audience for something besides the staple song and dance routine—this became conventional wisdom for the television industry and, increasingly, the press.

Suddenly newspapers and magazines were full of gossip, lifestyle stories and fashion features. Non-entities attractively packaged and paraded as celebrities occupied centre-stage. New dailies emerged with giant crosswords and entire pages were devoted to cartoons, films and fashion (a new Marathi eveninger actually called itself 'Time Pass'). And spurious concepts such as 'infotainment' (basically film trivia masquerading as news) gained ground.

The trend was acutely visible on television and its coverage of what were generally considered serious areas, such as politics. On random shows I watched slick-haired heroes and giggly starlets being asked to analyse the political situation in the country. The handful of politically inclined programmes *(Aap Ki Adalat, Ru-Ba-Ru)* were designed less for discussion of issues and more for light entertainment. Even the 1996 Parliamentary elections, though awarded saturation coverage, were treated more like a giant cricket match with scorecards, expert comments and speculation on the outcome.

Just a decade before, observers of the media scene had sounded a death knell for the press claiming that television would attract its best talent and render it superfluous. Their predictions were totally off the mark. By the 1990s it was clear who the new kingpins on television were. They were businessmen, entrepreneurs, producers, actors, directors and cameramen. As in the press, so on television, the journalist had been completely marginalised.

The decline of the journalist and the emerging power of the salesman, the technician and the entertainer was a clear and unequivocal statement of the attitude that was already shaping the Indian media and would continue to do so in the future. It was an attitude that indicated a preference for fantasy over facts; packaging over content and profit over achievement.

ANGRY AND ADDICTED

ONE DAY IN EARLY SEPTEMBER 2015, Uday Prakash, a reputed Hindi writer and journalist posted on Facebook that he was returning the prestigious Sahitya Akademi Award, a literary honour from India's National Academy of Letters, conferred on him in 2010. He was doing so, he wrote, to protest against the murder of a Kannada scholar and rationalist M. M. Kalburgi a few days before by 'Hindutva forces'. For some years, random mobs, professing allegiance to Hindutva had been attacking journalists and writers in their homes, vandalising cinema halls, media offices and libraries and forcing reputable publishers to withdraw books and manuscripts that they construed as inimical to their beliefs. Emboldened by the BJP's victory in the 2014 national elections, the assailants stepped up their attacks. Earlier that year, an activist and writer, Govind Pansare was killed by members of a radical Hindu group. And on 28 September 2015, a 52-year-old Muslim man named Mohammed Akhlaq was beaten to death for allegedly stealing and slaughtering a calf by a mob of Hindu cow-protection vigilantes in rural Uttar Pradesh.

Prakash's post and his decision to return his award gave voice to a widespread revulsion caused by the sustained violence. Describing the Kalburgi murder as part of a series of attacks on and instances of disrespect shown towards writers, artists, thinkers and intellectuals, he wrote: 'This cowardly act of terror shook me. This is not the time to remain silent to protect oneself. Silence will only embolden such forces.' His words and his step triggered a spontaneous wave of resistance. Other writers, including an octogenarian novelist Dalip Kaur Tiwana and journalist and author, Nayantara Sahgal, returned their awards. Documentary filmmakers, photographers and scriptwriters came forward as well, turning in their state-conferred honours. A writer's epiphany had spawned a movement.

It was no small thing for a community of intellectuals and artists, with scant sources of income to sacrifice their hard-won recognition. The growing list of artists announcing their solidarity by offering up their awards gave heart to a public that was feeling emasculated and helpless against the relentless assaults. It was an aesthetically powerful moment too, I thought, imagining it playing out in a dark theatre with a gurgling cascade of names in the background and a soft spotlight falling on one brave pen-wielding solider after another. And yet, for all its stark beauty and rightful anger, I felt that the movement was symbolic and fated for futility. It was a late, late move in a game that had already been fixed.

***

The beginning of the twenty-first century was marked by the emergence of the 'K' serial. The K serial (so-called because each of the titles that fell into this category started with the letter 'K'), was a series of top-rated daily soaps made for the Star Network by Balaji Telefilms, including the wildly popular *Kyunki Saas Bhi Kabhi Bahu Thi* which launched in 2000 and ran over 1,833 episodes for eight years. The serials (which accounted for 23 of the 50 most watched serials in cable and satellite homes in 2001) were the brainchild of Ekta Kapoor, Creative Director of Balaji Telefilms. Daughter of the 1970s film star, Jeetendra, Ekta had been an overweight child, given to spending long, solitary hours on a couch eating chocolates and watching soaps on television. She had grown into a successful but eccentric adult: a workaholic, a punishing taskmaster and prone to extreme anxiety from which she sought relief in a heightened religiosity and faith in superstition. She was known to set herself arduous tests to prove her faith such as walking through wilderness and rolling on tar. On airplanes she could be seen surrounded with holy figurines chanting as the plane readied for take-off. Pictures showed her usually in track pants or a business suit, with a thick smear of ritualistic powder on her forehead.

The tele-world that emerged from her unusual psyche was of the domestic politics of multi-generational families set in an ethos that was overtly and exclusively Hindu. These families and the enormous mansions they occupied were set in a nowhere land, lodged between Bollywood notions of an extravagant rustic zamindari lifestyle with flamboyant interiors, a tulsi plant in a courtyard and women covering their heads in silk, and a metropolitan one. The style was melodramatic, relying heavily on tearful close-ups and schmaltzy background scores.

Stereotypical characters repeated stock phrases and facial expressions ad nauseum. Plotlines regurgitated familiar moments of tension and release. And at a fixed time, every weekday this loud, maudlin fare pounded into millions of households drawing viewers into its sticky-sweet web. Opinions were divided over whether Ekta Kapoor's female characters, typically housebound but feisty under their covered heads, were deeply regressive or agents of change within a conservative, patriarchal society. What was not in dispute however was the consumer friendliness of this artificial world. It was a world which existed almost exclusively inside houses elaborately furnished and peopled by bejewelled women and men in designer ethnic wear. Male characters periodically left the cloistered environment of the studio house to travel abroad for business deals, and the women, to shop. The gaudy interiors, the sumptuous celebrations of festivals and heavy finery set fashion trends for aspiring middle-class viewers. The lower socio-economic classes were blanked out and did not make an appearance, not even as domestic help, an erasure which, alongside other features led historian Uma Chakravarti to observe that the serials, despite their claim to traditional and family values, were firmly moored in a globalising India.

Alongside the K serial another form of programming which had captivated Indian audiences around this time was cricket. In a 1995 ruling, the Indian Supreme Court ended government monopoly over the airwaves. The subsequent entry of private broadcasters into the profitable business of telecasting live cricket turned the game from a mere sport into a mega industry. Sony Entertainment Television paid over ₹10 billion ($220 million), for the rights to telecast the 2002 and 2007 International Cricket Council (ICC) World Cup and expected to earn over twice as much through endorsements and advertisements. The craze for cricket saw the size of television audiences soar. Samsung estimated sales of as many as 300,000 new television sets in a few weeks before the 2007 World Cup. The apparently limitless supply of advertising revenue to be tapped saw the game itself swell and balloon into a mammoth machine. New forms of cricket such as Twenty20 evolved. New tournaments came to be held, often in non-cricketing countries with a large South Asian diaspora. The populous subcontinent, particularly India with its massive fan base, came to exercise greater control over the sport. The culture of the sport also changed. The polite 'gentlemen's game' came to be celebrated raucously by spectators with painted faces, dhol-beating, bugles and whistles. Aaron Smith, professor of Sports Business at the British Loughborough University described the new culture in his observations on the Indian Premier League, an inter-city competition started in 2008 by the Board of Control for Cricket in India as, a 'perfect storm of sporting entertainment with elements of the Champions League, professional wrestling and a touch of Bollywood'. This mixture of sport, pantomime and entertainment offered viewers much more than mere sporting action. Gambling had become widespread among television viewers. Viewers gambled on match outcomes, on runs per over, on every ball. Huge betting syndicates came up, run by underworld figures operating through a network of agents on mobile phones.

The gambling mania and colossal monies that came into the game had engendered corruption with allegations of match fixing, spot fixing and pitch doctoring becoming routine. But spectators seemed unaffected by the tainted nature of the sport and its surfeit. 'People ... get so overwhelmed by just an advertisement or music of IPL, which is the very strategy of the organisers: to set up a cricket fever among the audiences' wrote a blogger. Fervour, adulation and a blind frenzy had always surrounded cricket in India but the scale was ratcheted up many times over by its expansion and consequent ubiquity. Even if people were fatigued by too much cricket they wanted more and more.

An important feature in sustaining this heightened obsession with the game was a phenomenon that stemmed from circumstances outside the sporting arena which was the background of hostility between India and Pakistan. Both countries, important members of a sport that had about a dozen serious contenders in the world, were also traditional political foes locked in a never-ending battle over the ownership of the northern state of Kashmir. Raging antagonism laced confrontations between the two teams on the field with a special significance which tournament organisers exploited to the hilt by pitting them against each other as often as they could. 135 million Indians watched the World Cup semi-final between India and Pakistan in 2011 and 288 million watched the opening match between the two at the 2015 World Cup. Political opposition to cricketing ties had affected official cricketing tours between the two countries but the two faced off at the World Cup, the ICC World Twenty20, the ICC Champions Trophy, the Austral-Asia Cup and the Asia Cup. Sport as politics and politics as sport: I thought of the kids laughing at the fake scuffles in the wrestling ring in Chapter 9 ('Let's Play Life') and of the lone wide-eyed boy who insisted 'It's all true!'

**

26 November 2008. With an early morning train to catch from Mumbai Central the following day, I had gone to bed early. The phone rang around 11. 'Turn on the TV,' my caller said, 'Something is happening. They are calling it the biggest terrorist attack ever.'

I turned on the TV. A strange, eerie visual lit up the screen. Flames were licking the high windows of the Oberoi Trident hotel on the Mumbai seafront. On the promenade across the street where families sauntered and lovers necked, were overturned carts and peanut vendors with their hands up in the air in a gesture of surrender. Terrorists arriving by sea had taken over the city. In those early hours nobody had a clear idea of the numbers involved and the scale of the operation. Like in the 1993 bomb blasts, the attacks appeared to be simultaneous and widespread. A device had reportedly killed a taxi driver in the suburb of Vile Parle. A visual showed a car streaking past a traffic intersection between Metro cinema and the Press Club downtown, spraying bullets. Under the gothic dome of what was once known as the Victoria Terminus and now renamed the Chatrapati Shivaji Terminus, blood was visible on the floor, amidst strewn luggage. Footage from security cameras showed shadowy figures with machine guns prowling the streets. The senior-most officers of the Anti-Terrorist Squad were dead, surprised by a gunman in a back alley. A reddish haze hung over the dark streets. Friends called through the night from across the seas expressing concern. In a few hours, the sun would set on their homes and rise above ours. But for the 60-odd hours of the siege it seemed as if the only light that mattered was the blue neon of the television screen. The security forces arrived, the Rapid Action Force, Marine Commandos and the National Security Guards. Someone trapped in one of the hotels spoke to a reporter on a cellphone. Leaders came, made statements. Things proceeded at a snail's pace, but we were transfixed.

***

Indigenous news television channels began to appear in India at the beginning of the 2000s. By 2008 the genre was well established with a plethora of channels in several languages. Free from state interference, professionally managed and fiercely competitive, these channels had come to dominate the media landscape beaming familiar presences into drawing rooms every night. The print media too was thriving. Apart from the closure of some prominent general features and news magazines, television did not seem to have affected the press with over a 100,000 publications being registered with the Registrar of Newspapers for India. Cellphones and the internet had arrived. Plasma and LCD or Liquid Crystal Display screens had transformed the television viewing experience. Cable continued to make inroads into peoples' homes. Radio had come back into fashion with a dozen new FM channels starting up in every major city. The advertising industry meanwhile, which had grown as much as 25 times between 1976 and 1994 (from ₹1,160 million to ₹30 billion), had surged to 129.6 billion in 2004 and from this high perch, the advertiser called the shots more vigorously than ever before. The quantum of media exposure to cricket, films, fashion, products, parties and money escalated. The expansion of space awarded to lifestyle and finance reflected, to some extent, the interests of a society with increased leisure and money, yet the volume was out of all proportion to its expected audience. A mere two per cent of the population invested in stocks for instance, yet dozens of business channels sprouted up and their main job was to monitor the daily action in the stock market.

Editorial policies reflected the need to provide an upbeat environment to encourage consumerism. One newspaper got rid of older columnists to project youthfulness; another decreed that its front page should reflect only positive news. These policies were put in place alongside a growing rash of outright corruption. Talk of individual journalists and media houses being bribed by public relations professionals acquired a touch of credibility after 2010, when an investigation by a committee of the Press Council of India found that certain newspapers had sold news space to political candidates standing for elections, a practice that came to be known as 'paid news'. More proof of declining mores came from a letter N. Ravi addressed to the board of Kasturi & Sons, publishers of the respected Chennai-based daily, *The Hindu*. Writing the letter in 2011 when he resigned after 20 years as Editor in Chief, Ravi expressed shock 'that some of the board members should want to run a media institution like a company producing plastic buckets with purely commercial considerations and unethical practices overwhelming editorial interests and values'. In an article released a few weeks later he commented on the state of the media in general, bemoaning the increasing coverage given to subjects of interest to advertisers such as lifestyle, cinema and celebrities and the 'relative downgrading of the traditional serious content that is of historical significance, including democratic deliberation on policies and livelihood issues'.

It was not just issues but entire sections of the population that were being excised from the media gaze. The rural populace, the labouring class and the poor had all but disappeared from the media, a phenomenon that fit political scientist Leela Fernandes's term 'Politics of Forgetting' ('a political-discursive process in which dominant social groups and political actors attempt to naturalise these processes of exclusion by producing a middle-class-based definition of citizenship'). The shift was evident across the board. For the first time a substantial portion of advertising revenues had flowed to regional media. Many national dailies had also started city supplements at this time. But rather than producing diversity, the effect was one of greater homogeneity with regional and local media following national trends in exaggerating metropolitan and consumer-friendly coverage. So what was covered was significant in shaping perceptions and setting priorities. And then there was the matter of how it was covered.

Following CNN's non-stop coverage of Operation Desert Storm in 1991, the saturation relay of a single event had become standard practice for news organisations. The event could be a major global story or one of local human interest: the death and funeral of Princess Diana in 1997, the Kargil war in 1999, the 2001 attack on the Twin Towers and the rescue of a five-year-old boy from a village well in Haryana in 2006 were some stories that received round-the-clock treatment. Space allocation by subject, prioritisation of news by significance which once characterised the editorial decision-making process gave way to arbitrariness. News editors could suddenly lose their minds over an event such as an accident or a suicide involving a minor celebrity and carpet bomb what was once considered precious news space with it. In the year 2000 for instance, the hospitalisation of a Mumbai fashion designer was covered with daily bulletins, interviews with colleagues, heartfelt tributes, so on and so forth, occupying reams and reams of column-space for days in the mainstream press. The obsessive focus on a single issue did not necessarily translate into an exhaustive approach. In fact the media actually withdrew from its earlier responsibility of educating the viewer and provoking reflection through investigation, supplementary features, perspective and analysis and restricted itself to providing the best ringside view to the audience at home while offering a commentary on things they could already see.

In the print media I saw a similar move in the keenness news editors suddenly demonstrated for carrying boxes alongside articles. Unlike in the past when boxes were used to provide additional information or to convey depth and perspective to the story they accompanied, the new boxes carried lists or summaries whose aim was not to deepen and broaden understanding but to jog the memory. This apparently minor but in reality, significant development showed how media space, which could have been used in an expansive manner was instead being used as a reiterative device. This trend of endless, repetitious coverage without introducing context or societal relevance took its cue from strategies that were becoming common in the marketing world at the time. Promoters of new film releases for instance worked on creating a media blitz by placing very slightly altered content in different formats: star interviews for television, reviews and articles for the press, behind-the-scenes clips and quizzes on the internet and so on. For the 2007 ICC Cricket World Cup, Pepsi launched a new drink in a bottle the colour of the golden trophy, VISA composed a team song and LG Electronics launched a limited-edition 'official world cup television set'. This fetishisation of the event or product was to hook the reader-viewer in a manner very similar to the cloying clasp of the K serial. The techniques of addictive marketing spread across the media and into the arena of news and current affairs. An event or controversy would find itself pitched across media formats: television, broadsheet, tabloid, Facebook, Twitter, Whatsapp and radio with only a slight variation of content. An obsessed public having devoured every jangling, eye-catching piece of the same information capsule in different places, down to the last desperate mite, would experience fatigue with the mindless consumption and most likely as not swear off the media. But almost as soon as the decision was made, the craving would start all over again, for a media fix.

***

On 29 November, after the last gunman was taken out and rescue operations completed, I turned off the TV and headed downtown. If streets could grieve, Mumbai's did. At every turn one found reminders and markers of the recent attacks. Photographs of the slain Anti-Terrorist Squad chief, Hemant Karkare and his colleagues were displayed at Shivaji Park. At Worli, an ambulance stood outside the large glass windows of an art gallery: the owner's businessman husband had been killed at the Trident. As I got out of the cab, the driver and I wished each other a safe day. People were out on Colaba Causeway glad to be let out of confinement. The manager of a delicatessen urged customers to pick up complimentary loaves of bread. 'We have so much left over.' A group of tired firemen rested in one of the lanes, helmets by their sides. A guard let me into the cordoned-off streets leading to the Taj Mahal hotel. The display windows of the once-elegant shopping arcade which ran around the side of the hotel were in darkness. There was soot on the towers and a white sheet hanging from a broken window. A pillow lay on the pavement. It was dark all along the seafront but as I approached the historic basalt archway, the Gateway of India, the surroundings took on the surreal look of a fair with lights blazing from countless OB vans parked all the way to the Regal Cinema Circle 500 metres away. Within the arc of brightness, television anchors were waiting with microphones while notables from Mumbai's social circuit were being powdered to face the lights.

In the aftermath of the attacks, motley Mumbaikars interviewed by the English news television channels spewed rage at politicians for making the city vulnerable to attack. A mass public gathering at the Gateway of India a few days later was marked by a similar mood of belligerence against the political class, which many national commentators found disturbingly naive. Like the latter I too was troubled by the public response of Mumbai's social elite but not surprised. Since liberalisation, discussion of politics and political issues regarding the state or the city had almost disappeared from newspapers while consumer-friendly reports, glamour and coverage of parties and product launches had become a staple. At the same time, like other parts of India, Mumbai was being projected in the national media in a way that suited narrowly focused, often sensation-seeking, correspondents and editors in Delhi. A routine monsoon day in Mumbai became a flood on television raising alarms and warnings to schools. Lacklustre state assembly elections in Gujarat were tom-tommed by the national media as if the event was taking place in the capital. The narrative seemed to come down from the top rather than from the ground up. In this environment, Mumbai, once seen as an accumulation of many peoples, classes and aspirations was branded by the Delhi-based news media as a city of business and Bollywood. Nobody had asked Mumbaikars to comment on national affairs for many years and the lacuna created by the neglect showed glaringly at a time when the spotlight sought out the city, the commercial heart of the country.

The anti-political sentiments of Mumbaikars however was also to my mind an indirect consequence of another phenomenon which had occurred inconspicuously over the preceding two decades: the centralisation of media in Delhi. As the political capital, New Delhi had of course always enjoyed precedence over other places but in the past, editors with a national influence such as Rusi Karanjia (*Blitz*), Girilal Jain (*Times of India*), S. M. Moolgaonkar (*Indian Express*), Vinod Mehta (*Sunday Observer, Indian Post*), M. J. Akbar (*The Telegraph*) and N. Ram (*The Hindu*) were scattered across the major metros, Mumbai, Kolkata and Chennai. National magazines such as the *Illustrated Weekly of India, Imprint* and *Onlooker* from Mumbai, *Sunday* from Kolkata and

The Week from Kochi contributed to the national discourse. By the end of the twentieth century, however, many magazines had shut down and editors of any influence had moved to Delhi. Over time, many newspapers would base their operations in Delhi keeping only a skeletal team in other metros. As opinion makers at the national level, other parts of the country, not just Mumbai, were marginalised. The national networks, speaking in the pan-Indian languages Hindi and English, as against regional networks, came to be based in Delhi. This and a subsequent boom in the English-language book publishing industry, with several leading international houses setting up shop in the national capital led to a staggering concentration of media power in one location.

This phenomenon, unnoticed and unremarked upon, had a massive impact on shaping media culture. One significant impact was an overwhelming focus on politics, that is, a literal interpretation of politics without the leavening effect of the social, the cultural, the historical and the regional that may have provided a more complex and thoughtful perspective. At one time, magazines from other cities, carried features: interviews, profiles, analyses and thoughtful long-form articles. Now they had shut down and a reporter's necessary focus on the immediate, minute-by-minute unfolding of events determined the dominant content and treatment of events. Under the media's newly contracted gaze, national politics became a business of daily power-broking and controversies. What complicated the situation further was that the media now was also part of the community it reported on.

Ethical practice in an earlier time was about boundaries: between editorial and marketing, between journalists and their subjects. But now, media houses sold cars, entered the public relations business, organised glitzy stage shows, socialised and hosted chat shows that required a cheery bonhomie and interdependence between journalists and politicians, policemen, film stars and business moghuls on a sustained basis. The consequences of blurring the lines became apparent in a dramatic fashion in what came to be known as the Nira Radia Tapes controversy. Nira Radia was the proprietor of a public relations firm, Vaishavi Corporate Communications whose roster of clients included leading Indian industrial conglomerates such as the Tata Group and Reliance Industries Limited. In 2008–9 the Income Tax Department tapped Radia's phone lines as part of their investigations into possible financial malpractice and tax evasion. Transcripts of the recorded conversations found their way to several media offices where they were ignored till a couple of publications carried them opening a can of worms and exposing a disturbing state of affairs in the Indian media. On the tapes, Radia could be heard offering scripted interviews and columns favouring her clients to prominent journalists and then laughing and exulting with a colleague about her success. In other conversations she was heard urging a well-known journalist to use her access to politicians to lobby for a ministerial berth for a candidate favourable to her business clients. Radia's drawling voice, assertive, gossipy, wheedling, familiar and confidential by turn was like the expert play of a juggler balancing some of the country's most influential voices. Her consummate ease and confidence suggested a questionable level of closeness between the media, industry and politics. The tapes created a scandal and damaged reputations within the media fraternity but led to little reflection on how the situation had been arrived at.

And it was perhaps unrealistic to expect a deep reflection on journalistic practice when journalism itself was in peril. More and more, people in senior editorial positions, particularly in news television were talking about the unaffordable cost of doing journalism. 'It's very difficult for channels to invest in hardcore reportage. I see this as the beginning of the end of reporting,' Bhupendra Chaubey, national affairs editor for CNN-IBN told the tabloid *Mid-day* in May 2014. Why it was unaffordable or difficult for media houses, many publicly listed and with a turnover running into crores of rupees, expensive studios and printing presses to send a few reporters out to the field was never explained. Alternatively, why a news media that openly proclaimed its inability to invest in newsgathering should continue to exist was also never explained. And nobody asked. Perhaps it was the dampening effect journalism (sans the thrill of a natural disaster or cricket match) might have on the advertiser that was the problem. Perhaps a growing intolerance of media freedom was the reason why journalists were being turned into what a 2018 book, *The Post-truth Media's Survival Sutra: A Footsoldier's Version* called 'clerical coolies'.

Meanwhile and somewhat contradictorily it would seem, the media was serving as an outlet for a melange of voices unfiltered by professional editorial discretion. In the age of internet anybody could have their say, in blogs, or as online feedback to articles in the press. Media houses were opening up to the trend of 'citizen journalism' encouraging ordinary people to send in photographs and reports of events they might have witnessed.

If non-professionals were getting a taste of the media's power, the media itself was becoming a noisy place, swelling with opinions. The source of this cacophony was the new format that had become a staple of news television which was the primetime debate. Modelled on American talking heads shows, the primetime debate (which soon extended beyond prime time) brought together guests of varying persuasions to debate the issue of the day. Guests were chosen on varying grounds, for the positions they occupied to the views they held. Familiar faces acquired a caché regardless of the value of their opinions and channels vied to get them into their studios. Guest co-ordination became a primary function on television. As *Mid-day* reported: 'Channels are increasingly investing in hiring good coordinators with access to the corridors of power, at high salaries—sometimes higher than mid-level editors.'

The primetime debate was loud and cantankerous. Since the aim of the show was not to foster understanding or agreement but to showcase a fight between various fixed positions, the format encouraged belligerence and extremism. Conversations became increasingly heated, sometimes personal and decibel levels flared with the journalist-host often fanning the flames. Commenting on the American media in their 2013 book *The Outrage Industry: Political Opinion Media And The New Incivility*, Jeffrey M. Berry and Sarah Sobieraj proposed that political polemics had become a business, a business they termed the 'outrage industry'. 'Individual enterprises, ranging from enormous media empires to lone bloggers have collectively generated political mudslinging on a scale unprecedented in American history with a view to attracting viewers, listeners, readers, voters, members or donors by providing compelling political shows or stories, the common denominator for "compelling" in politics being "what makes you angry ...".'

A certain section of India was conspicuously angry. The daily barrage of invective and the exposure of scams and corruption scandals by the then ruling Congress party were reasons enough for anger. But underlying conditions were also hospitable for stoking public anger. In Chapter 3 ('The Middle Class Strikes Back') I wrote about the discontented middle class, its frustrations arising from an absence of economic mobility and its feelings of marginalisation because of the rise of the plebeian politician after independence. The middle class wanted liberalisation and it was granted its wish. But the opening up of the Indian economy, while it grew opportunities for financial advancement, also created inflation and raised aspirations which were not met, creating new frustrations. Leela Fernandes doing interviews in Mumbai was told by some of her respondents: 'Anger. The major feeling is anger. The interests of the middle classes are not being represented by politicians.'

The simmering rage of the middle class found a target in the surging high-handedness and venality of the political class. Spontaneous public rallies such as one in 2006 to protest the acquittal of the son of a Congressman who shot and killed a Delhi model and in 2008 against the above-mentioned terrorist attack in Mumbai took on a strongly anti-political hue. In April 2011 a respected activist, Anna Hazare, began a hunger strike in New Delhi for tough anti-corruption legislation sparking off a countrywide movement that saw non politicians taking centre-stage.

Some of these, most prominently a former bureaucrat, Arvind Kejriwal, would become the new political contenders of the times. Another strain contributing to the public rage had its roots in a concurrent phenomenon.

A political mobilisation of the Hindu community through the unifying effect of the televised Ramayana and the Rath Yatra as described in Chapter 6 (*The Rath Yatra*) and the mobilisation of a socio-cultural opposition to the effects of runaway modernisation (*The Backlash*, Chapter 10) had created volatile mobs that were both the product of modernisation and its anti-thesis. The sensation-seeking media publicised the violent activities of these mobs in turn, encouraging them to ratchet up their attacks both feeding off each other. In the studios of news television channels the BJP, closely aligned with many of these demonstrators outshouted its political rivals conducting a daily referendum on the ruling Congress party and determinedly steering the conversation towards its socio-cultural vision for the country. Against this tumultuous backdrop came the landmark 2014 election which saw the BJP, a party at odds with the commitment to secularism enshrined in the Constitution, win a majority on its own at the centre for the very first time under the leadership of Narendra Modi.

***

Around 2009–10, while researching a book on Ahmedabad I found myself in a room in the Gujarat Secretariat complex in Gandhinagar surrounded by stacks of publications. They were booklets, pamphlets and brochures brought out by various government departments. They all had Narendra Modi's photograph on them. It was not one photograph repeated over many items but several photographs, each in sync with the category it illustrated. On the cover of a pamphlet on security for instance, I noted how the chief minister's face and gestures were set in grim resolve and how they softened for publications on the girl child and the environment.

From an acquaintance I received another stack of publications brought out by assorted entities, many of them associated with the state government. The Gujarat Chamber of Commerce's Exim Directory for 2009 claimed an inflow of billions of dollars worth of foreign investment in recent years ('Today Gujarat has become the most happening place in the world and lately even House of Commons of UK has appreciated Vibrant Gujarat by the highest votes ever achieved in the history of Great Britain', it said) and opened with a picture of a laughing Modi. A 2007 publication in two volumes titled 'Pragati nu Panchamrut' (Nectar of Progress) had a printed price of ₹700. Volume One had 212 pages of which 27 had full page pictures of Modi alone and 62 had Modi addressing a crowd or in other ways, interacting with people and about a dozen pictures were of people responding to him. Volume Two had 16 solo pictures of the Gujarat chief minister and 54 group pictures. Narcissism was not unusual in Indian politics and it was common to find images of leaders splashed across hoardings and government press material but the pictures of Modi were very different from conventional political propaganda. These pictures appeared to involve the kind of styling that went into commercial photography for the advertising industry with attention paid to costuming, colour palettes, backdrops and moods.

In one picture Narendra Modi was writing in a large journal with a gold pen, possibly copying from a thick open book, veins bulging on his hand. He was in an office but the kind that resembled a set in a film rather than a messy government space. There was a table covered with an embroidered cloth, a bowl of colourful flowers, and a small Indian flag on a stand. The beige wood, striped furnishings, the journal with its beige pages and orange cover, the walls and the napkin on the back of the chair were all colour co-ordinated, perfectly matching Modi's white kurta and orange jacket. The scene was bathed in a soft light. In another picture, Modi's hand caressed his cheek bringing into focus his rings, one with a star shaped diamond and another, a square stone. In yet another he stood to attention with a black RSS cap on his head and in yet another picture where he was all in white the red tip of his pen cunningly matched a red thread around his wrist. The paper, layouts and imagery were also akin to commercial publicity material rather than government propaganda. The paper was thick, glossy or handmade, all in colour with special effects like sepia and embossed lettering. Brochures of the Gujarat Maritime Board displayed aquamarine seas, golden sunsets, mango coloured beach umbrellas, chequered tiles, cruise ships, shiny white sailboats and Toyotas rolling off a glistening ferry. Other brochures showed futuristic cities with palm trees, multiple lane highways, glass edifices and burnished blue skies.

In Chapter 2 (*The Big Leap*) we saw the role played by television in transforming Rajiv Gandhi's image from a political upstart into that of a responsible statesman-like figure capable of leading the country at a time of personal loss and national crisis. Three decades later the media had the heft and pervasiveness to be an even more effective political marketing tool. Unlike Rajiv Gandhi, Narendra Modi did not come from a distinguished political family. He was by his own claim a tea seller in his youth and a functionary of the RSS who happened to find himself as the chief minister of a state where the most virulent episode of communal violence possibly since Independence, broke out, months into his term. The episode widely known by the year of its occurrence, '2002', was often referred to as India's first 'televised' riot. Never before had television cameras and crews been present at the site of an outbreak of communal mass violence. This was still the early days of news television in India with fewer channels and the fervid sense of competition and sensationalism was yet to enter the business. The rough-edgedness of the reportage and non-stop coverage involved the viewer in the event in a way that had not been possible before. The fact that the coverage gave substantial expression to the terror and vulnerability of victims (unlike CNN's war coverage which spent a considerable amount of time in the skies watching missiles being lobbed at targets below) invoked a responsibility which, combined with the fact that the violence occurred under the watch and with the alleged collusion of a ruling party openly committed to a majoritarian agenda, gave the violence an unprecedented significance. It also made Modi at once the most reviled as well as the best known regional politician in the country.

By any standard, Narendra Modi's rise to power in 2014 was meteoric. Observers, fixated on old frameworks of political analysis failed to understand the powerful role of the media in his rise. At one level, the role was a literal, conscious enterprise. As Gujarat chief minister in the aftermath of 2002, Modi projected intense criticism from the national and international media as an assault on Gujarati asmita or pride. He asked his fellow Gujaratis for co-operation in avenging this 'insult' and was able to implement a fast-track developmental exercise which he would later showcase nationally as the 'Gujarat Model'. To the gushing Gujarati media he offered tidbits of biographical anecdotes. He talked for instance about how he moved about in disguise during the Emergency, sneaking late night meals at the house of a supportive activist. Stories of him fighting alligators surfaced. His claims of incorruptibility became the talk of the town. Pictures of him in outfits designed by local designers were splashed across the media. He spoke directly to the public at political rallies and published books of poetry. This mode of self-projection was not unknown in political marketing. Meaghan Morris commenting in *Ecstasy And Economics: American Essays for John Forbes* on the inordinate charisma of Paul Keating wrote: 'something unusual about the figure of Keating is its simultaneous availability to me in several affective registers. Widely distributed over time in differing networks of cultural production—conversation, newspapers, radio, news and talk-back, daytime "women's" TV variety shows ... prime-time family news ... as well as heavily masculine late night "analysis" shows ... and weekend magazine programs. The figure of "Keating" is a constellation of anecdotes accessible to me equally and *convergently* as an enthralling political drama, as an unsettling ideological problem, as an enigmatic object of analysis and ... as a sentimental folktale.'

In Modi's case, a politico-religious appeal was also encoded in his image. It drew strength from his role in 2002, casting him in the light of a protector of Hindus, which he augmented through various references in his public appearances. One of his first acts after winning the 2014 Lok Sabha elections was to visit the holy town of Varanasi where he had contested the elections from. He offered prayers at the famous Kashi Vishwanath temple and participated in the Ganga Aarti at Dashashwamedh Ghat. The aarti was relayed by several television news channels. The moment of conflation, politics mixing with religion on television screens was reminiscent of Indira Gandhi's funeral in 1984 where Indian audiences empathising with the grieving son also saw the new prime minister, Rajiv Gandhi, through the haze and din of ceremonial rituals. Unlike that moment, brought about accidentally by the assassination of a long-serving prime minister, the Ganga aarti was a deliberate act, intended to signal the arrival of new, avowedly pro-Hindu dispensation in a constitutionally secular nation.

For many Hindus, the familiar elements of ritual, the massed flowers, flaming lamps, poured unguents and chanting priests touched an emotional chord and revived a longstanding debate about the form of secularism that was best suited to India and whether the existing one was too dry and devoid of religiosity in a deeply religious country. In his article, 'How Modi Defeated Liberals Like Me' in *The Hindu* (22 May 2014), Shiv Vishwanathan dwelt on this subject. 'At first he wrote the message ("We don't need to be ashamed of our religion") irritated me and then it made me thoughtful. A colleague of mine added "you English-speaking secularists have been utterly coercive, making the majority feel ashamed of what was natural." The comment, though brutal and devastating, was fair. I realised at that moment that liberals like myself may be guilty of something deeper.'

Over time however and with the unfolding of events another interpretation also seemed to be possible. In his book, *It's a Sin: Postmodernism, Politics and Culture*, Lawrence Grossberg described the New Right's project in the US working 'powerfully through a war of affect waged in and as popular culture'. The war, according to him, aimed to reconstruct an American national-popular by divorcing common sense from faith and from emotional investment. The BJP had long argued for faith over history and legal processes at various times and most consistently in its demand for a temple at the site of the Babri Masjid on the grounds that it was the birthplace of Rama. Attempts by various spokespersons allied to the BJP or Hindutva to undermine modern scientific and historical practice by making claims based in belief about ancient India post 2014 when seen in conjunction with the televised rituals at Dashashwamedh Ghat made it possible to perceive the latter in another light: not as an event by itself but as part of a campaign of affect to prioritise faith over rationality.

Whichever interpretation or mix of interpretations one applied to the televised Ganga Aarti, there were lessons to be drawn about Modi's talents as a communicator from it. Both the spectacle and its emotive content showed how well Modi understood the power of the media but also

the very charged ecology of a media age filled as it was

with images and sensory affects. In 1989, David Harvey in *The Condition of Postmodernity* noted that an 'image dominated aestheticizing regime is displacing a mode of ethical apprehension'. Media visibility had a power to create icons out of thin air. It was a power that was used by advertisers of consumer products, by dictators, by the likes of Paris Hilton and Kim Kardashian, by political fixers, by socialites and bloggers. 2002 may have presented Narendra Modi negatively but the media gaze itself was a precious commodity and useful in drawing attention to his 'Gujarat Model', a mantra picked up by excited television anchors, building brand value with every repetition. For the parliamentary elections in 2014, the BJP projecting Modi as the prime ministerial candidate, spent a reported ₹5,000 crore on publicity. Modi spread himself over all available media including the emerging social media demonstrating flashes of his flair as a stylist when he emerged from the polling booth for instance, dressed in starched white, holding a small white lotus, the party symbol in his hand. A quarter of a century had passed since the opening up of the Indian economy. Among the voters was the first generation of voters born after liberalisation and the arrival of satellite television. Modi positioned himself not just as a leader, but also as an object of mass consumption.

***

Mid-August in the year 2012 an eerie silence lay over the buzzing offices of the television channel IBN 7. For a week, TV18 Broadcast Ltd which ran a bouquet of channels including IBN7, had been handing out termination letters to journalists, camera crew and sales personnel. Three to

269

four hundred people had been retrenched, about 30 per cent of the 1,300 staff. The restructuring or 'bloodbath' as staffers called it was the most dramatic the industry had ever seen and there was talk of it being engineered by Reliance Industries Ltd which had acquired indirect control of the influential media company the previous year. Over the next four years it became abundantly clear that Reliance chairman Mukesh Ambani, India's richest man, had emerged as a dominant player in the news media business. *Caravan* magazine examined filings with the registrar of companies in the ministry of corporate affairs and found that five leading Indian news media companies—NDTV, News Nation, India TV, News 24 and Network18—were indebted either to Mukesh Ambani or to his associate. Industrialists had owned media before and used their clout as media owners to advance their business interests. But at the beginning of the twenty-first century, corporate houses were seen to be closely allied with the state and the party in government. And news television came to be seen as partisan, supporting either the ruling dispensation or the opposition. In other words, rightly or wrongly, audiences began to see television coverage not as an objective view of events but as ideological positioning. One could say that regardless of the plethora of channels, this took India right back to the time of state-run and monopolised television.

And like it was then, in the 1980s (See Chapter 4 'The New Guerrillas'), technological innovation threw up possibilities for an alternative conversation. These possibilities were felt across the world. Early in 2011, the death of a fruit seller in Tunisia sparked off a wave of anti-government protests in the Middle East that came to be known as the 'Arab Spring'. Mohamed Bouazizi was unable to find a job and started selling fruit by the roadside. When a municipal inspector confiscated his wares, he immolated himself. Social media played a significant role in bringing people out on the streets—in 2011 there were almost 30 million users of Facebook in the Arab world—and in sustaining the movement. Inspired by the Arab Spring, a leftist Canadian magazine, *Adbusters* published a blog post urging tens of thousands to converge on Manhattan's financial district to 'set up tents, kitchens, peaceful barricades and occupy Wall Street for a few months'. The Occupy Wall Street movement, aimed at protesting economic inequality demonstrated by moves such as the US government's decision to bail out large banks at the time of the financial crisis of 2008, spawned similar movements in other countries and gave rise to other influential movements in the US such as the anti-racist 'Black Lives Matter' campaign.

More recent interventions by social media included the 'Yellow Vests' movement against rising fuel prices and inflation in France which started with an online petition in November 2018 and the stirring coverage provided on social media to a march by drought-hit farmers to Mumbai from rural Maharashtra around the same time. If social media emerged as a powerful tool for organising protests and creating solidarities around issues blanked out by the mainstream media, a rash of online publications provided opportunities for showcasing socially-conscious journalism that had diminished in other media. The conflict between powerful, vested interests and representatives of the vulnerable and powerless for control of the message continued. But the challenges too were growing.

***

In August 2007, visuals of a furious mob beating up a woman in Delhi were beamed across the media. The woman, a 40-year-old school teacher called Uma Khurana, had been identified as a procuress in a sting operation aired on television and the mob spent its ire by also damaging cars and attacking police personnel on the scene. The only problem was that the television programme was concocted. A journalist with a small Noida newspaper had been persuaded to make allegations posing as a former student and victim of Khurana's alleged criminal activities. The whole thing was a set up by a personal acquaintance with a grudge against the schoolteacher. The Uma Khurana case was not the first instance of fake news in Indian journalism. There had been cases in the past including a false newspaper story planted by a disgruntled hospital trustee about a spate of deaths in the ICU of a well-known Mumbai hospital in the 1980s. What was of concern in the new scenario was first of all, the hugely expanded terrain occupied by the media which made it harder to control. In India at last count, there were 188 million television homes, 183 million of them equipped with cable and satellite, 857 licensed television channels, almost half devoted to news and 82,000 registered publications of which 14,000 were daily newspapers. India also had 500 million internet connections, scores of FM Radio channels, 240 million active users of Facebook (the largest country audience in the world), 67 million Instagram users and 30 million on Twitter.

In Chapter 12 (*The Age of Infotainment*) I wrote about how the decline of the journalist and the emerging power of the salesman, the technician and the entertainer indicated a preference for fantasy over facts. The acute anxiety of the marketing industry regarding viewers' attention levels and the immense pressure on newspersons to be perpetually entertaining could not but affect the approach to news gathering. Journalism in the past meant a pursuit, however imperfect, of the truth. This placed a certain responsibility on the editor, the copy desk and the reporter and photographer on the ground to investigate and discover facts, to verify and cross-check them and represent them with the greatest accuracy possible. In the changed scenario where the audience had to be entertained, for a large part of the media, the news came to mean facts that supported a story. Story meant the important role of narrative. Since its inception the advertising industry had used stories to sell products: children, hungry after play and a mother who cooked up a meal in two minutes; a boy who could not eat ice cream because of his weak teeth and his friend who could because of his toothpaste; a TV service repairman who drove over rugged terrain to get to his client on time; a girl who supported her elders and taught them gender equality. By stoking commonly shared emotions these stories created bonds between strangers and forged communities of consumers. Many Indian news television channels came to adopt a similar approach to editorial content, perceiving news as an instalment in a pre-decided narrative which played on familiar political biases. News could be slanted through headlines, announcements, tickers. Occasionally news of dubious veracity whipped up a tornado in the real world.

A well-known instance of this happening was in the United States at the time of the closely fought 2000 Presidential race in America between George Bush Junior and Al Gore. Fox News called the election for its candidate, Bush, on the closing night of the polls. The announcement was premature and the network would retract it later but by then it had dragged other networks into imitating it, thereby creating an investment in the outcome: in the controversy following the Florida vote, the television blunder would make Al Gore seem like a sore loser for demanding a recount. Similarly, in 2016 an incident involving media interference caused a political storm in India. On 9 February, Zee News telecast footage from an event at Delhi's Jawaharlal Nehru University, protesting the hanging of a Kashmiri separatist convicted in a 2001 terrorist attack. The channel identified incoherent sounds on the footage as slogans in support of India's bête noire, Pakistan, by placing captions on the screen and screened the footage repeatedly. The Delhi Police filed an FIR on the basis of the footage and arrested JNU Students' Union president Kanhaiya Kumar for allegedly seditious activities. The arrest snowballed into a confrontation between right wing allies of the BJP and university students. Later, questions emerged over the veracity of the footage. Vishwa Deepak, an Output Producer at Zee News even resigned claiming that captions had been added to give the story a slant which the footage did not merit.

Allegations of doctored footage from a mainstream news channel should have provoked widespread outrage. They produced barely a ripple of criticism from commentators. Even a move to ask writers to boycott the Zee-sponsored Jaipur Literary Festival, a few weeks later, produced a lukewarm response. Presumably, a public which had once demanded television autonomy and vociferously condemned press censorship during the Emergency was resigned to instances of extreme irresponsibility on the part of the media. Or, the indifference towards declining media ethics was part of a larger indifference towards democratic rights. The Indian middle class had increasingly bought into an argument that recommended surrendering ordinary rights for economic gains, reflecting a global trend towards authoritarianism. It was this shift that encouraged corporate houses and governments to push for increased surveillance and data harvesting, disregarding concerns of privacy. The increasing pressure for Indians to register under Aadhar, the world's largest biometric ID system by the BJP government after 2014, was a case in point. The potential for abusing access to data was exemplified by the discovery in 2018 that a company, Cambridge Analytica, had harvested personal information from millions of Facebook profiles without consent as data for Donald Trump's US presidential election campaign.

Declining public support in turn also increased the vulnerability of the media in India, or at least those sections of it that still believed in the media's role as a guardian of citizens' rights. At the beginning of the twenty-first century a steady denigration of the media was in evidence. And the freedom of the journalist appeared to be in greater peril than ever before. News of journalists being harassed by online trolls, pressurised to change or retract stories, intimidated with expensive law suits and so on, became routine. At least three journalists were murdered in 2017 in connection with their work. Among them was a

55-year-old editor and publisher, Gauri Lankesh, who was a vocal advocate of secularism and a critic of a right-wing political ideology. People were arrested for lampooning politicians or expressing critical opinions on Facebook. In 2018, India was ranked a dismal 138 out of 180 in the World Press Freedom Index put out by Reporters Without Borders, below countries like Israel, Bhutan, East Timor, Kenya, Ukraine, Palestine and Afghanistan. Prannoy Roy, co-founder of NDTV and a pioneer in television, said India was experiencing 'an aggressive variant of McCarthyism against the media'. Journalist and writer Shanta Gokhale called contemporary India a 'Republic of Fear'.

This state of vulnerability did not come about overnight. It was preceded and fostered by a process of trivialisation and dumbing down. The process occurred and snowballed over three decades and was driven by a relentless and single-minded pursuit of profit which was and is a motoring feature of the hyper-capitalist economic policies shaping India and much of the contemporary world. This trend has not extinguished the truth-telling impulse. Indeed surveying the contemporary landscape one finds that, despite the limitations of their times, many journalists, writers and artists continue to pursue their vocations with diligence and integrity. But their efforts occupy an ever diminishing space in a vast, expanding enterprise.

Today we are surrounded by hoardings, blinking LED screens, Youtube videos and insistent cellphones. The rapidity with which the cellphone, in particular, has spread across the world—two-thirds of the world's 7.6 billion inhabitants have a mobile phone—is awe-inspiring. With over a billion cellphones, India is part of what media analysts are calling the 'fastest, most capillary technological revolution in human history'. This trend of 'always connected' devices like smartphones, tablets and others has freed the exchange of information from the fixed time and place to which television and the PC were limited. And soon they will give way to a new paradigm of internet-meets-body termed 'bio-hypermedia'. Accompanied by the pervasive capabilities of new technologies such as near field communication, object-oriented internet and augmented reality.

Protecting the media's purpose to advance the human urge for truth and justice in the new ethos is a challenge for our times.

INDEX

20th Century Fox, 218

ADMAR,133
AIDS, 16–18
A Kiss Before Dying, 147
ATN, 134
Aap Ki Adalat, 124, 242
Adhikaar, 186–187
Advani, L. K., 29, 91–92, 106, 108
Afternoon Despatch & Courier, 125
Agence France Presse, 208
Agnivesh, Swami, 170–171, 173, 176
Air Time Committee of India (ATCI), 126–127
Airhostess, 186, 189
Aiyer, Mani Shankar, 202
Ajinkya, 98
Akbar, M. J., 29
Akhil Bharatiya Patni Atyachar Virodhi Morcha, 190
Akhtar, Javed, 110
Ali, Sikandar, 191
All Assam Students' Union, 30
All India Anti-Video Piracy Organisation, 61
All India Democratic Women's Association, 195
All India Radio (AIR), 7, 11, 172, 222
Alter, Tom, 49
Ambani, Dhirubhai, 45, 217
Ambedkar, 34

Anantrarn, S., 182
Adhein Choohein, 54
Antigone, 47
Apache Indian, 81–84
Application Technology Satellite, 9
Arranged Marriage, 81, 86, 145–147, 149, 152, 185
Arya, Arjun, 70
Arya Sabha, 170
Asian Games 1982, 13, 15
Asianet, 227, 230, 232
Assam Accord, 30
Associated Press, 208
Athavle, Manohar, 146
Atyeo, Don, 78
Aung San Suu Kyi, 74
Aur Bhi Hain Raahein, 187
Aurelius, Marcus, 202
Aweke, Aster, 81
Azharuddin, Mohamad, 219

BBC, 4, 80, 105, 108–109, 111, 15, 207, 237, 239–240
Baaki Itihaas, 49
Bamigar, Babri Masjid/Ram Janmabhoomi dispute, Babur, 95
Bachchan, Amitabh, 47, 132, 219
Basu, Jyoti, 206
Baum, Richard, 224
Baywatch, 162
Bedi, Nikki, 142, 174–175
Bedi, Pooja, 140

Begal, Uday, 201
Benegal, Shyam, 134
Bhalla, Surjit, 46
Bharatiya Janata Party, 20–21
Bharatiya Sanskriti Manch, 171
Bhatt, Pooja, 140–141, 193
Bhaye Prakat Kripala, 97
Bhimani, Vinod, 45
Bhindranwale, Jarnai1 Singh,
    12, 25
Blue Prints, 63
Bold and the Beautiful, 133, 169,
    188
Bombay, 175
Bonded Labour Liberation Front,
    170
Boom Shak-A-Lak, 82, 85
Bose, Subhash Chandra, 174
British Broadcasting World
    Service, 77
Broadcasting Corporation of
    India, 11
Buruvaad, Buniyaad, 52, 89,
    275
Business India, 134
Byrne, David, 81

Cable News Network (CNN),
    75–76
Cable Television, 59, 61, 100,
    126, 133, 172, 226
Celia Chong, 79
Chaaya Geet, 4
Chalmers, Patrick, 80
Chandra, Subhash, 124
Chandralekha, 235
Channel V, 196–197, 201, 203,
    241
Chastity, 141
Chatterjee, Basu, 54
Chatterjee, Upamanyu, 202
Chawla, Juhi, 155
Chopra, Yash, 202
Christie, Agatha, 54
Chugh, R. P., 190–191
Chung Ching, 54

Cinema, 202, 219, 234
City's Cable, 111
Clarke, Arthur C., 75
Coleridge, Nicholas, 216
Communal violence in
    Bombay, 265
Congress, 11, 20, 24–25, 29,
    56–57, 66, 70, 93, 101,
    115–116, 119, 206, 229,
    261–262
Consumer trends, and television,
    2–10
Count of Monte Christo, 4
Current Opinion and Future
    Trends, 146

D' Cunha, Jean,192
Dabholkar, Bharat, 199
Dangerous, 95, 104, 121, 171, 175,
    235, 240
Darr, 154
De, Shobha, 50, 139–140
De Mello, Melville, 5
De Souza, Merlyn, 181
Debonair, 140, 152
Deepika, 90
Deo, K. P. Singh, 127
Deodhar, P. S., 127
Deol, Sunny, 155
Desai, Morarji, 175
Desai, Murli, 164, 195
Desai, N., 182
Devi Lal, 57, 63–64, 120
Dhanraj, Deepa, 186
Dharmendra, 140
Dillagi, 137
Dilwale Dulhaniya Le Jaayenge,
    202
Donahue, Phil, 133, 139
Doordarshan. *See* Television
    Doordarshan International,
    230
Dubashi, Jay, 46
Dubey, Satyadev, 49, 54
Dutt, Kamalini, 118
Dynasty, 52, 136

El TV, 137
ESPN, 207
Economic Times, 216
Economist, 44, 46, 118, 210
Ek Khahani, 52, 68
Ekshuf, 49, 54
Eyewitness, 175

Fantasy, 141
Far Eastern Economic Review,
    208
Film and Television Institute,
    Pune, 4–8
FM Channel, 222, 250
Forster, E. M., 138, 197
Foundation for Organisational
    Research (FORE),
    166
Fun, 141

Gama, Vasco da, 83
Gandhi, Indira, 10–11, 15, 17–18,
    27–34, 205, 267
Gandhi, Mahatma, 1, 38, 93, 142,
    173–174
Gandhi, Maneka, 19
Gandhi, Rahul, 19
Gandhi, Rajiv, 15, 18, 23–26, 29,
    31, 37, 56, 93, 107, 119, 205,
    264–265, 267
Gandhi, Sanjay, 15, 38
Gandhi, Sonia, 19, 30
Gandhi, Tushar, 173–174
Garware Plastics and Polyester
    Limited, 62
Ghai, Subhash, 48
Ghosh, Shashank, 201
Gilani, Benjamin, 49
Gill, S. S., 27, 51
Glad Rags, 141
Godfather, 134
Gokhale, Mohan, 135
Gujral, Inder, 10
Gupta, Neena, 140
Gupta, Urmila, 238

Hai Mera Dil, 54
Hamare Kamgar Hamare
    Udyog, 6
Hanneman, Paul, 218
Hema Malini, 47, 140
Here's Lucy, 4
Hindustan Thompson Associates,
    39, 62
Hitler, 92
Hogan, Hulk, 156
Home Box Office, 177
Hong Kong Foreign
    Correspondents' Club, 75
Hong Kong University, 73
Hum Aapke Hain Kaun, 202
Hum Log, 40, –51, 89
Humraahi, 188
Hussein, Saddam, 174

Imprint, 33, 256
Inamdar, Shafi, 49, 51, 54
India Today, 26, 123, 132,145,
    148, 154, 167, 237
Indian BPs, 63
Indian Copyright Act, 61
Indian Documentary Producers'
    Association, 120
Indian Express, 29, 217, 256
Indian Institute of Management,
    8
Indian Peoples' Theatre
    Association, 49
Indian Post, 53, 55, 256
Indian Space Research
    Organisation, 8
Infotainment, 226–242, 273
INSAT 1B, 26, 76, 117
International Monetary Fund
    (IMF), 37
Irwin, Christopher, 207

Jackson, Michael, 171–172, 200
Jaffrey, Javed, 196
Jagriti Mahila Samiti, 176
Jain, Girilal, 217, 256
Jain, J. K., 56, 97, 134

Jain, Samir, 215–216
Jain TV, 134, 137, 193, 232, 240
Jaitley, Arun, 238
Jalaram, 174
Jana Sangh, 20, 93
Janata Dal, 170
Janata Party, 11, 21, 37
Jayalalitha, 234–236
Jennifer, 46
Jodi Purottam, 233
Johnny Mera Naam, 130
Joshi, Mahendra, 49
Joshi, P. C., 118
Jungli Toofan Tyre Puncture,
     199

Kabhi-Kabhi, 202
Kalani, Dhunichand, 70
Kalani, Narain, 72
Kalani, Pappu, 66, 68, 70
Kamala, 156
Kamasutra, 151
Kante, Mary, 90
Kanwar, Anita, 49, 51
Kapoor, Mohan, 137, 176
Kapoor, Prithviraj, 46
Kapoor, Shakti, 141
Kapoor, Shashi, 46, 132
Kapur, Anjali, 193
Kapur, Pankaj, 49–50
Kapur, Shekhar, 134
Kapur, Steven, 81
Karamchand, 51
Karat, Brinda, 195
Kashmakash, 186
Kaushik, Meena, 169, 181, 184
Kavi, Ashok Row, 142, 174
Khaled, 81
Khan, Feroz, 49
Khan, Salman, 140
Khan, Shahrukh, 155
Khandaan, 52
Khanduri, Ramesh, 42
Khanna, Harish, 127
Khelaiya, 49
Khirwadkar, Suren, 42

Khoj, 52
Knott, Alan, 5
Kohli, J. S., 227
Kojak, 59
Kothari, Prakash, 139, 153
Krishi Darshan, 6
Krishna Iyer, V. R., 123
Kulkarni, Mamta, 139, 176, 193
Kulkarni, S. D., 146
Kya Scene Hai, 137

Lerner, David, 8
Li Ka-Shing, 77
Liberty, 192
Lloyd, Clive, 5
Look Back in Anger, 54
Love, in changing trends, 143
Lu, Ping, 74
Lumet Sidney, 182

Madras Family Court, 150
Mahabharata, 89–90
Mahadevan, V., 148–149
Main Chup Nahin Rahungi, 191
Mallya, Vijay, 218–219
Mansukh, 231
Maran, Kalanidhi, 232
Marg, 145, 148, 154
Marx, 167
Mass Media and National
     Development, 8
Mastaan, Haji, 131
Masud, Iqbal, 55, 121
Mazumdar, Roabin, 62
McDonald, Hamish, 208
McGill, Danny, 79
McLuhan, Marshal, 27
Media Advocacy Group, 181, 188,
     203
Mehta, Harshad, 169, 227
Mehta, Vinod, 28, 256
Menezes, Margeret, 81
Menon, Raji, 227
Metro Channel, 126, 134, 222,
     230
Metzger, Geoff, 78

Michael, George, 274
Midnight's Children, 199–200
Mitra, Amitav, 184
Monopolies and Restrictive
    Trade Practices Act
    (MRTP), 35
Mortimer, John, 49
Mousetrap, 54
Movie, 202
Mr. Ya Mrs., 52
MTV, 77–79, 82, 85, 132, 139,
    196–197, 207, 221–222
Mukherjee, Kalidas, 43
Mukherjee, Sushmita, 51
Murdoch, Rupert, 207, 218

Naik, Vikram, 43
Naipaul, V. S., 197
Nair, Shankaran, 15
Namedia,118
Narayan, Jayaprakash, 34
Narayan, R. K., 88
Nasreen, Taslima, 189
National Aeronautics and Space
    Administration (NASA),
    USA, 9
National Council of Applied
    Economic Research
    (NCAER), 210
National Front, 119
National Institute of Design, 8
National Institute of Mental
    Health and Neuro Sciences,
    Bangalore, 165
National Satellite
    Communication Group
    (NASCOM), 8
National School of Drama,
    48
Nehru, Jawaharlal, 10, 16, 93,
    171, 274
Network, 182
New Times, 92
Newstrack, 175, 239
Nigam, Rekha, 137, 184
Nikki Tonight, 142, 173–175

No Full Stops in India, 90
Nonie, 78

Oedipus Rex, 49
Operation Desert Strom, 252

Palkhivala, Nani, 12–21
Pan Am Sat, 257
Panandikar, V. A. Pal, 44
Paper Tigers, 216
Parthasarathi, Vibha, 160–161
Passage to India, 138, 197
Patel, Haresh, 66
Patel, Karsan, 39
Pathak, Ratna, 49
Patil, Babulal, 68
Patil, Raja, 44
Patil, Ranjana, 69
Patil, Rinku, 68
Patwardhan, Anand, 63
Pawar, Sharad, 66
Phadke, Vimal, 146, 148
Phool Khile Hain Gulshan
    Gulshan, 4
Pinter, Harold, 49
Playways, 141
Prabhavalkar, Nirmala, 189
Prabhudeva, 202
Pran Jaaye Par Vachchan Na
    Jaaye, 98
Prasad, Mahesh, 123
Prasad, Rajendra, 7
Prasar Bharati Bill, II, 119, 122
Pride and Prejudice, 4
Parikh, Rajish, 139
Prime Sports, 77–78, 156
Prithvi Theatre, 46–48, 53
Priyanka, 19
Probe, 44, 46
Purie, Aroon, 238

Raghuvanshi, Manoj, 238
Raheja, Dinesh, 141
Rai, Gulshan, 130
Rainmaker, 54
Raj TV, 232

Jain, Samir, 215–216
Jain TV, 134, 137, 193, 232, 240
Jaitley, Arun, 238
Jalaram, 174
Jana Sangh, 20, 93
Janata Dal, 170
Janata Party, 11, 21, 37
Jayalalitha, 234–236
Jennifer, 46
Jodi Purottam, 233
Johnny Mera Naam, 130
Joshi, Mahendra, 49
Joshi, P. C., 118
Jungli Toofan Tyre Puncture,
    199

Kabhi-Kabhi, 202
Kalani, Dhunichand, 70
Kalani, Narain, 72
Kalani, Pappu, 66, 68, 70
Kamala, 156
Kamasutra, 151
Kante, Mary, 90
Kanwar, Anita, 49, 51
Kapoor, Mohan, 137, 176
Kapoor, Prithviraj, 46
Kapoor, Shakti, 141
Kapoor, Shashi, 46, 132
Kapur, Anjali, 193
Kapur, Pankaj, 49–50
Kapur, Shekhar, 134
Kapur, Steven, 81
Karamchand, 51
Karat, Brinda, 195
Kashmakash, 186
Kaushik, Meena, 169, 181, 184
Kavi, Ashok Row, 142, 174
Khaled, 81
Khan, Feroz, 49
Khan, Salman, 140
Khan, Shahrukh, 155
Khandaan, 52
Khanduri, Ramesh, 42
Khanna, Harish, 127
Khelaiya, 49
Khirwadkar, Suren, 42

Khoj, 52
Knott, Alan, 5
Kohli, J. S., 227
Kojak, 59
Kothari, Prakash, 139, 153
Krishi Darshan, 6
Krishna Iyer, V. R., 123
Kulkarni, Mamta, 139, 176, 193
Kulkarni, S. D., 146
Kya Scene Hai, 137

Lerner, David, 8
Li Ka-Shing, 77
Liberty, 192
Lloyd, Clive, 5
Look Back in Anger, 54
Love, in changing trends, 143
Lu, Ping, 74
Lumet Sidney, 182

Madras Family Court, 150
Mahabharata, 89–90
Mahadevan, V., 148–149
Main Chup Nahin Rahungi, 191
Mallya, Vijay, 218–219
Mansukh, 231
Maran, Kalanidhi, 232
Marg, 145, 148, 154
Marx, 167
Mass Media and National
    Development, 8
Mastaan, Haji, 131
Masud, Iqbal, 55, 121
Mazumdar, Roabin, 62
McDonald, Hamish, 208
McGill, Danny, 79
McLuhan, Marshal, 27
Media Advocacy Group, 181, 188,
    203
Mehta, Harshad, 169, 227
Mehta, Vinod, 28, 256
Menezes, Margeret, 81
Menon, Raji, 227
Metro Channel, 126, 134, 222,
    230
Metzger, Geoff, 78

Michael, George, 274
Midnight's Children, 199–200
Mitra, Amitav, 184
Monopolies and Restrictive
    Trade Practices Act
    (MRTP), 35
Mortimer, John, 49
Mousetrap, 54
Movie, 202
Mr. Ya Mrs., 52
MTV, 77–79, 82, 85, 132, 139,
    196–197, 207, 221–222
Mukherjee, Kalidas, 43
Mukherjee, Sushmita, 51
Murdoch, Rupert, 207, 218

Naik, Vikram, 43
Naipaul, V. S., 197
Nair, Shankaran, 15
Namedia,118
Narayan, Jayaprakash, 34
Narayan, R. K., 88
Nasreen, Taslima, 189
National Aeronautics and Space
    Administration (NASA),
    USA, 9
National Council of Applied
    Economic Research
    (NCAER), 210
National Front, 119
National Institute of Design, 8
National Institute of Mental
    Health and Neuro Sciences,
    Bangalore, 165
National Satellite
    Communication Group
    (NASCOM), 8
National School of Drama,
    48
Nehru, Jawaharlal, 10, 16, 93,
    171, 274
Network, 182
New Times, 92
Newstrack, 175, 239
Nigam, Rekha, 137, 184
Nikki Tonight, 142, 173–175

No Full Stops in India, 90
Nonie, 78

Oedipus Rex, 49
Operation Desert Strom, 252

Palkhivala, Nani, 12–21
Pan Am Sat, 257
Panandikar, V. A. Pal, 44
Paper Tigers, 216
Parthasarathi, Vibha, 160–161
Passage to India, 138, 197
Patel, Haresh, 66
Patel, Karsan, 39
Pathak, Ratna, 49
Patil, Babulal, 68
Patil, Raja, 44
Patil, Ranjana, 69
Patil, Rinku, 68
Patwardhan, Anand, 63
Pawar, Sharad, 66
Phadke, Vimal, 146, 148
Phool Khile Hain Gulshan
    Gulshan, 4
Pinter, Harold, 49
Playways, 141
Prabhavalkar, Nirmala, 189
Prabhudeva, 202
Pran Jaaye Par Vachchan Na
    Jaaye, 98
Prasad, Mahesh, 123
Prasad, Rajendra, 7
Prasar Bharati Bill, II, 119, 122
Pride and Prejudice, 4
Parikh, Rajish, 139
Prime Sports, 77–78, 156
Prithvi Theatre, 46–48, 53
Priyanka, 19
Probe, 44, 46
Purie, Aroon, 238

Raghuvanshi, Manoj, 238
Raheja, Dinesh, 141
Rai, Gulshan, 130
Rainmaker, 54
Raj TV, 232

Rajni, 52
Ramayana, 87–90, 96, 187,
    262
Ramayana *Retold,* 88
Rangeela, 199
Rao, N. Bhaskar, 159
Rao, N. T. Rama, 206
Rao, P. V., Narasimha, 205
Rapid Action Force, 105, 250
Rashtriya Swayam Sevak Sangh,
    93
Ratnam, Mani, 202
Ray, Ashis, 208
Razdan, Karan, 135
Reddy, D. Narayana, 153
Rahman, A. R., 202
Research International Observer,
    167
*Reuiew of Studies on Middle
    Class Women's Entry in to
    the World of Work,* 182
Richard, Li, 77
Rijhwani, Gopal, 64
Rogers, Everett, 52
Row Kavi, Ashok, 142, 174–175
Ru-Ba-Ru, 242
Rushdie, Salman, 174, 199

SEWA, 63
SITE, 9, 76
Saanp Seedi, 137
Sabido, Miguel, 51
Sagar, Ramanand, 88–90
Sainath, P., 120
Santa Barbara, 133, 136, 180,
    188
Sapre, Madhu, 194
Sarabhai, Vikram, 8, 226, 279
Satanic Verses, 174
Sathe, Vasant, 12
Schramm, Wilbur, 9
Scindia, Madhavrao, 20, 23
Scindia, Vijay Raje, 20
Seth, Vikram, 200
Sex, attitude towards, 239
Shah, Dhiren, 43

Shah, Naseeruddin, 49
Shahani, Kumar, 120–121
Shanker, Shailendra, 7, 12, 15
Sharma, Shiv, 14, 187
Sheshadri, Shekhar, 165
Sheth, D. L., 181, 194
Shiv Sena, 92, 95, 98, 104, 116
Siddiqui, A., 107
Simon, Paul, 81
Simpson, O. J., 222
Singh, Archana Puran, 137
Singh, Kalyan, 101
Singh, Nalini, 239
Singh, Zail, 18
Singhal, Arvind, 52
Sippy, N. N., 130
Sircar, Badal, 49
Soman, Milind, 193
Sony Entertainment, 246
Sophiya, 85–86
Sputnik, 75
Srinivasan, A. C., 150
St. Valentine's Day, 143–144, 147
Star Ferry, 73
Star Plus, 77, 79, 139, 142, 162,
    174
Star TV, 75–78, 122–123, 133,
    144, 168, 204, 207, 218
Star Trek, 74, 76, 78, 80, 82,
    84, 86
Stardust, 138, 141, 176
Star's Prime Sports, 156
State Council of Educational
    Research and Training, 158
Subah, 52
Sun TV, 204, 228, 232–233
Sunday, 4–5, 18, 23, 32, 40, 46,
    87, 91, 141, 163, 256
Sunday Times, 23
Superhit Muqabla, 213
Swatantra Party, 34
Sword Sultan, 96

Tagore, Sharmila, 140
Tamas, 96
Tanzeem Allaho Akbar, 107

Tara, 136
Tarkovsky, 48
Television, Advani's rath yatra, 92, 106
  backlash, 172–194, 262
  beginning of, I 224
  changing attitude of woman and, 183
  consumer trends and, 209
  expansion of, 210
  impact on, social life, 160
  students, 154–155, 159–160
  Indian lifestyle, 212
  infotainment, 226–242
  metro, 126, 134, 222, 230, 249
  middle class entertainment, 35–53
  new channels and, 126–127, 136
Tendulkar, Sachin, 219
Thackeray, Bal, 91, 104, 111–112, 114, 124, 175
Thakur, Dinesh, 49, 54
Three Is Company, 59
Times, 215–216
Times of India, 53, 171, 215, 218, 256
Tully, Mark, 90, 109
Turner, Ted, 76
Twain, Mark, 225

UNESCO, 7
Udaya TV, 204, 228

Ulhasnagar Sindhi Association, 65
United Liberation Front of Assam (ULFA), 30
Upendra, P., 120, 122

Vajpayee, Atal Bihari, 22
Varadan Committee, 126
Venkataraman, Janaki, 232
Venugopal, G., 231
Video, 58–64
Video Cassette Recorders (VCRs), 37, 57
Video piracy, 61, 130
Vijayan, K. M., 235
Vishwa Hindu Parishad, 56

Wadia, Nusli, 217
Walesa, Lech, 224
Whose News—The Media and Women Issues, 186
World Wrestling Federation, 156

Yadav, Laloo Prasad, 206
Yadav, Mulayam Singh, 106
Yeh Jo Hai Zindagi, 51–52
Yokozuna, 156
Yudh,136

Zee TV, 176, 199, 204, 230, 233

ABOUT THE AUTHOR

Amrita Shah is the author of the award-winning book *Ahmedabad: A City in the World* (2015) and a biography *Vikram Sarabhai: A Life* (2007). She has been a journalist and a writer for several decades. She has worked for *Time* magazine, edited features magazines *Debonair* and *Elle* and has been a contributing editor with *The Indian Express*. Ms Shah has received fellowships from the New India Foundation, the Homi Bhabha Fellowships Council and the Fulbright Program. She is an alumna of the Institute for Public Knowledge, New York University and has been Visiting Faculty at the Centre for Contemporary Studies, Indian Institute of Science, Bengaluru.